Mob Law on Delmarva

Cases of lynchings, near-lynchings, legal executions, and race riots of Delaware, Maryland, and Virginia

1870-1950

By Linda Duyer

Mob Law on Delmarva
Cases of lynchings, near-lynchings, legal executions,
and race riots of Delaware, Maryland, and Virginia
1870-1950

Copyright © 2014 Linda Duyer

All rights reserved. This book or any portion thereof may not be reproduced or used in any manner whatsoever without the express written permission of the publisher except for the use of brief quotations in a book review or scholarly journal.

First Printing: 2014

ISBN 978-0-9915540-0-3

Edited by Cynthia Byrd, Ph.D.

Ordering Information:
This book can be purchased through www.lulu.com or from the author.

Dedicated to
Wallace Duyer and Polly Stewart

I dedicate this book to my father for his faith and pride in my historical work, and for his passion for history and all its implications.

And I dedicate this to Polly Stewart for her commitment to folklore and her work with oral histories. Her tolerance and enthusiasm for people was likely unmatched. The spirit of Polly Stewart seemed to follow me throughout the production of this work.

"It is difficult at this day to realize the state of public opinion in regard to that unfortunate race which prevailed in the civilized and enlightened portions of the world at the time of the Declaration of Independence, and when the Constitution of the United States was framed and adopted; but the public history of every European nation displays it in a manner too plain to be mistaken. They had for more than a century before been regarded as beings of an inferior order, and altogether unfit to associate with the white race, either in social or political relations, and so far unfit that they had no rights which the white man was bound to respect."
Chief Justice Roger B. Taney, *Dred Scott v. Sanford*, 1857

"In the argument, it was said that a colored citizen would not be an agreeable member of society. This is more a matter of taste than of law."
***Dred Scott v. Sanford*, dissent by Justice John McLean, 1857**

"It is evident that the Negro has no rights in Delaware which a white Governor is bound to respect."
***Philadelphia Times* editorial, 1878, on the executions of Samuel Chambers and George Collins**

"Violence can only be concealed by a lie, and the lie can only be maintained by violence."
Aleksandr Solzhenitsyn

"…guilt is often assumed before innocence can be proven."
Miguel Syjuco

"Citizens got to participate in ridding their community of something unwanted, be it by pulling a rope, throwing a stone at the victim, taking home a souvenir, or simply yelling encouragement."
Philip Dray (2003, 146)

"Incidents like the 1903 lynching of George White in Wilmington, Delaware almost defy interpretation. Historians, sociologists, psychologists, social critics have offered a range of interpretations for why lynchings occurred, why they persisted in American history. When you look at incidents like the death of George White close up, no interpretation suffices to get at that element of human decision-making and tragedy. It is as if, the novelist Walker Percy once said, that we have the angel and the beast warring inside of us. And what incidents like the Wilmington lynching demonstrate is too often the beast has won out."

Dennis Downey, Ph.D., Professor of History, Millersville University
In the Dead Fire's Ashes, The Lynching A Town Forgot, film by Stephen Labovsky

Table of Contents

Acknowledgements 1
Preface 3
Introduction 7
Chapter 1. About the Referenced Material 10
Chapter 2. Examining Our Personal History 13
Chapter 3. Howard Purnell Tells a Story 17
Chapter 4. Crime and Punishment 21
    A Legal Execution 22
    The Pillory & the Whipping Post 25
    The Almshouses 28
    Last Hanging at Old Elkton Jail 31
    The Spectacle of Lynching 35
Chapter 5. The Dangers of Excursions 41
Chapter 6. A Townscape: Princess Anne 43
Chapter 7. The Ku Klux Klan 57
Chapter 8. The Outside World Looks In 67
Chapter 9. More to Learn, Mysteries to Solve 73
Chapter 10. The Race Riot Cases 76
    Cape Charles Violence, 1887 76
    Wachapreague Riot of 1899 77
    Onancock, Regulators 1890 77
    Wilmington Riot of 1903 78
    Camden Riot of 1904 79
    Southern Delaware Riots of 1905 80
    Southern Delaware Riots of 1906 84
    Onancock Race Riot of 1907 86
    Pocomoke City, Maryland 1907 90
    Rehoboth, Delaware Riot 1908 92
    Wilmington Riots of 1910 93
    Laurel, Delaware Race Riot of 1911 94
    Seaford, Delaware Race Riot of 1911 97
    Crisfield, Maryland Riot of 1912 98
    Delmar Riot of 1914 98
    Seaford, Delaware Riot of 1915 100
    Wilmington, Delaware Race Riot of 1915 101
    Middletown, Delaware Race Riot of 1915 102
    Wilmington, Delaware Riots of 1919 103
    Centreville, Maryland Riot of 1919 104
    Ridgely, Maryland Violence of 1931 105
    Princess Anne, Maryland Rioting of 1934 106
Chapter 11. Eastern Shore Cases 111
    Jacob Hamilton 111
    John Holden 113
    William "Obie" Evans 114
    William Wilson, William Wells, Frank Rounds and George Bailey 114
    Unidentified Man 118
    John Jones 119

Ernest Smith	122
George Wheeler and George Hines	124
Jenkins Showell	127
Samuel Chambers and George Collins	130
William Neal	131
James Redden	132
George Lake	133
Frederick Cephas	135
Charles Williams	136
James Stevens, alias Sewell Wright	139
Alexander Moses	140
George Smith, alias William Black	141
Magruder Fletcher	142
Asbury Green	145
James Taylor	147
Dr. Hill's Murder	151
Henry Taylor and Arthur Courtney	154
William Jackson	158
Isaac Kemp	160
Taylor Rowlett and Richard Everitt	164
William Andrews	166
Garfield King	169
Samuel Jones	172
Adam Stewart	172
George White	175
Eugene Harris	179
Leander Moore and Joseph Shockley	180
Fletcher Hollis	181
Oliver Cephus	182
William Lee	183
John Henry	186
Charles Conley	188
Edward Watson	191
James Reed, Lemuel Showers, Hildred	193
Moses Driver, James Pitt, Arthur (Artemus) Miles	197
Henry Taylor	199
Charles Anderson (Granger)	200
Wesley Miles	202
Norman Mabel and James Paraway	205
James Dutton	207
Aloysius "Wish" Sheppard	210
Aaron Johnson	211
Robert J. Smith (or James Smith)	213
Bailey Jonabe	215
Harry Paynter	216
Isaiah Fountain	217
George Chelton	221
Howard, Gunby, Mills, Wise, and Cutler	223
Carroll Gibson	226
Harry Merrill	228
Wilbur Barnes	231
Joshua Tiller	232
Henry Butler	234
Unidentified Man	236

    George Davis 237
    Euel Lee, Matthew Williams and George Armwood 240
    Sam Jones 255
    Howard McClendon, alias Harry Flemming 258
    James E. Bowland 259
    William Holland 260
    Arthur Collick and Charles Manuel (Pilchard Murder) 261
Chapter 12. Other Notable Cases 265
    Benjamin Goslee (Darby Case) 265
    Dennis and John Frank Furbey 266
    Luther Moore 270
    Junius Evans 270
    William Randall 271
Chapter 13. Reflection 273
Bibliography 275
Index 279

List of Figures

Figure 1 Sheriff house and jail, Chestertown, Maryland 15
Figure 2 Site of burning of Matthew Williams, Salisbury, Maryland 20
Figure 3 Pillory and whipping post, Delaware 25
Figure 4 Waterloo Almshouse Farm, Somerset County, Maryland 28
Figure 5 Almshouse, wooden structure Somerset County, Maryland 29
Figure 6 Almshouse, Worcester County, Maryland 30
Figure 7 Almshouse, Kent County, Maryland 30
Figure 8 Execution of John M. Simpers, Elkton, Maryland 31
Figure 9 Piece of the rope used to hang Matthew Williams 38
Figure 10 Princess Anne, Maryland, circa 1930s 43
Figure 11 The 1877 Maryland Atlas of Princess Anne 45
Figure 12 Newspaper ad of 1839, "Cash for Negroes," Princess Anne 46
Figure 13 Cash for slaves advertisement, 1839 46
Figure 14 Postcard "Looking for the negro, Princess Anne, Md." 49
Figure 15 Newspaper ad for the movie The Birth of a Nation 52
Figure 16 Crowd in Princess Anne following release of suspects 55
Figure 17 Ku Klux Klan newspaper articles and advertisements 65
Figure 18 "The Putrid Eastern Shore" 67
Figure 19 "The Eastern Shore Kultur" by H. L. Mencken 68
Figure 20 "Maryland, My Maryland" lynching cartoon, 1931 69
Figure 21 Listing of 1897 Lynchings 72
Figure 22 Advertisement for the Tasley Fair, Tasley, Virginia 89
Figure 23 Old courthouse, Princess Anne, Maryland 168
Figure 24 Map of Princess Anne structures at time of Andrew lynching 168
Figure 25 Map of vicinity of George White lynching 177
Figure 26 Image of souvenir hunters at site of George White lynching 178
Figure 27 William Lee 184
Figure 28 Images from William Lee Execution 185
Figure 29 Postcard of 1907 lynching of James Reed 193
Figure 30 Matthew Williams 243
Figure 31 Image of Salisbury courthouse and sign near site of lynching 246
Figure 32 George Armwood being transported following arrest 249
Figure 33 Body of George Armwood at lumber yard 252
Figure 34 Lillian Black Collick and daughter Martha 264

Acknowledgements

I would like to thank some of those who glanced at some of the material in this book and said "yes, it has to be done" at times when I doubted the necessity of the project. Compiling hour after hour accounts of lynchings, murders and threats got to me at times, blinding me and causing me to wonder if there was a point to this. So I thank the people who emphatically said it should be printed. So thanks to Phillip Hesser, Mike Dixon and Kate Clifford Larson. Thanks to Debbie Phelps Mano for listening to me at a low point when I wondered how I might respond to questions of why study this history, and she smartly said, "Because it is dangerous not to."

Thanks to the Edward H. Nabb Research Center for Delmarva History and Culture at Salisbury University, Salisbury, Maryland, for indulging my frequent hours at their computers searching the university online newspapers. Thank you Dr. Ray Thompson and Dr. Clara Small for their encouragement and assistance, and particularly Clara for helping me to locate the extraordinary photograph of James Reed. Thanks too to Jason Rhodes of Salisbury University and for his father Frank Rhodes who contributed the photograph.

A thanks and a hug to my mentor and friend Dr. Lee Ann Fujii, of the University of Toronto (and formerly from George Washington University) for her encouragement and support, and for keeping me sane throughout incessant delving into the peculiar histories of lynchings, near lynchings, and all other manner of murder and violence. Mostly, I have appreciated Lee Ann for being a sounding board for thoughts and insights into the subject, for helping me to look at the history from new angles.

It was such a wonderful relief to have the editorial assistance of my friend Dr. Cynthia Byrd who took the time to make this work better. Whatever remaining errors or omissions grace these pages are my own.

Thanks again to historian Mike Dixon and the Historical Society of Cecil County, Maryland for invaluable information contributed. Thank you Eldon L. Hayman, Sr. for contributing a chilling history written by his late sister, Carlyn Juanita Hayman-Bingham (1916-2003) describing her experience in Princess Anne, Maryland on the day George Armwood was lynched in 1933.

Mob Law on Delmarva

A special thanks to Dr. Kirkland Hall of the University of Maryland Eastern Shore. His work and love for his community, in particular his dreams for his community, inspired this book.

Still others have contributed information that did not get into the book due to sections left on the cutting room floor. I have hung on to the information in case there are opportunities to share the material.

And I shall slip in a special nod to a certain coffee shop in Salisbury, which I will not name but you know who you are. Some readers may know as well, as I could be seen sipping many a coffee while hovered over my laptop computer with considerable angst trying to get this book done.

Thank you all who have not been mentioned or I may have overlooked. And finally, thank you to family and friends who have put up with my focus on this book, I owe you all my gratitude.

Preface

This book came about after decades of researching Eastern Shore African American history and contemplating issues of segregation, intimidation, hate, and violence towards African Americans.

I am not an accredited historian. My background is more like that of a genealogist – not of families, but of communities. I collect stories for the enjoyment of learning and sharing them, as a way of giving back to the storytellers who have enriched my life. Not all of my collected stories are of blood and guts, even if it seems that way to some. Still, there must have been some foreshadowing, because my studies began with documenting African American cemeteries. This I did for the purpose of trying to learn more about the people I never knew growing up in Salisbury, Maryland. This was difficult for a person who was horrifically shy for the first few decades of her life. At first it was easier to research cemeteries, books and old newspapers than it was to actually confront the shyness and ask. Eventually I did ask and now it seems I cannot stop asking. The interest in history was a journey of exploration and a late realization that maybe I should have pursued this earlier.

The fun for me is in documenting and sharing history little known to others. And I found that because little is understood of certain aspects of local history, misconceptions continue. But I also know my limitations – I can never know fully what life was like for people other than myself. But I try. My reward is when someone says, "I didn't know that" or "I never looked at it that way."

In 1997 I researched and documented African American burial sites in Dorchester and Wicomico Counties as part of a grant with the Maryland Museums Program and produced the publication *One Kind Favor, See That My Grave's Kept Clean, African American Burial Sites of Dorchester and Wicomico Counties, Maryland*. My 2007 book, *'Round the Pond, Georgetown of Salisbury Maryland*, was based on research of the history of Georgetown, the earliest African American neighborhood of Salisbury. I have written several articles, conducted numerous oral history interviews, and researched a wide range of topics – all for the sheer joy of it.

So why did I create this book? It started after assisting Dr. Kirkland Hall as he organized an historical program in 2011 at the University of Maryland Eastern Shore about the history of the 1933 lynching of George Armwood in Princess Anne. I was not new to the subject, as I had known about it ever since my early years of microfilm-viewing old newspaper articles. But my experience as both an assistant and as a spectator of the program, along with other related projects, resulted in new questions.

People began to ask me just how many lynchings had taken place on the Eastern Shore. I knew of a few, certainly, and the Maryland Archives had online listings. But in considering the whole region of Delmarva, I did not know the answer. So I set out to compile a list. I knew there would never be an accurate number because of undocumented lynchings and because of the ill-defined nature of the term.

The listing did not take long to compile. But during the process, which involved searching online historic newspapers, I was struck by the occurrence of references to near-lynchings, so I began collecting those stories to add to my list, then limiting the time period to about 1870 through the 1940s. I knew many of those near-lynchings ended with legal executions, so I began also listing the executions of African Americans on Delmarva. Some people refer to executions of that time period as "legal lynchings" because of the nature of criminal system at that time which provided few if any protections for African Americans. I do not like that term because it trivializes the term "lynching." Both lynchings and legal executions, mostly by hanging on the Eastern Shore for that time period, were certainly horrific menaces to the community. But lynchings were distinctly different from legal executions. It can be hard to imagine, but there could be far worse than a legal death by hanging.

During the search of newspapers, I encountered a number of so-called race riots of the Eastern Shore during this time period. The term "race riot" was widely used by newspapers to include racial violence of different types. The term may or may not have been meant to describe black-on-white crime. I became curious about what I was reading, so they too were included in the compilation.

Reflecting back on the work, I know that this effort was my response to the comments, implied or otherwise, that "things weren't so bad" on the Eastern Shore. I knew that, yes, they were bad, but I wanted to find a way to show it. The work does not at all include a full picture of what was endured and suffered during this time period, but it is my hope that the material makes people think, to look at history from a different point of view, to ask questions, and to look further into this history.

Why is it important to delve into such painful history? Because to not discuss this history can be to deny it. I once interviewed a survivor of two World War II concentration camps and a death march. He felt it

Preface

important to know and recognize the signposts of societal actions based hate in order to prevent violence and death before circumstances rise to a level making it impossible to stop. I am not so sure that if confronted with those signposts, we as a society are able to effect change. But I feel strongly that the uglier parts of our history, of us, need to be examined and taught.

Our actions for the present and the future are often based on our feelings and our knowledge of the past. We make our choices – of who we associate with, interact with, how we vote, how we live our lives – based on what we know of other people and of the past. If what we know is incorrect or lacking, then we cannot change our point of view enough to affect our decisions for our future. If we cannot confront this difficult past, we cannot be strong or knowledgeable enough to affect change.

Finally, the guilt and innocence of the person lynched is something we are quick to ponder. I also get caught up in what did or did not happen. But then I remember that some were lynched, many nearly so, and far more were put through mock judicial treatment. Acts of lynching render the question of guilt or innocence moot. Due process was denied. To dwell on the alleged acts of the lynched victim is to ignore the fact that someone was brutally and horrifically murdered. Instead we should focus on the long-term psychological and cultural impacts of this historical practice.

As you read case after case, consider what it must have been like to live in a time and place where, at any moment, these things could happen to you or to people you know. Imagine how you would react to the circumstances around you. A little empathy could go a long way.

Mob Law on Delmarva

Introduction

What follows are stories of violence or threats of violence toward African Americans of Delmarva, the peninsula encompassing Delaware and parts of Maryland and Virginia on what is described as the Eastern Shore of the Chesapeake Bay.

Chapter 1 of the book includes information about the scope and limitations of the project and the nature of the referenced material, what is included, what is not.

Chapter 2 includes reflections on my personal experience and about some of the stories that influenced me and this work. This is included to encourage others to reflect on their own histories.

Chapter 3 is an account by the late Howard Purnell of the lynching he witnessed as a young adult. There are few first-hand witnesses remaining who can describe a lynching or similar violence if they wanted to. Because of the limited nature of the scope of this book, the most glaring omission is the lack of description of the victims as people, individuals who had lives, families, and friends, regardless of guilt or innocence of the crimes of which they were accused. In an era when the fate of an accused African American was a foregone conclusion, there was little description or concern for African Americans as people, because often they were not thought of as people. The story of Howard Purnell describing his experience is included to represent the many stories that could not be included nor openly shared.

Chapter 4 describes some aspects of crime and punishment. Included are a couple of example cases of legal executions and a description of Delaware's practice of using the pillory and the whipping post. Also included is a review of almshouses which were sometimes the sites of executions, and reflections on the spectacle of lynching.

Chapter 5 describes mob violence at was reported as a race riot in Rehobeth, Delaware.

Chapter 6 describes some of the cases from the perspective of a townscape, that of Princess Anne, Maryland. Cases identified in this book affected communities all over the Eastern Shore. The effort of looking at the racial violence of Princess Anne over time and describing the town can be applied to communities throughout the region.

Chapter 7 describes some of the activities of the Ku Klux Klan on the Eastern Shore during the 1920s.

Chapter 8 provides a reflection on the responses of outside newspapers on the violence of the Eastern Shore.

Chapter 9 provides a few reflections on the mysteries surrounding some of the stories or cases detailed in this book. Not every case included in this book goes into much depth or detail. Yet every case has a story – known, yet-to-be known, or perhaps never to be known. Also included are a few cases not included earlier in the book because of the scope of the topic. These are included for researchers who may be interested in in the detail for further study.

Chapter 10 includes the so-called race riots, in chronological order. These are followed by Chapter 11 of the individual cases, approximately in chronological order.

Chapter 12 describes several other notable cases that do not appear to meet the criteria of mob violence but are interesting for their context. Chapter 13 concludes with final reflections on the content of the book.

The time period is roughly between 1870 and 1950, an era of Civil War reconstruction and the period described as Jim Crow, before the Civil Rights struggles of the modern era enjoyed television as the newest form of historical documentation.

It is important that historical research contributes to a body of work that examines the psychological and sociological impact of violence on people, particularly African Americans. Author Douglas A. Blackmon writes about this aspect of historical research.

> There was no acknowledgment of the effects of cycle upon cycle of malevolent defeat, of the injury of seeing one generation rise above the cusp of poverty only to be indignantly crushed, of the impact of repeating tsunamis of violence and obliterated opportunities on each new generation of an ever-changing population outnumbered in persons and resources (2009, 6).

As you read some of these accounts and if you delve into your own research about these and other cases, I urge you to ponder what hate looks like, and its effect on people.

Consider the sources of all that you read. The cases provide a renewed sense of awe of what is possible. If you think evidence cannot be planted,

Introduction

then look at the Sam Jones case of 1934. If you think Delmarva was not capable of burning down homes and businesses and driving people from their homes, then look at the race riot cases.

Imagine a community where white ministers throughout the Maryland Eastern Shore in 1923 introduced the Ku Klux Klan to crowds on Sunday afternoons, just hours after Sunday services.

Imagine having to walk past white neighbors on the way to church two days after a lynching, and worse, having to return to jobs on the following Monday. Imagine having to instruct children in a form of social etiquette no person should have to learn.

This book may include only cases of the Eastern Shore that received newspaper coverage, but the full picture of race relations throughout that era and the effect on the survivors and their descendants is far bigger and more complex. Think twice about the notion that things were "not so bad" on the Eastern Shore.

Chapter 1. About the Referenced Material

Limits of Research and the Material in the Book
The purpose of the overall research was to identify cases involving reported racial violence or the potential for violence identified for the Delmarva region for the period of 1870 through the 1940s. But this book is limited in scope to cases of mob violence; in particular, mob violence that could be identified largely through newspaper accounts. I recognize that there could have been more mob violence than printed or located in newspapers. Some newspapers reported vague speculation but no specific description of mob violence, so most of those cases although identified were not included.

My detailed research to specific cases has been limited to the cases of the lower Maryland Eastern Shore during the early 1930s, specifically the 1931 lynching of Matthew Williams in Salisbury, Maryland and the 1933 lynching of George Armwood in Princess Anne, Maryland. The remaining cases were identified solely through a search of historic newspapers. There was not an extensive search of studies or articles of books by others who may have researched these cases, but a few were identified and referenced.

Focus on African Americans
This book focuses on African Americans – of lynchings, near-lynchings, legal executions and other violence. There were whites who were lynched and legally executed by hanging, but the vast majority were of African Americans, the subject of this book.

There were some notorious cases of lynching and legal executions of whites on the Eastern Shore. In 1895, a white man, Marshall E. Price, was lynched by an angry mob, which dragged him from the Denton jail in Caroline County, Maryland, and hanged him by a tree three days before his scheduled execution for murdering 13-year-old Sallie Dean.[1] The Price case has been described Christine Arnold-Lourie (2008, 1031-1045).

In September of 1915, an Italian man, Frank Grano was arrested for the murder of Levin P. Robinson, his wife, and their farm hand, Alonzo Redden, on the Robinson farm near Snow Hill in Worcester County, Maryland. Grano was returned to Snow Hill to stand trial, and on October 18th, he was convicted of the murder of Alonzo Redden and

---

[1] *The Baltimore Sun*, "Price Lynched. The Murderer of Sallie Dean Hanged at Denton. A Mob Of Masked Men," Jul. 3, 1895

Chapter 1. About the Referenced Material

sentenced to hang. He was not tried for the murder of Levin P. Robinson and Robinson's wife.[2] (*See page 22 for more information.*)

White-on-Black Violence
The cases included here involve mob violence or violence inflicted on African Americans. There were cases of black-on-black crimes reported in newspapers. These cases were not included in this compilation.

Newspaper Articles
Most of the cases and information referenced in this book are from newspaper articles. Some points about the inclusion of this material:

- **Not every newspaper was searched.** Due to constraints of time, extensive research for most cases is lacking. Readers interested in learning more about what was printed about these cases are urged to search for more articles.

- **Not all newspaper articles are referenced or quoted in their entirety.** For some cases a lot more material was located than was included in this publication. Many of the articles include a great deal of detail, but duplicate information from other articles. In some cases, whole articles are included, and in others, only excerpts are used. Researchers interesting in knowing which newspaper articles were compiled can contact me for more information.

- ***The Baltimore Sun* is the most frequently referenced source.** At the beginning of the project, the primary purpose was to identify as many cases as possible with the means available. I searched keywords of *The Baltimore Sun* online as a basis from which to start. Other newspapers were reviewed only if they were readily available. The Somerset County Library in Princess Anne had their microfilm collection of newspapers digitally reproduced for viewing. That collection included *The Crisfield Times* and the *Marylander and Herald*. Other newspapers were reviewed, but not for all newspapers or all available issues. Some newspapers were searched and had a wealth of information; others searched had little or none.

---

[2] *The Baltimore Sun*, "Triple Murderer To Die, Frank Grano Convicted of Slaying Alonzo Redden – Not Tried on Other Charges," Oct. 19, 1915

The Ku Klux Klan
Reports about the activity of the Ku Klux Klan were located during the course of the search. The inclusion of their activity in newspapers was a surprise to me. There was no extensive research of KKK activity on the Eastern Shore; but descriptions have been included from the articles that were located during the course of the research.

The Riots
Little or no effort was made to research the identified riots in any detail. The Onancock riots have been researched by Brooks Miles Barnes and the reference has been included.

Case Descriptions
Naturally, not all the information about each case identified in this book could be included. The space for the descriptions of cases was limited. The selection of what to include was limited to descriptions which illustrate violence or the threat of it. There are many cases for which no other information was located.

Missing cases
A number of cases were identified during the course of the research project but were not included because there was no reported evidence of mob violence. Also, no doubt cases were overlooked whether or not they were reported in newspapers. So this compilation cannot be considered definitive for the inclusion of all cases.

Legal executions
Not all legal executions are identified in this book. Generally the only legal hangings included were about cases for which newspaper accounts identified evidence of actual, threatened, or rumored mob violence.

Other Notable Cases
Some cases may not have fit the criteria of mob violence but nonetheless are powerful stories about which researchers may wish to further investigate. The definition of mob law may not or may not apply to some of these cases. These cases have been included at the end.

Chapter 2. Examining Our Personal History

After years of looking at the concepts of hate and racism, I have not been able to come to terms with their meanings or to fully understand them.

Perhaps the closest we can come to understanding their meanings is to examine not the history of strangers, but to take a closer look at what racism has meant in our lives and in those of our families. Sometimes that takes a hard look, a step that we're not willing to take. I'm not sure if even I can. But perhaps if we can try and look at racism as it has manifested itself throughout our family history, and try to do so by suspending our temptations to judge, defend, condemn, or justify the actions of our ancestors, then maybe we can begin to look at how history has impacted our own personal histories and outlooks on life.

Years ago I sat in on a training class for people working as mediators for conflict resolution, and they were specifically addressing race and racism in that particular session. One of the most interesting exercises had people pairing off, with each student telling the other their earliest recollection of race or racism affecting them. I was just watching as a bystander, but naturally I began thinking back on my early years.

My first recollection was of grade school. A neighborhood friend, also in my class, was at my home asking me to review her short essay for class the next day. I cannot recall the nature of the assignment, but in her essay, she relayed a comment made by her mother, expressing an obvious hatred of "niggers." I remember that I froze with shock at seeing the word. I must have heard the word before and knew its meaning for this to shock me, but it was never used in our household, and I was never told not to use it. I somehow just knew it was wrong and that it was a term of hate. I remember being so frozen that I could not comment.

I do have vague recollections of the segregated movie theaters in Salisbury. I recall once as a young child meandering throughout one of the theaters and noticing stairs to the balcony. I remember going up to see what was up there, only to find a sea of dark faces throughout the balcony lobby. I quickly exited but recalled that they seemed to be having so much more fun up there than those on the lower level.

A few years later, as a young teenager, my mother took me to the hospital. My mother had for years hired a black woman to clean her home every few weeks, because my mother worked at two jobs. Lola was the woman's name. Well, Lola was sick and was in the hospital. She had phoned my mother with a few requests, and I accompanied my mother to the hospital. Until then I did not know that hospitals were segregated; I didn't even know what that meant until I saw Lola in a huge ward of only black people. "Why did Lola have to be in this huge room? Why was everyone in it the same color? And why didn't she have her own room," I wondered. This also became a favorite, funny memory because I watched as my mother pulled out a brown paper bag from her large purse, open some bottle within the bag, insert a straw and help Lola drink whatever was hidden in that bag. My mother said it was beer and that Lola had asked for it. I remember thinking, "Mother!!" My mother was also a nurse, so it shocked me that she should be secretly serving beer to a friend in the hospital! But it is also a fond memory because it showed my mother's compassion. She did not care whether or not it was wrong, she did it because Lola asked and she knew it would be a small thing to ease the woman's pain and circumstances.

Throughout the work with this book, my thoughts go to my father, who passed away in February of 2013.

One of his most often-told stories to me (one that got more frequently told as his memory got worse later in life) has been on my mind since he passed and while compiling this book. It was a short story, but I long ago groaned at having so often heard it. The story was simple enough. As a band and music instructor throughout Wicomico County, Maryland, for a time he had a routine. After school let out, he would go to some bar for a beer. He particularly liked it when it was crab season, for he would enjoy his favorite seafood.

But one particular time, as he sat at the bar, he noticed a black man enter the bar and order sandwiches to go. It was a time when no black person was permitted to eat in for a meal or take a drink. So this man was doing what most did, what they could only do, follow the rules. He ordered his sandwiches or meal to go. But then the man was barked at by the server or owner and rudely told to wait outside. My father had watched this, something so ordinary and everyday. I do not know if this was the first time my father saw this everyday slice of life, but this time, it sickened him, so much so that he left and repeated his recollections throughout the rest of his life.

He was no stranger to segregation. My father was born in Chestertown, Maryland, into a relatively poor Irish family and without a father. For a time he lived downtown in a house right next to the jail. And he would tell me that even though he was there as a child, he did remember hearing

Chapter 2. Examining Our Personal History

"discussions" held out back of that jail, of whites deciding just what to do with certain black people. He would not specify those discussions. My father had an uncle or some relative who was a reporter for a Baltimore newspaper, a man my father described as mean and fiercely racist. So there may well have been some history of mob vengeance in my family, I do not know.

Figure 1 Sheriff house and jail, Chestertown, Maryland

Old Chestertown Sheriff house and jail located on Cross Street next to the historic courthouse. Maryland Historical Trust Online Inventory of Historical Properties.

Soon my father moved with his family to across the river, but he would spend every available moment exploring historic Chestertown. It became his escape from a troubling childhood, escaping back over the bridge, exploring the historic buildings and getting to know the people.

He did not leave Chestertown until World War II broke out and he was able to join the Navy band and travel the world. In Chestertown and at school at Church Hill he developed his love of music. And from the beginning he was the music organizer, participating in jazz and swing bands, combos, the Fire Department community band. As a teenager and young adult he looked like a young Bing Crosby.

Mob Law on Delmarva

At that time and place, even the musicians were segregated. All the bands or combos he played in had only white musicians. It was the way things were. But in all things music, my father was color blind. Musicianship trumped race, or anything else for that matter. All my life my father was quick to comment that some musician was particularly excellent.

He was also a born organizer. So when the jazz band he performed with in Chestertown suddenly had a drummer drop out in an emergency, he was called to action to find one. This he continued to do for the rest of his life, always working to line up musicians for this gig or that. And at that early age, this was no different. They needed a drummer and it was his job to find one. He got the best available drummer he knew. But the drummer was black. My father managed to arrange it somehow. I cannot remember where the group was to play, but it was in some building downtown, possibly a commercial building of some sort.

"He was a good drummer," would be all my father would say. The occasion had no significance to my father at the time, but it certainly did to the black residents in town. When they were practicing and performing, curious black residents congregated outside of the building and peered into the windows in the hope of seeing this wondrous new thing, one of their own playing drums in a white jazz band.

There was a lot I didn't see growing up in Salisbury. The blinders, the shyness, limited curiosity, and my white world made it so that I saw and understood little. And even though the 1931 lynching of Matthew Williams in Salisbury was written about, I never even knew about it until a friend described what he knew about it to me. He did so just as I was preparing to move from the area during my college years. I still remember it. I still remember most of what he said and his manner of saying it. So if my friend sees this book, he will roll his eyes and chuckle at the strangeness of me still thinking about it, after all those years.

My purpose for including these stories is my hope that we all examine our own histories and ourselves more, to understand our own context in the world in which we and our families have lived. Keep re-examining the stories, because there just may be something new learned, even after hearing it a million times.

Chapter 3. Howard Purnell Tells a Story

Howard Purnell didn't intend to do it, but back in the early 1990s he told the story of his witnessing a lynching. He never expected to tell the story to a virtual stranger, but he did, to me.

In researching her 2007 book, *On the Court House Lawn*, Sherrilyn Ifill met Howard. According to Sherrilyn, unlike his friends and co-workers who witnessed the 1931 lynching of Matthew Williams in Salisbury, Maryland, he took his memories of the lynching to his grave. Well, it turns out that it was not so. And it wasn't until I read the account in her book that I realized just how privileged I was to have heard his story. Mr. Purnell did indeed talk about it, a few years before he met Sherrilyn, and I have never forgotten it.

Howard never intended to talk about it; I am fairly convinced of that. So when the words came out of him, it's as if I had bumped into him, jarring him, so that the words mistakenly fell out beyond his control. We were both stunned and surprised.

I had not long known Mr. Purnell. He had started attending a few meetings held back in the early 1990s at the home of Elaine Brown of Salisbury, where a group of us history buffs assembled to discuss the history of the old black neighborhoods of the town. I had wanted to learn about these neighborhoods and Elaine was gracious to introduce me to people she strong-armed to participate. There were only a few meetings but they became forums of people interested in talking about their memories. Nearly every one of those assembled have since passed, including Howard.

Howard was particularly enthusiastic, along with his friend, the late Robert Hudson. The two of them visited a woman who had lived in the old Salisbury neighborhood known as Georgetown. They interviewed her and reported back. They drew up a map identifying who had lived where in the Georgetown neighborhood, and they returned to share what they had learned. He and the late James Jolley were so inspired by some information I shared about the old Houston Cemetery in Salisbury, that they secured funds to restore and protect it. In fact, I stood on the sidelines of the dedication day, watching as Howard read from a speech he had written based on that history. I watched as he held back tears for his love of this history, speaking to the crowd gathered for the ceremony. I had to turn away afterwards because I began to cry, having seen Howard's show of emotion as well as his effort to honor history. For a soft-spoken man, he spoke well. I did manage to walk up to him and asked if I could have his written speech. I still have it.

But at the time of his admission I had only known Howard a short time. At those meetings I purposely did not mention the Williams lynching even though it occurred during the time period we were discussing. I had only started to know these people, so I made it my rule to discuss the difficult topics only if they brought them up. In the beginning, they seldom did. Though I had two thick notebooks of old newspaper clippings of the lynching and other related history, I did not discuss them.

But that night, following one of our meetings, I broke my rule.

I simply could not resist. I knew he had been a young adult at the time of the 1931 lynching of Matthew Williams and that Howard had been working at the Wicomico Hotel, located directly across the street from the courthouse grounds and the tree where the hanging occurred. The meeting was over, and everyone had left except for Howard and James Jolley. Elaine was in the kitchen cleaning up. I was seated and the two rose to leave, heading toward the door, when I asked. "Mr. Purnell. I have a question for you...." They both stopped, and Howard looked at me. "Where were you on the night of December 4, 1931?"

He stared at my face for a few seconds, then said, "What do you mean, the lynching?" I must have nodded yes, but he just looked, then suddenly said, "I was there! I saw it!" Another few seconds passed, then, "And you know what really sticks in my craw, it was my mother's birthday!"

I think my mouth dropped. At some point soon after, they both sat down, with Howard next to me on the sofa, James on the chair opposite us. And Howard began his description. Watching him was just as amazing as the story itself. It was if he was possessed in the telling of it. The words simply fell out, as if he could not prevent it. And I had the feeling he had never told this story before, at least not to a stranger. At the end of this description, all three of us just sat there, transfixed, with Howard looking straight ahead, as if looking at some distant world. It was then that Howard heard a sound and looked down. The tape recorder I had had with me for our meeting was still running; I had never turned it off and had forgotten about it. But the look on his face was one of raw emotion, of sudden fear. It was this look of fear that struck me, for the emotion on his face looked just as it might have looked nearly sixty years before, when it all had happened.

Chapter 3. Howard Purnell Tells a Story

Sherrilyn didn't have it quite right, as it turns out. Howard was not working the night of the lynching. He had switched hours with someone so that he could have the evening off to catch a movie. Working at the Wicomico Hotel was a good job, somewhat. Howard once explained to me that the staff had to work seven days a week. He and a few of the others got together, crunched the numbers, and convinced management that they could hire one other person so that the staff could get one day off a week, without any additional expense.

But on this night, Howard got to go see a movie, on Main Street, right down the street from the hotel and the courthouse. I do not know how much he knew before going to the theater, but inside word began to circulate about what was going on outside. People began leaving the theater, African Americans leaving their seats in the segregated balcony section of the theater, racing for the relative safety of their homes.

For most leaving the theater, safety meant walking towards the west side, across the bridge to the neighborhoods on that side of town. But not so for Howard. He lived in the Georgetown neighborhood, in his parents' home on Cathell Street, very near Main Street. Today, Cathell Street is gone. The location of his home is just north of the intersection of Main Street and Salisbury Boulevard (Route 13). Ordinarily, walking home meant leaving the theater and walking east, past the courthouse and hotel, to the street's intersection with Cathell, turning left, and entering his home. But on this evening that meant walking into the mob congregated at the intersection of Main and Division Streets, mostly on the Main Street side nearest the hotel.

On this night, he walked to that corner and saw his classmate, Matthew Williams, being strung up on a tree. Howard had to encounter the mob but made a quick left turn at the intersection to rush north along Division Street, then right on Church Street and down to Cathell and his home. As he passed the courthouse he heard members of the mob string up Williams several times. I cannot imagine what it must have been like, and what might have happened if he had been nabbed in his rush past the mob to get home. But when he did get home, he found his father looking out of a second story window, watching the mob from this vantage, his rifle near him, just in case any of the mob decided to head to their neighborhood.

After Matthew Williams was hung on the courthouse lawn, his body was dragged a couple of blocks to a vacant lot adjacent to the Georgetown neighborhood and set afire. From the vantage of the Purnell's second story window mob members could be seen dashing into a nearby garage, obtaining gallons of gasoline, and returning to burn the body in full view of many of the residents.

Figure 2 Site of burning of Matthew Williams, Salisbury, Maryland

Photograph taken the day after the lynching, at the site where Matthew Williams' body was burned. Baltimore News American Collection, Special Collections, University of Maryland.

He gave a few more details, of his friend Stanley Pinkett seeing Williams being kicked as he was taken from the hospital to the hanging and of stories of what happened later to families of some of the mob members. But the discussion did not last long, it ran its course. I asked few questions, for I was transfixed absorbing this stunning story.

I visited Howard a few more times, but I never again asked about the lynching. I am not sure why I didn't. Maybe I didn't want to again induce that look of fear or cause more pain. Not pressing was my payment for the great gift that was his story. But I asked Howard if he was interested in seeing the newspaper clippings about the lynching and other violence of the time. He was interested in them so I gladly let him borrow them. He later told me that his brother had come for a visit, from Philadelphia. And the two poured over the newspaper clippings and reminisced literally all night long. I miss my visits with Howard, of sharing time in his living room and listening to a few more of his memories. But the memories he related in Elaine Brown's living room are the ones I cannot forget.
(See page 242 for more detail about the lynching of Matthew Williams.)

Chapter 4. Crime and Punishment

Although the subject of this book is mob law, I would be remiss if I did not describe the different forms of executions or punishment of a time when legal protections were at best minimal and at worst non-existent for African Americans.

Most of the specific cases identified in this book were for capital offenses of the time. Perhaps it was mostly those which stirred the mob violence, or perhaps the nature of the crimes which achieved enough notoriety to be reported in newspapers.

The criminal assault of white women, was the most prevalent of the cases reported here. There were alleged murders and other offenses, but the specter of rape inhabited the newspapers. The offense required the least amount of evidence, making it the easiest among the scapegoat accusations. But even in the cases of alleged murder, it didn't take much more than pointing a finger of accusation to kill an African American. Some authorities might have focused their interrogations of prisoners as to the nature of sexual assault on women, but it might have been only to determine if the convicted got life imprisonment or execution, or perhaps to have evidence enough to justify execution, even if interrogations were coerced or falsified.

Of the cases of sexual assault and murder, there were a few acquittals, not many. And of the sexual assault cases, a few of the convicted got life imprisonment. It seems that of the life sentences imposed, most were not before a juried court.

Some of the sentences of execution were commuted, with considerable backlash. Convicted prisoners pardoned by governors were secreted away, sometimes under the cloak of darkness, to the safety of faraway penitentiaries in an effort to avoid lynching. The issues of guilt or innocence are not delved into here. In the case of lynchings, guilt or innocence means little in the face of lawless violence. And for some capital offense cases, evidence of innocence or of considerable doubt meant nothing.

Some legal hangings were accompanied by large numbers of spectators. Some authorities feared disruption at legal hangings and undertook measures that limited the number of spectators or arranged for private executions. In 1923, the State of Maryland changed the practice by requiring all executions to be held in the state penitentiary in Baltimore.

A Legal Execution

Murder, legal or otherwise, could be one of spectacle and ritual. Prisoners condemned to capital punishment spent their last days in a ritual almost like theater, the details of which newspapers would report to readers eager for the description. The reporters described the prisoners' visitors, last meals, how they spent their time, and interviews provided. All detail of the scene surrounding each execution was described.

An example of this is that of the November 1915 execution of the white man previously mentioned, Frank Grano, always identified in the press as "the Italian." *The Baltimore Sun* describes the spectacle near Snow Hill, Maryland.

> With between 3,000 and 3,500 men, women and children crowding around the gallows, Frank Grano, the Italian, was hanged here at 9.30 o'clock this morning...
>
> The crowd, which assembled from this, Somerset and Wicomico counties, Md., Accomac and Northhampton counties, Va., and Sussex county, Del., was an orderly one and seemed bent only upon getting in the best possible position to see the triple murderer pay for the penalty for his crimes.
>
> The crowd began arriving in town long before daylight in automobiles, horse drawn vehicles, on horse back and on foot. Several hundred machines were parked around the woods in which the execution took place. Every vantage point was occupied by onlookers and the trees in the neighborhood of the gallows were loaded down with the morbidly curious.
>
> The scaffold was erected in a strip of woods on the almshouse farm about three miles from this town. Influenced by the demands of many residents of this county that the hanging be private Sheriff Bishop had first intended to have the gallows enclosed by a high board fence and to admit only the legal witnesses. The certainty, however, that the fence would be torn down by the mob was done on a former occasion, led the County Commissioners to authorize a public execution.
>
> Grano was taken from the jail at 8.45 o'clock. He was accompanied to the gallows by the Sheriff Bishop, Deputy Sheriff Richardson, the special guard, Herman J. Lewis and a number of special deputies. The Rev. George M. Garlarneau, of the Protestant Episcopal Church, who had been Grano's spiritual adviser, also accompanied him on his march from the jail and ascended the scaffold with him....[3]

---

[3] *The Baltimore Sun*, "3,500 See Grano Hanged, Mob Crowds Around Gallows Erected In Woods Near Snow Hill, Trees Filled With Onlookers," Nov. 27, 1915

Chapter 4. Crime and Punishment

The same article reports that amid the traffic hurrying to the hanging, an accident occurred at Queponco, when a son of farmer Ernest Laws "was caught between an automobile and a motorcycle and his skull fractured."

However, this manner of execution was not the first choice, for Grano had narrowly escaped lynching as well. The *Marylander and Herald* reports that "the Italian" was "chased by a mob through several Eastern Shore counties, from Snow Hill to Salisbury, thence to Cambridge, from which place he was brought at night to Baltimore for safe keeping in the City Jail."[4]

---

[4] *Marylander and Herald*, Princess Anne, MD, "The Lynching Spirit," Sep. 14, 1915

Mob Law on Delmarva

The Pillory

His head and arms locked in the pillory
His soul in the pillory
the pillory, the pillory
He got sixty minutes
in the Wilmington pillory
as another got whipped
beneath his feet

Not the stocks of the colonies, not the era of dirt and dark
But the fall of 1903, in the century of motion and light

As they secured him in the pillory
His soul in the pillory
the pillory, the pillory
he knew at the end
       of one long hour
he would face the feared
Red Hannah

He hung his head slumped in the pillory
His soul in the pillory
the pillory, the pillory
Looking down at the faces in the yard
Spectators' eyes on the whipping post
the whipping post, the whipping post
       one lash, a yelp, then another
       cries and blood from the lashes
       over and over and over

At the end of the hour
he descended the wooden ladder
and hugged the pole
hands in an iron brace

He took thirty lashes at the whipping post
the whipping post
the whipping post
Thirty lashes at the whipping post
How many minutes
do thirty lashes
take?

                                            Linda Duyer 2013

Chapter 4. Crime and Punishment

The Pillory & the Whipping Post

Some might be surprised to learn that one form of legalized punishment commonly remembered as a familiar part of colonial history existed on the Eastern Shore into the twentieth century – Delaware's use of the pillory and the whipping post. Delaware was one of the last states to abolish the practice.

Figure 3 Pillory and whipping post, Delaware

Photograph (c. 1900) from Delaware Archives Online, showing a two-story pillory and whipping post located behind the New Castle County Courthouse.

The Delaware Archives provides the following description.

> The whipping post and pillory have a long history in Delaware. Whipping was first sanctioned as a form of punishment in 1717. By the 1840s,

> there was some opposition to its use and many thought reforms were needed. The Legislature did revise the code and in 1852 there was a provision that no more than sixty lashes or more than one hour in the pillory would be executed for all sentences combined. The code also stated that whippings were to be well laid on the bare back and in public with the post and pillory near the jail of each county. The pillory was abolished in 1905, but the whipping post was law until 1972. The post was last used as a form of punishment in 1952. (Delaware State Archives, Enforcing the Law 2010)

As described by author Yohuru Williams, "The use of the whipping post against Black defendants was so common that African Americans appropriately christened the device Red Hannah" (2001, 8). The use of the pillory and the whipping post were applied regardless of color although blacks were disproportionately punished.

Maryland restricted the punishment of whipping in 1882 by changing its code so that only the offense of wife-beating was punishable by whipping and was administered as late as the 1940s. (Delaware State Archives, An Ancient Punishment -- The Whipping Post Last Used in Cecil in 1940 2008) According to the Delaware Archives online. (2011),

> There were three whipping posts: one in each county. The Kent County whipping post was located at the east side of the Old State House on the Dover Green, and was relocated to the Morris Correctional Facility in the 1930's. The one in New Castle was located at the New Castle County Jail then moved to the New Castle County Workhouse. And the one in Sussex County was in Georgetown at the Jail.

The Baltimore Sun, in a 1903 article provided the following.

> Wilmington, Del., Sept. 26 – The most severe whippings ever known in Delaware since the whipping post was re-established were meted out to offenders at the New Castle County Workhouse this morning, when the lash was administered to 15 culprits for various crimes by Warden Meserve. Those whipped and their sentences were:
>
> Frank Ward, 10 lashes, 15 months' imprisonment.
> Thomas Campbell, 10 lashes, 15 months.
> Theodore Walcott (colored), 10 lashes, 6 months.
> Edwards Filkins, 10 lashes, 15 months.
> George Clayton (colored), 10 lashes, 6 months
> James Hunter (colored), 10 lashes, 1 month.
> Thomas Mullin, 40 lashes, 6 years.
> Henry Pitts (colored), 30 lashes, 1 hour in pillory, 10 years.
> Alfred Spencer, 40 lashes, 1 hour in pillory, 6 years.
> Charles Wallace, 10 lashes, 1 month.
> William Darsey (colored), 10 lashes, 1 hour in the pillory.
> George Compton, 10 lashes
> Percy Coleman (colored), 10 lashes, 15 months.

Chapter 4. Crime and Punishment

> Alfred Turner (colored), 20 lashes, 11 months.
>
> Between 300 and 400 persons saw the whippings. The crowd was so great that it was necessary to close the gates, and several times Warden Meserve, who applied the lash, had to request order. About a dozen women were in the crowd.[5]

In the above account, Henry Pitts was sentenced to 10 years in jail, 30 lashes and one-hour pillory for assaulting a white woman. Pitts was arrested during the turbulent time in the months following the June 23, 1903 lynching of George White who was burned at the stake. In an article with the heading "Another Negro In Danger," *The Baltimore Sun* describes the arrest and arraignment of Pitts.

> Wilmington, Delaware: Aug. 5 -- Henry Pitts, a negro about 27 years old, had a hearing before the Magistrate Hollis this morning on the charge of attempting assault upon Mrs. Ella Ruth, wife of Theodore Ruth, a farmer of Brandywine Hundred. He was held in $2,000 bail for the Court of General Sessions and immediately thereafter was taken to the county workhouse to prevent the culmination of what appeared like a demonstration against him.
>
> Mrs. Ruth testified that the negro, who was a farmhand on the place, took advantage of the absence of her husband, who passed the night in the barn, and went to her room between 1 and 2 o'clock this morning. She said she fought him off after a severe struggle, and that the negro returned to his own room and slept there until he was arrested by a policeman about 5 o'clock this morning. Pitts denies the charge against him.[6]

In the newspaper report of his punishment, Henry Pitts "took his punishment harder than any of the others. He tried to climb the post and wrenched his hands free from the iron braces and had to be put back." Pitts commenced his prison sentence. There is evidence Pitts may have died in jail a few years later of tuberculosis.[7]

---

[5] *The Baltimore Sun*, "14 Culprits Whipped, Severe Punishment At Post And Pillory In Delaware, Big Crowd Sees Blood Flow, Two Highway Robbers Get 40, 'Well Laid On'— Others Given 10 Licks – Some Cringe And Grovel," Sep. 27, 1903
[6] *The Baltimore Sun*, "Another Negro in Danger," Aug. 6, 1903
[7] Ancestry.com, Delaware Death Records, 1811-1933, identifies an African American male, Henry Pitts, age about 1879, located at the New Castle County Workhouse, died of tuberculosis on November 2, 1906.

The Almshouses

Almshouses, in addition to being government-operated residence facilities for the elderly, poor and the so-called insane, were sometimes the sites of executions and burials.

The county almshouse became the site of executions as well as an area potter's farm. Located outside of Princess Anne, the almshouse comprised historic property known today as Waterloo. The structure is an amazing piece of architecture for one used as an almshouse. The property was first known as *Carey's Purchase*, patented in 1666, and later known as *Waggaman's Purchase* for Henry Waggaman who bought the 1,000-acre plantation property and constructed the historic home that by the 1860s became known as "Waterloo." In 1864, Waterloo was purchased by the Trustees of the Poor of Somerset County to be used as the county almshouse, and referred to as the Almshouse Farm. The county owned and operated the building as an almshouse until the property was sold in 1948.[8]

The pre-Revolutionary War plantation house built circa 1750 remains as an impressive piece of architecture, a two-story Georgian period brick house with Flemish bond walls, serving for a time in the shadow of legal executions and burials at unmarked gravesites. The main structure was used for the superintendent and the white patients, "with a wooden building for the colored insane and paupers."[9]

Figure 4 Waterloo Almshouse Farm, Somerset County, Maryland

Photo taken in 2013 by author.

---

[8] *National Register of Historic Places Inventory – Nomination Form, Waterloo, Somerset County, Maryland*, Item 8, page 5, prepared by Paul Touart, Architectural Historian, 1985
[9] *Report, Maryland Lunacy Commission*, Baltimore: The Sun Book and Job Printing Office, 1899, page 33, available online at Google Books

Chapter 4. Crime and Punishment

The 1878 execution of Hiram Fooks, aged about 35, is an example of such executions at the almshouse. Fooks had been tried and convicted of murdering a black male, Jack Tyler. Executions could draw a crowd. Fooks was delivered to the almshouse grounds by carriage.

> The carriage arrived on the grounds, where 2,000 people had assembled at twenty minutes past 12 o'clock. When the prisoner, sheriff, deputies and preachers had taken their places on the scaffold, the Rev. Nathan Young sang, in loud, clear tones, the hymn beginning, "Show pity, Lord, O Lord, forgive." The prisoner and the crowd congregated around the gallows joined in the singing."

After the singing, Fooks made a speech professing his innocence and implicating another. Following his speech, he was hanged.

> He was taken down at 1.21, placed in a stained pine coffin, with shavings for a pillow, and buried in the almshouse lot.[10]

The Maryland State Lunacy Commission in 1908 began photographic documentation of almshouses. The descriptions and photographs are available for view online.[11]

Figure 5 Almshouse, wooden structure Somerset County, Maryland
Maryland State Archives, available online

---

[10] *The Baltimore Sun*, Baltimore, MD, "The Scaffold, Hanging of Hiram Fooks, in Somerset County, Md.," Jul. 13, 1878
[11] *Preliminary Report: Exhibits portion*, The Maryland State Lunacy Commission, Oct. 6, 1908, available online

Mob Law on Delmarva

Almshouse Farm at Waterloo was the site of other Somerset County executions and burials. Today there is a cemetery with markers at the site but are of early white ancestors who occupied Waterloo; there are no visible markers or indication of the location of the unmarked graves.

It is not clear if all almshouse properties were used for executions or burials, and likely not. Below are samples of other Maryland Eastern Shore almshouses from the 1908 report.

Figure 6 Almshouse, Worcester County, Maryland

The Worcester County almshouse consisted of two buildings, from the 1908 preliminary report of the Maryland State Lunacy Commission, the wooden structure used to house male and female African Americans. Maryland State Archives, available online.

Figure 7 Almshouse, Kent County, Maryland

Maryland State Archives, available online.

Chapter 4. Crime and Punishment

Last Hanging at Old Elkton Jail

Sometimes an innocent man gets executed or narrowly so. The last hanging at the Old Elkton Jail in Cecil County, Maryland, was that of John Simpers, a white man, executed for the 1904 killing of prominent Cecil County lawyer Albert Constable, Sr. But for circumstances, the last hanging may have been of two black men, John Holland and William Hopps, who lived near the site of the murder.

Figure 8 Execution of John M. Simpers, Elkton, Maryland

The 1905 execution of John M. Simpers in Elkton, Maryland. Courtesy Historical Society of Cecil County.

Constable was reportedly shot, robbed, and left for dead during a robbery on August 18, 1904 on a public road on the top of Grays Hill early in the evening. Even the earliest located account, the August 19th edition of *The Baltimore Sun* reported that, "Mr. Constable was unconscious when found by John Holland, colored, who hastened to town and spread the report.

Mob Law on Delmarva

Upon the arrival of Drs. John H. Jamar and H. Arthur Mitchell, Mr. Constable regained consciousness and told of the shooting."[12]

There were other suspects, but nonetheless, attention narrowed on Holland and he went on trial in January of 1905. Had Constable died without describing his assailant, chances are that Holland would have been found guilty, even though early on he was shown to come to Constable's assistance.

It was reported later that Holland had been approached at his home by a white man who had said a sick man down the road needed attention.[13] When doctors arrived, Constable regained consciousness and told of being robbed and shot at three times, two of the bullets striking him. And he was robbed of his gold watch. In a few days he died from his wounds. Both the board of county commissioners and Maryland Governor Warfield offered rewards for the arrest of the then unknown assailant.

There was a flurry of activity trying to locate the culprit. George Kirwin Linton (sometimes reported as spelled Litton) was arrested in Wicomico County on August 30th because he had tried to dispose of a gold watch a few days after arriving at White Haven on a steamer and hiring himself out for farm work. In Wilmington, Delaware, Walter Wilson, also white, was held for questioning; the man was already arrested for drunkenness.

At the same time, a black suspect, Frank Mitchell, was arrested in Easton, Maryland, under suspicion for the crime against Constable. According to *The Baltimore Sun*, "the arrest was made through information received from Edward Douglass, of Preston, who about 8 o'clock called to Sheriff Gannon by telephone and advised him to be on the lookout for a suspicious-looking colored man who had boarded the 9:15 A.M. westboard train of the Baltimore, Chesapeake and Atlantic Railway at Preston, heavily armed with pistols and cartridges." Reportedly, when authorities searched the train and the suspect escaped but a man was later apprehended. But it was suspected that the man was not Constable's killer but one of several prisoners who had recently escaped from the jail in Georgetown, Delaware.[14]

---

[12] *The Baltimore Sun*, "Robbed and Shot," Aug. 19, 1904
[13] *The Baltimore Sun*, "State of Maryland, John Holland And Wm. Hopps, Colored, Presented, Murder of Mr. Constable, Both To Be Indicted Today—Trial Will Take Place After Christmas, May Have New Evidence," Dec. 16, 1904
[14] *The Baltimore Sun*, "An Arrest in Easton: A Mulatto Suspect Who May Be A Jailbreaker," Aug. 31, 1904

Chapter 4. Crime and Punishment

Litton was cleared and released due to multiple alibis of his story. There were other unsuccessful leads to the whereabouts of the gold watch.

Word surfaced at the end of September of two black suspects, John Holland and William Hopps, reportedly from a man who had overheard a conversation about the crime.[15] Both Holland and Hopps were held for questioning. In October, John Simpers, white, was reportedly under suspicion for the crime; he had been arrested and jailed in Elkton, charged with stealing horses in Cecil County. He reportedly confessed to being in Cecil County and stealing horses but denied being at the site of the Constable crime.[16]

During the trial of John Holland in early January, the doctor who had treated the dying man testified, as reported in *The Baltimore Sun* of January 10, 1904.

> Dr. H. Arthur Mitchell, who attended Mr. Constable after he was shot, stated that during the night of the assassination Mr. Constable at his home said:
>
> "Art, I can't see why I could not say what color the man was. He was a white man, for I had a little chat with him."
>
> The witness then said to Mr. Constable: "You don't mean to say he talked with you?"
>
> "Yes," answered Mr. Constable; "he said he wanted my money. I then said:
>
> "'You are not going to let me die here alone?' and then asked him to go and tell the colored people on the hill to come down to me. He said he would."[17]

On January 11, John Holland was found not guilty for the murder. The next day, William Hopps, who had been indicted along with John Holland, was declared not guilty.[18]

The mystery of the murder would continue. By the end of the month, suspicion was placed on a white man, John M. Simpers, alias, Simmons, 22, a former resident of Elkton who had recently been sentenced to eight years for horse stealing. Officers covering the crime had located two black women who had identified the white man near the scene of the crime.

---

[15] *The Baltimore Sun*, "Evidence in Constable Murder Case," Sept. 24, 1904
[16] *The Baltimore Sun*, "Constable Murder, A Young White Man in Jail Under Suspicion," Oct. 20, 1904
[17] *The Baltimore Sun*, "Mr. Constable's Murder," Jan. 10, 1905
[18] *The Baltimore Sun*, "'Not Guilty' of Murder, Verdict of the court in the case of John Holland at Elkton," Jan. 12, 1905, and "Hopps Declared Not Guilty," Jan. 13, 1905

Mob Law on Delmarva

Circumstances and a tip from a prison official led to further suspicion of Simpers. Further witnessed accounts put Simpers at the site of the crime. After investigation, indictment and conviction, Simpers was found guilty and sentenced to die. Simpers was executed by hanging in the jail yard in Elkton on October 20, 1905.[19]

Not wanting to die alone, Constable specifically asked for help from black residents he knew lived near by. He identified his assailant as white, yet the ones who came to his aid were jailed for several months before being tried even in the face of Constable's own testimony.

---

[19] *The Baltimore Sun*, "Meets Fate Bravely, Simpers Goes To The Gallows With Smiling Face," Oct. 21, 1905

Chapter 4. Crime and Punishment

The Spectacle of Lynching

As Philip Dray notes, "The term *lynching* has always been somewhat ambiguous." The number of perpetrators involved in the killing varied among the definitions, ranging from two or more and up to five or more (2003, viii). Researchers have referred to the "spectacle" lynchings involving large crowds and events widely recorded in the newspapers. As the term morphed into something almost synonymous with the illegal killing of African Americans, it seems that there was some spectacle in every sort of lynching.

The lynching definition may or may not be applicable to the unidentified man, found murdered following the December 4, 1931 large-scale lynching of Matthew Williams in Salisbury. How many were involved in the killing is unknown. But a carload of white males were known to have inquired the next day as to if the man had been located, possibly indicating two people may have been involved. Perhaps gloating or the sharing of the story was part of the spectacle nature of such a killing. Ritualistic tendencies may have proved a part of all lynchings.

Philip Drey describes the large spectacle lynching

> ...a kind of ritualized affair that could take almost an entire day to enact in which a suspect was seized, brought to a large place that had been chosen for the fact that it afforded as many views as was possible, lumber had been piled up, excursion trains might have been run from the nearest big city, so that city folk could come out, wagons could be pulled up, food could be sold. Basically it would become like a daylong picnic. And these could involve as many as ten or fifteen thousand spectators centered around this core of activists who were actually carrying out the lynching.

> They often occurred close to the site of the murder. It was believed to be important to carry out the execution near where the original crime had taken place. This wasn't always possible for one reason or another....

Drey further describes the rituals of allowing family members of the victim of the original crime to be allowed to exact vengeance, pressuring the lynching victim for a confession, then the lynching itself, followed by the collection of souvenirs (In the Dead Fire's Ashes, The Lynching A Town Forgot 2004). Souvenirs could take the form of body parts, pieces of ash or trees, or postcards commemorating the events.

Mob Law on Delmarva

Most lynchings were hangings, but lynchings could be killing by gunfire, or by beatings. Others were killings by burning. For many of the lynched African American victims, the rituals included added components to the spectacle-mutilation and overkill. It was not enough to kill, many of the bodies were hung many times, then burned, and the burnings could last for hours.

The Delmarva lynchings identified for the period of 1870–1950 are as listed.

> John Jones, Cecil County, Maryland, 1872
>
> Magruder Fletcher, Accomack County, Virginia, 1889
>
> Asbury Green, Queen Anne's County, Maryland, 1891
>
> James Taylor, Kent County, Maryland, 1892
>
> Isaac Kemp, Somerset County, Maryland, 1894
>
> William Andrews, Somerset County, Maryland, 1897
>
> Garfield King, Wicomico County, Maryland, 1898
>
> George White, New Castle County, Delaware, 1903
>
> James Reed, Somerset County, Maryland, 1907
>
> Unidentified Man, Queen Anne's County, late 1920s
>
> Matthew Williams, Wicomico County, Maryland, 1931
>
> George Armwood, Somerset County, Maryland, 1933

Earlier lynchings were not specifically researched but three were identified during the course of the project and include the following.

> Jacob Hamilton, Smyrna, Delaware, 1861
>
> John Holden, Pungoteague, Virginia, 1866
>
> William "Obie" Evans, Leipsic, Delaware, 1867

Most of the above were killed by hanging, with the exception of Isaac Kemp, George White, the unidentified victim found after the lynching of Matthew Williams, and possibly James Reed. Isaac Kemp was shot to death in his jail cell, his body riddled with bullets. George White was killed by being burned at the stake. The unidentified victim mentioned above was killed from beatings. James Reed was hanged but not until after his skull was reportedly crushed. He may have been dead by the time his body was hanged.

Chapter 4. Crime and Punishment

Magruder Fletcher was mutilated then killed by hanging. He was shot multiple times after being hanged. James Taylor was hanged but there were reports that following the hanging, some in the crowd implored that the body not be shot. Garfield King was hanged outside of the jail, his body riddled with bullets. Gunfire was fired into George White's burned body.

James Reed's body was later dug up from his grave and set on fire. Following the hangings, the bodies of Matthew Williams and George Armwood were dragged to other locations and set on fire. In the case of Matthew Williams, a considerable amount of gasoline was procured for the burning. The body of George Armwood was left on the pyre for at least three hours.

Two victims, Jacob Hamilton and William Andrews, were grabbed from authorities as they left the courthouse where they were tried, and lynched from trees.

Some of the victims were beaten and/or mutilated before being killed. And for some, there was mutilation following the killing, some described, some not described. There were reports of souvenirs taken. An ear was sliced off of George Armwood. A foot was hacked off of George White, and his body struck by spectators.

Writes Dennis Downey, "When the deputy coroner arrived late that afternoon to collect White's corpse for an official inquest, he found few recognizable body parts" (2013, 242).

> The newspapers reported a prominent Wilmington physician had retrieved White's skull and right foot, and set them on display in the window of a Market Street saloon. Another man was seen placing a piece of backbone in his pant pocket as he raced to the waiting trolley. According to the *Evening Journal*, every automobile returning to Wilmington brought back some kind of keepsake....

After hangings, usually the rope was measured off and pieces were cut and distributed. Pieces of wood from the hanging trees would be kept as souvenirs, as were ashes and body parts from the aftermath of pyres.

Some of the lynchings were expected well in advance, enabling people to arrive from long distances. Extra train cars would be pressed into service for the purpose. These cases evoked ritualistic, arguably festive gatherings. In the case of George Armwood, his existence in the county jail was known since he was brought back from Baltimore in the early hours before sunrise. Crowds congregated on street corners, in front of businesses, and near the jail. An out-of-towner was told of the upcoming lynching and came into town to witness what was going on. The lynching did not occur until after sundown.

The lynchings seldom occurred as isolated forms of violence. There would be secondary murders, such as the victim found following the Williams' lynching. Some of the reported episodes of violence or riots described in this book followed not long after the spectacle lynchings.

A sample of the oil-soaked rope used by the lynchers.

Figure 9 Piece of the rope used to hang Matthew Williams
December 12, 1931, *Baltimore Afro-American.*

The near-lynchings seemed to have ritualistic qualities as well. There would be the use of large-scale, organized posses. African Americans were arrested and rushed successfully to safekeeping with mobs fast on the heels of the authorities, demanding inspections of jail cells, and traveling long distances. And in one case described in this book, a mob failing to find the arrested suspect at a jail grabbed two women and attempted to take them to a place to be lynched.

Spectacle and ritual might be considered a part of most legal killings. Executions require an audience. Condemned prisoners are provided meals, spiritual advisors, and a chance to speak. There may well be

Chapter 4. Crime and Punishment

lynchings not identified here, perhaps smaller, little-known or unknown killings that never reached the grandeur of full spectacle lynchings, with details of the illegal murder of human beings.

Some writers have described "good" lynchings as ones where the victim was alive when hung. The issue of whether or not the prisoner was alive or dead by the time of the hanging might fuel speculation, for a dead man hanged was a "bad" lynching. Watching the prisoner suffer was part of the ceremony. Confessions could be rituals. Prisoners were encouraged to confess, whether or not they'd previously offered a forced confession.

What follows is a different kind of souvenir as described by *Baltimore Afro-American* reporter Ralph Matthews.

Matthews covered the story of the 1931 lynching of Matthew Williams in Salisbury, Maryland, as well as the 1933 lynching of George Armwood in nearby Princess Anne. It is not clear if he covered other violence like these; it could be that the Williams' lynching was his first.

Williams was killed in the style of many lynchings. He was dragged to the site where he was hung, on the courthouse grounds, a common location, a symbol of community sanctioning. His body was taken down and dragged to a spot where gallons of gasoline was secured and used to burn the body in full view of one of the black neighborhoods.

The next day another black man was killed, a fact not printed in white-owned newspapers but reported by the *Baltimore Afro-American*. To this day the identification of this second victim was not publicly determined; his name is given as unknown on his death certificate and he was buried in the Salisbury Potter's Field. His body was horrifically beaten and delivered to the local black undertaker. It was believed that a carload of white men had participated in the killing. The *Baltimore Afro-American* described the wounds of both Williams and the unidentified man, and Ralph Matthews, Sr. was likely the reporter who wrote the accounts because he indeed saw the bodies. The news accounts did not identify Matthews in the bylines, but he had a different column, one that he contributed weekly to the newspaper on a wide range of topics, usually social events.

The December 12, 1931 issue was filled with the reporting of the December 4th lynching. But after Ralph Matthews finished his contributions to the news stories, it was time for him to sit down to do his column which typically did not relate to the issue's news. But this time, he could not shake the trauma of what he had witnessed and just finished reporting, nor the bitterness. All of what he wrote weighed heavily on his mind. Back to the usual ordinary world. His column began,

"Watching the Big Parade" with the subtitle:

"The Show Must Go On"

> Often after a newspaper fellow has rushed off suddenly to investigate a lynching or the like, such as happened on the Eastern Shore Friday night, column writing is indeed a problem.
>
> The question one naturally asks is, shall I attempt to write an article under the stress and strain or shall I merely leave a large gaping white space with the advice, "See next week's paper"?

The column then meanders through the absurdity of whether to devote the price of the ink to the endeavor, what money might be saved if he didn't bother with his column. He adds to the column about hunger marchers passing through Baltimore en route to Washington, D.C., describing the "parade" of people as Christmas neared. Attempting to make sense of life and his seemingly incongruous remarks, he approached the end of his column. He wrote,

> This isn't a very good column, although I presume it is about as good as the average.
>
> Even as I write, I am twiddling a leaf that I lifted from the charred remains of one Matthew Williams who was hanged and burned in Salisbury, Maryland. Before me lies a bit of garment that I snatched from the unidentified man whose mutilated body was found not far from the lynching scene.
>
> My observations on these tragedies are elsewhere in the paper, but this column must be filled. I must think up jokes, with these gruesome spectacles floating before my eyes — the show must go on.[20]

Souvenirs serve a purpose. They have meaning, they provide proof. And when witnessing the disfigured bodies of acts of brutality difficult to understand, souvenirs can prove that what was experienced was real and not imagined – proof of the unimaginable. So Ralph Matthews' column, forlorn and extraordinary, prompts readers to imagine the African American reporter sitting at his desk, fiddling with that leaf and piece of cloth, trying to make sense of the loss of two lives.

---

[20] *Baltimore Afro-American*, Baltimore, MD, "Watching the Big Parade, The Show Must Go On," Ralph Matthews, Dec. 12, 1931

Chapter 5. The Dangers of Excursions

An excursion is a journey for pleasure, an outing away from home, a pleasure unlike any at home, a one-day vacation. Excursions involved travel – an experience with different dangers and outlooks for African Americans during this time period. And for many during the period of segregation and exclusion, the destinations of those traveling excursions were ocean resorts.

At an Atlantic City, New Jersey excursion of 1892, "scenes were enacted there during the afternoon and until late in the evening as are seen but once a year in Atlantic City….The grounds around the Excursion House resembled nothing so much as an old-time camp meeting scene" and that before returning home, "the travelers indulged in dancing and competitive cakewalk contests well into the night (Alnutt 2005, 73)." Often, travel was along excursion trains.

Not all excursions were to seashore resorts. The July 9, 1892 edition of the white-owned newspaper, The *Salisbury Advertiser*, mentions a train excursion to Salisbury.

> About 200 colored people from Cambridge came to Salisbury last Tuesday on an excursion over the B. & E. S. railroad for a day of pleasure and recreation. They were met by our colored citizens and escorted to their park on Lake Humphreys where they indulged in innocent pastime during the day. They were accompanied by a colored cornet band. In the afternoon they witnessed a game of baseball by our amateurs. They marched through the streets led by their band followed by a crowd; all very orderly.[21]

Travel on excursion trains could be reminders of segregation that permeated lives. A Salisbury, Maryland resident described her experience taking the train from Salisbury to Ocean City, Maryland. When the train stopped at stations along the way, the blinds of their car were lowered. White people on the platform waiting to board the train were not to be troubled with the sight of black people traveling on their train, even if they occupied a separate car.

No doubt the excursions to the seashore resorts were most memorable, for those who got to go. A woman from Somerset County described not being permitted by her mother to go with friends to Ocean City during those special excursion days. She long resented the memory of being denied as a young person an experience shared by her friends. She would

---

[21] *Salisbury Advertiser*, Salisbury, MD, Jul. 9, 1892

come to understand her mother's feelings against being "permitted" to enjoy a resort only on certain days yet be restricted from using it all other days of the year. The young daughter only knew the confusion and pain of a day at the seashore with her friends.

One might reflect on the train's literal and figurative place in history, particularly for African Americans. Trains were used as a means of long-distance transportation for most people. But sometimes trains were commissioned for other purposes. Historian Brooks Miles Barnes, in his book on the near-lynching of William Lee describes how the train was boarded by "thirty to forty armed civilians" traveling from Somerset County, Maryland, to Northampton County, Virginia, to retrieve their presumed prisoner (1906, 13). In other instances, trains were pressed into service for the express purpose of delivering people to locations where a lynching was expected. In other cases, train stations would be sought out and searched in anticipation that authorities who were moving their prisoners to other locations for safekeeping might use this form of transportation. Authorities were known to avoid the railroad stations, knowing mobs would be waiting. Blacks could be harassed or attacked at railroad stations simply for being at the wrong place at the wrong time.

At the seaside resorts at the end of the line of these railroad excursions, anything could happen. In 1908, violence erupted at the seaside resort of Rehoboth in Delaware, among white soldiers and excursionists. The resort was crowded with excursionists and National Guard soldiers. But a minor incident erupted into widespread violence, ending the day for the July 31st excursionists. Only one newspaper account was located about the Rehoboth violence, but the reports were horrific. Whatever the actual circumstances, one white soldier's skull was reported as crushed during what was described as a fight, presumably from a thrown brick. A black waiter was described as "badly bruised and injured internally." An aged man hid to avoid a threatened lynching, and a man was beaten and thrown from the pier. (*See page 92 for more detail about the 1908 violence in Rehoboth.*)

Chapter 6. A Townscape: Princess Anne

Figure 10 Princess Anne, Maryland, circa 1930s

From *The Great Depression*, Program 6, "To be somebody," PBS television, 1993.

Princess Anne, Maryland, like a number of Eastern Shore communities, is steeped in history. The town is one of many throughout the region where life occurred in the few square blocks where little has changed. You can walk the town's center today and see a town that looks much as it did over a hundred years ago. And today, while walking or riding through the streets of Princess Anne, that sense of history might make one wonder what the place and people looked like during certain moments in time. For those still living and having a past with the town, memories might include Princess Anne Days activities, perhaps parades, New Year's Eve celebrations, and touring cyclists passing through the town. Some may recall the rioting during the 1960s. But for the years before that time how did the town's people interact and how did they feel during some of the most disturbing periods of their history?

This chapter puts some of the violence identified in this book in its community context. Any community of the Eastern Shore could have been selected to do this. Princess Anne was selected, however, because of my knowledge of the area and the historical information acquired during research projects conducted over the years. This is an exercise in viewing a community's violent past from a chronological perspective. Singling out Princess Anne does not mean it experienced any more or less racial violence than other towns.

I am of the firm belief that the people of Princess Anne can face all of its history -- confront it, present it, and through this process become a stronger community for it. In fact, I know the community has begun that process in positive ways that other communities have not; I know this because I have witnessed it. Every community has some aspect of their history that can be difficult to face. Communities which take the steps to face it should be applauded.

Olde Princess Anne

Founded in 1733 as Princess Anne Town from 25 acres of the Beckford Plantation and named for the daughter of King George II, Princess Anne's central position, at the head of the Manokin River and as a crossroads of transportation, made it a natural market center with its designation as the seat of Somerset County, a county which at that time covered a far larger expanse of the lower Maryland Eastern Shore.

The Presbyterians had a meetinghouse at Manokin as early as 1680, the first reportedly about thirty feet in length. By 1764, the meetinghouse was found to be too much in decay and too small and a second building was planned and the order went out "to build a new one of brick, 50 by 40, in the clear, 16 feet from the water table to the plate, to be covered with cypress shingles, to have a gallery at each end for Negroes, with such windows, doors, pews and other matters, as shall be convenient." In 1872-73, for a period of fifteen months, the church underwent extensive repairs and major changes. "The galleries, which at one period in the history of the congregation were essentially for the servants of the families worshipping here," were removed. There must have been a gallery for slaves before these, as in 1747, the congregation paid for some repairs to the meetinghouse and for the erection of a gallery "for Negroes to sit in." (Ford 1910)

Beckford originated from the 500-acre patent issued in June of 1664. The precise date of the Beckford structure is uncertain, with estimates ranging from the late 1700s to the early 1800s. The Beckford plantation and Teackle mansion likely figured prominently in the lives of local African Americans. And as a center of commerce, so too was Princess Anne to be a center for the commerce of human trafficking, of the enslaved.

St. Andrews Episcopal Church also served as a focal point in the area's history. The Somerset Parish is one of thirty parishes established in Maryland in 1692. The original parish church was built near the Almodington plantation near the community of Champ; the remnants of the structure lies beneath the waters of the Manokin River. The second church, All Saints Church, was built at the "Old Monie" site at Venton, a structure destroyed by a storm and replaced in 1868. St. Andrew's, built in Princess Anne in 1770 was erected as a "chapel of ease" for All Saints Church but over the years because the center for the parish. According to church history of the Metropolitan Methodist Episcopal Church, slaves had worshiped in the balcony of St. Andrews until the black community organized their own church.

Chapter 6. A Townscape: Princess Anne

Like most of the Eastern Shore, Princess Anne's history is steeped in slavery and freedman history. The town was in the business of owning slaves, using slaves, and the sale of slaves. It is strange to know of a town so old but to not know much about its enslaved people, other than the images of enslaved women helping out in meal preparations at Teackle Mansion, an image portrayed throughout the town's history, in its reenactments and even its modern day walking tour brochure.

We can only imagine what pre-Civil War Princess Anne must have looked like and wonder who later lived on "Low Alley" close to Teackle Mansion. Where there were county seats, courthouses, jails and slave auction sites, there were slave dealers who came to town to stay in the local hotels or taverns or perhaps stay with a known local resident. Within a few short blocks were all of those. What must have the town looked like as the enslaved, freedmen, and later the freed African Americans went about their business of working in a town steeped in history?

Metropolitan United Methodist Church has a physical relationship to slave history. The church's history began with the formation of a separate church in 1842. A frame building was erected on the farm of Georgia Jones in that year and was named John Wesley Methodist Episcopal Church, located west of the town. The congregation grew and in June of 1884, land was purchased from Thomas Dixon, the site of the old county jail and slave auction block. The cornerstone for today's structure was laid on September 30, 1886, the church named Metropolitan Methodist Episcopal Church.

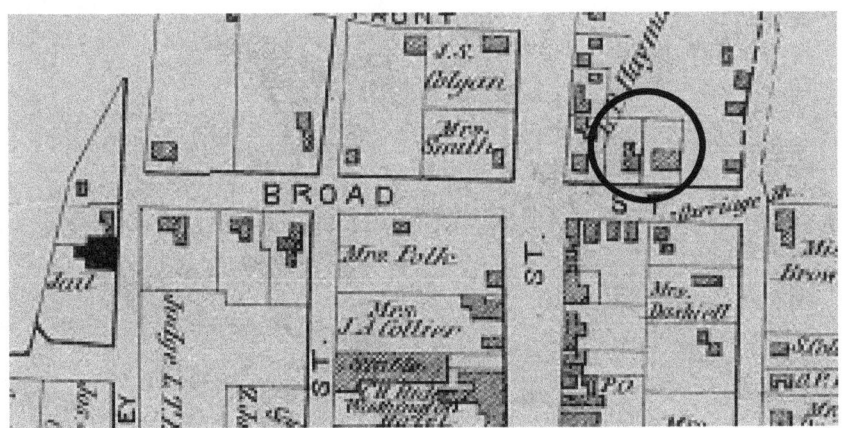

Figure 11 The 1877 Maryland Atlas of Princess Anne

The 1877 atlas shows the new jail and the site of Metropolitan Church before it was construction, the site of the old jail and slave auction block

Mob Law on Delmarva

The "new" jail was built in 1857 at the other end of Broad Street and was known as the "*Grey Eagle*" for its distinctive gray color of its stone façade. The 1877 Atlas shows the new jail and the properties in the vicinity of the land purchased in 1884 for Metropolitan Church. Could the structures shown had been the abandoned old jail and slave auction block?

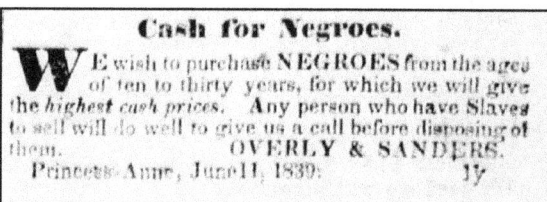

Figure 12 Newspaper ad of 1839, "Cash for Negroes," Princess Anne

Ad from the *Somerset Herald* of Princess Anne, Maryland, November, 19, 1939

The *Somerset Herald* same newspaper edition listed sheriff sales, including,

> By virtue of a writ of Venditioni Exponas, issued out of Somerset county Court at the suit of Jonathan Riggin against Elijah Robertson, and to me directed, I have heretofore seized and taken in execution the following property to wit: -- One Negro Man named Israel, two Horses, ten Cattle, and a Tract of Land called "Robertsons Delight," containing 150 acres more or less, the goods and chattels, lands and tenements of the said Elijah, which I shall proceed to sell at the Court House door in the Town of Princess Anne on Friday the 29th November instant, at the hour of 2 o'clock, P. M., to the highest and best bidder for cash to satisfy the above mentioned writ and cost. John S. Crockett, Sheriff, November 5, 1839.[22]

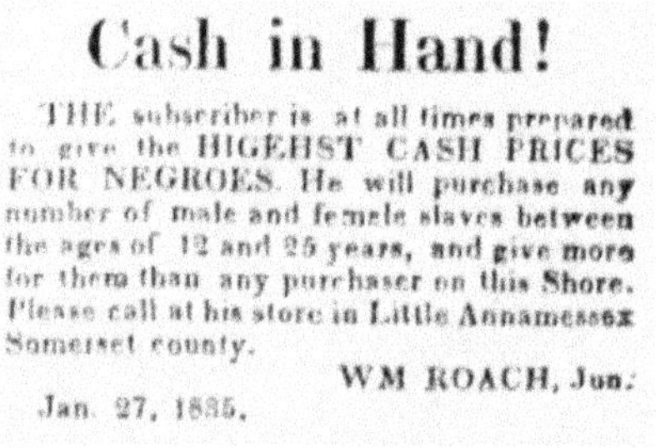

Figure 13 Cash for slaves advertisement, 1839

Advertisement from *The Village Herald*, Princess Anne, Maryland.[23]

---

[22] *Somerset Herald*, Princess Anne, MD, Nov. 12, 1839
[23] *The Village Herald*, Princess Anne, MD, Oct. 20, 1835

Chapter 6. A Townscape: Princess Anne

Four at the Gallows
On March 5, 1869, when William Wilson (later identified as Denby), William Wells (later identified as Linsey Wells), Frank Rounds, and George Bailey (later identified as Bryan) were executed by hanging before a reported crowd of four or five thousand. All were watermen working on the schooner, the *Brave*. They had been accused of the murder of the ship captain. (*See page 114 for more detail about this case.*)

James Stevens Execution
On February 25, 1887, a crowd of about 300 assembled at the jail yard to witness the execution of James Stevens, an African American convicted for the assault of an elderly woman. (*See page 139 for more detail.*)

Henry Taylor and Arthur Courtney Executions
Six years later, in December of 1893, another crowd assembled around the jail yard to witness two African Americans, Arthur Courtney and Henry Taylor from Virginia, executed for the crime of murdering a Deal Island boat captain. This crowd was reportedly much larger, with the crowded scaffold enclosure filled to capacity, forcing others to watch from rooftops or trees. (*See page 199 for more detail.*)

Isaac Kemp Lynched
The jail was the site of a lynching a year later, when on June 9, 1894, this time a mob killing of Isaac Kemp, arrested for the crime of murdering Constable Edward Carver. Kemp was in his cell when a mob reportedly of 75 men arrived at the jail, some of whom entered his cell where Kemp was riddled with an estimated 50 bullets from multiple weapons. (*See page 160 for more detail.*)

William Andrews Lynched
Three years later to the day, on June 9, 1897, the courthouse was the site of a crowd as William Andrews, arrested for assault of a white woman, was mobbed and lynched as he was being transported from the court. The crowd outside of the courthouse had been warned to act peaceably but when officials escorted the prisoner out the private entrance of the courthouse, the "maddened throng" rushed to grab Andrews and began hitting him. A deputy, reportedly in an attempt to separate Williams from the mob, seized Andrews and tried to drag him across a small ravine separating the courthouse yard from Church Street but was unsuccessful.

Mob Law on Delmarva

One of the mob members cut Andrews with a razor and he left a trail of blood along the path the mob members took to drag Andrews to be stung at a walnut tree. The body was taken by undertaker William H. Smith and was buried at the almshouse located several miles outside of town.
(*See page 166 for more detail.*)

William Lee

In 1906 Princess Anne became the scene of a near-lynching, when a crowd assembled for a trial which some expected might end with the lynching of William Lee. On June 20, 1906, crowds assembled at the Somerset County courthouse on Prince William Street for Lee's trial.

Lee, who had been arrested in Cape Charles, Virginia, as he fled south by hopping a train following an alleged crime in Somerset County, was taken first to Norfolk, Virginia. But Judge Page of Somerset County feared Lee would be lynched if arraigned and tried in Princess Anne. He knew firsthand the real danger of this after the 1897 lynching of William Andrews outside of the old courthouse located at the same spot of today's courthouse shown in this postcard. Wrote Brooks Miles Barnes in his 2006 book *Gallows on the Marsh*,

> Before light on the appointed day, white men began to assemble in Princess Anne. They came on foot and on horseback, by bicycle and by carriage. The trains brought men from the Maryland counties of Somerset, Worcester, and Wicomico and from Delaware and Virginia. By mid-morning a crowd of at least 2,500 had gathered before the two-and-a-half story, red-brick courthouse at the corner of Main and Prince William streets. ....
>
> When at 10.00 a.m. the bailiff unlocked the doors, 500 men rushed into the courtroom and as many more replaced them in the corridor. They jostled each other, invaded the space reserved for the members of the bar, and hoisted themselves onto windowsills. Those standing in the rear shouted, "Get down in front; we want to see, too!"

But the crowd was disappointed, as Lee never appeared. The hearing convened the jury, but the trial would be held in Baltimore. Barnes wrote the following.

> The spectators passed out of the courthouse and gathered in knots and clusters on the green and street corners. They were bitterly disappointed. They had expected Lee to have been present in court and they had expected to have lynched him. The men had come, wrote a reporter, "prepared to do business."

Judge Page anticipated trouble, and another prisoner, Edward Watson (sometimes referred to as Edward Carver), who had been arrested for a

Chapter 6. A Townscape: Princess Anne

crime and who narrowly avoided a lynching in Pocomoke and held in Princess Anne, was removed the day before the Lee arraignment and taken to the Salisbury jail for safekeeping. Barnes also wrote,

> Throughout the day Princess Anne's black citizens remained out of sight. Some of the hotel's guests went without dinner when the black waiters failed to appear. The only person, black or white, who seemed to enjoy himself was the town photographer who took numerous views of the scenes around the courthouse.

The photograph below is of a postcard believed to show the assembling crowd at the courthouse on June 20, 1906. Etched into the image are the words "Looking for the negro, Princess Anne, Md."

Figure 14 Postcard "Looking for the negro, Princess Anne, Md."

Postcard believed to be of the crowd assembled for the June 20, 1906 trial of William Lee. The words "Looking for the negro, Princess Anne, Md." are etched in this postcard which was not signed or mailed. Postcard courtesy of historian Mike Dixon.

So it seems the photographer had anticipated printing lynching postcards but instead had to settle for "Looking for the negro" postcards. I wonder if the photographer even knew the name of the young man who was given due process thanks to Judge Page (due process as dismal as it was for African Americans at that time), or if the photographer simply did not care to print it.

(See page 183 for more detail about this case.)

Mob Law on Delmarva

Wesley Miles Execution

Wesley Miles was executed in December of 1912, not in Princess Anne, but a few miles outside of the town, in a grove of trees near the county almshouse.

On June 2, 1912, Miles was quietly and secretly arrested and placed in jail. Officials anticipated attempts at lynching the prisoner and hurriedly placed Miles into a car to town. Miles was being escorted by Sheriff Tull, presumably to Salisbury. Throngs of men arrived in Salisbury in the hopes of grabbing the prisoner. People reportedly traveled by car and by train for this adventure. The plan was to place Miles in the Salisbury jail, but after a stop for gasoline in Fruitland, Sheriff Tull learned of mobs in Salisbury, mobs large enough to attempt to block all entrances to the town. Sheriff Tull drove around Salisbury and into Delaware hoping to use the train to deliver the prisoner to Baltimore, but that plan was dropped when he learned that crowds were awaiting in Delaware and still others traveling to other locations in search of the prisoner. Eventually the Sheriff and prisoner made it to the Baltimore jail. Miles was tried in Baltimore. Following his conviction he was returned to Princess Anne for the execution. *(See page 202 for more detail about the case.)*

A Parade of Draftees

On the afternoon of Tuesday, October 30, 1917, local African American draftees were honored in Princess Anne, Maryland, as a send-off for their service in World War I. After the men were checked in at the local examining board in the county courthouse, the group was turned over to Crisfield draftee-in-charge Gordon Byrd, who accompanied them on a parade conducted by community members in their honor. From the courthouse the men were paraded through town, from the entrance of the courthouse at Prince William Street, along Church Street and Washington Avenue, and down Main Street to Broad Street, a sort of loop that took them through most of the small downtown and past businesses such as stores, the movie theater and the Washington Hotel. The fanfare included two bands - the Princess Anne Silver Cornet Band and the Princess Anne Academy Band - and a throng of teachers, students, Civil War veterans, and community members assembled to honor them.[24]

---

[24] *Marylander and Herald*, "Colored Men Go To Camp Meade, Draftees Receive A Royal Send-Off By Members of Their Race," Nov. 6, 1917

Chapter 6. A Townscape: Princess Anne

Reports of how many Somerset County inductees were in attendance differ, with *The Marylander and Herald* of Princess Anne indicating there were 35, and *The Crisfield Times* indicating there were 54 men.[25]

The attending draftees were treated to dinner provided by members of the Red Cross under the leadership of Mrs. Hattie Nutter White. Following the dinner, the inductees were honored at Metropolitan Methodist Episcopal Church in a celebratory service led by master of ceremonies Princess Anne Academy Principal Thomas Henry Kiah. The choir sang "Faith of our Fathers," and a prayer was led by Rev. McDowell of Cottage Grove. The program also included a welcoming addresses by Rev. J. H. Nutter and Gordon Byrd; a solo of "Good by, Good Luck, God Bless You," by Mrs. Celeste Hayman; a duet called, "The Rosary" by Mrs. Mary Kiah and Alice Carrol; "Mary Go Toll the Bells" by the school male quartet; a patriotic song by the Academy students, and a rousing rendition of "The Star Spangled Banner" by the congregation. William L. Gale presented "The Military History of the Negro." Three Civil War veterans – John L. Dennis, Littleton Waters and C. W. Marshall – offered speeches.

Early Wednesday morning the honored men were served breakfast after which they reported to the courthouse for their orders. From there they marched to the train station where a crowd saw them off on their trip to Camp Meade. *The Crisfield Times* reported that the Somerset County inductees were joining others from the region including 38 men from Salisbury, 72 from Snow Hill, 68 from Easton and Cambridge and other areas of the Eastern Shore.

The courthouse was relatively new, only 13 years old, having been built on Prince Williams Street in 1904, replacing the earlier courthouse which had existed for over 70 years. Metropolitan Church is reputed to have been built on land purchased in 1884 from Thomas Dixon which was the site of the early local jail (1744-1831) and a slave auction block. The significance of three Civil War veterans giving speeches of encouragement and support from the site of a slave auction may or may not have had an impact on the crowd at the time.

---

[25] *The Crisfield Times*, "Colored Men Called to Colors Tuesday, Fifty-Four Men From Somerset County Respond," Nov. 3, 1917

Mob Law on Delmarva

Figure 15 *Newspaper ad for the movie The Birth of a Nation.*
Newspaper ad from *The Crisfield Times*, September 15, 1917.

Today looking back, the mind's image of a celebratory African American crowd parading their loved ones from the steps of the courthouse grounds contrasts sharply with more disturbing glimpses of history in Somerset County. Days earlier, the much anticipated movie *"Birth of a Nation"* arrived in nearby Crisfield, on September 20th at the Lyric Theater. The epic 1915 silent film by director D. W. Griffith based on the novel and play *The Clansman* both by Thomas Dixon, Jr. was known for its controversial portrayal of the Ku Klux Klan as a heroic organization, its depictions, and the Klan's aggression towards African Americans.

And nearly six years later, the same courthouse in Princess Anne would be the site of a different scene, far more disturbing than the celebratory fanfare of draftees on the streets of town, for the streets would be the site of spectators listening to the Ku Klu Klan.

George Chelton
George Chelton was executed in June of 1923, the first person executed under the new laws requiring executions to be held in Baltimore; there would be no more legal executions held in Somerset County. In January of 1923, George Chelton, accused of assault of a white girl, was removed to the Baltimore jail. But the proceedings leading to his execution still involved crowds in Princess Anne. The scene would once again involve the courthouse in April when Chelton would be tried, convicted and sentenced in the courthouse courtroom. (*See page 221 for expanded detail about the Chelton case.*)

Chapter 6. A Townscape: Princess Anne

Ku Klux Klan Event at the Courthouse

In the spring of 1923, a representative of the Ku Klux Klan from Georgia, Dr. J. H. Hawkins, was visiting various parts of the Eastern Shore, speaking to large groups and encouraging the creation of new chapters and enrollments to the national organization, as part of the second wave of growth and activity of the Klan.

On a Sunday afternoon on March 18, 1923, Hawkins spoke in Princess Anne, a week after speaking in Crisfield to a large, enthusiastic crowd. *The Crisfield Times* reported on the story of when the Klan came to town:

> Three thousand residents of Somerset County filled the court house green and the street in front of the court house in Princess Anne last Sunday afternoon, and were thrilled for more than two hours by Dr. J. H. Hawkins of Atlanta, Ga., who delivered a forceful lecture on the Ku Klux Klan and Americanism. Citizens from all parts of the county were in the large throng which cheered the speaker at different points in his discourse.
>
> The meeting had been advertised to be held in the Auditorium, which has a seating capacity of about 500. Long before the time appointed for the lecture, it became apparent that the Auditorium would not hold but a small portion of the crowd, and it was therefore decided to hold an open-air meeting. Many prominent citizens were on the court house plaza with the visitor, who was introduced by Rev. W. F. Dawson, pastor of Antioch M. E. church of Princess Anne.
>
> Taking 'Americanism' as his subject, Dr. Hawkins made a strong plea for the supremacy of American ideals and principles; and gave a detailed explanation of the origin of the Ku Klux Klan, the things for which it stood and the activities of the organization. He made a profound impression upon his large audience and his lecture struck a responsive chord in the minds of his hearers.
>
> At the close of the lecture application blanks for membership in the Klan were distributed, and it is understood that several hundred applications were signed and mailed in to the Baltimore office the following day.
>
> This is Dr. Hawkins' second appearance on the platform in Somerset, he having addressed a mammoth gathering in Crisfield a few weeks ago, which resulted in the organization of a large Klan in this city.[26]

The Crisfield Times reported the Princess Anne event. No editions of the 1923 Princess Anne newspaper, *The Marylander and Herald*, could be located to view for a local description of the event.

---

[26] *The Crisfield Times*, "Big Klan Meeting at Princess Anne, Three Thousand Countians Hear National Speaker, Dr. Hawkins' Address Thrills Big Audience," Mar. 24, 1923

Mob Law on Delmarva

Harry Merrill

Princess Anne and vicinity were a hub of activity when on Saturday, December 13, 1924, Deputy Sheriff Louis L. Dryden was found dead and policeman Orrie J. Carey wounded about five miles from Princess Anne. Soon after, Harry Merrill was being hunted for the crimes.

Following the death of Dryden, Merrill was identified as having entering a swamp two miles wide and nearly six miles in length. Assistant Fire Chief Raymond M. Carey sounded the fire alarm in town at the fire house, on Prince William Street, where State's Attorney Harry C. Dashiell appealed to the assembled to help search for Merrill. As described in *The Marylander and Herald*, hundreds of men responded, and along the roads surrounding this swamp could be seen "marching armed guards." The State's Attorney was busy ordering the procurement of trained bloodhounds that were reportedly delivered from Norfolk, Virginia by late Saturday night and utilized throughout Sunday. As the newspaper reported, "In the meantime the State's Attorney's office was a bee hive of activity, it being the headquarters of the different posses of citizens being formed and sent in many different directions searching and running down every report that came in." People were dispatched to areas in Delaware to watch houses of some of Merrill's friends. All forms of transportation were to be searched. By four o'clock Monday morning, exhausted and cold searchers returned to town. However, Merrill's whereabouts were located and after negotiations, Merrill was squired away to Salisbury and then on to Baltimore, avoiding a lynching.

On Tuesday December 16th in Princess Anne, the funeral procession for Dryden led to Antioch Methodist Episcopal Church. *The Marylander and Herald* reported that returning members of the two-day manhunt for Merrill "stood in silent tribute" to Dryden.

But Princess Anne would be denied the chance to try Merrill there. Instead, the trial was held in Cambridge, Maryland, on February 25, 1925. Merrill was found guilty of murder in the first degree before the full bench of the Judicial Circuit and sentenced to life imprisonment. Merrill was released to Somerset County Sheriff Luther Daugherty who transported the prisoner from Cambridge to Baltimore to begin his sentence.
(*See page 228 for more detail about this case.*)

Chapter 6. A Townscape: Princess Anne

George Armwood Lynching

In October of 1933 George Armwood was lynched in the streets of Princess Anne. The lynching and its aftermath would gain significant notoriety nationwide. Armwood was taken from the jail by a mob, dragged through the few blocks of downtown and into a residential area and hanged. His body was dragged back into the downtown area to Main and Prince William streets and set on fire. Armwood's body was left in the smoldering pyre for about three hours when finally a truck came by to take the body away. Reportedly, the black undertaker, when contacted to remove the body, refused, saying that it was the town's responsibility.

There were reports of mutilation and of the crowd singing and dancing at the burn site. After the body was burned, mob members measured out the rope used to lynch Armwood, cutting it into equal pieces for souvenirs. Weeks later, five suspects were arrested and transported to Baltimore. Within hours they were returned to Princess Anne. At a hearing, they were released, to the cheering of crowds assembled at the courthouse. (*See page 249 for more detail about this case.*)

Figure 16 Crowd in Princess Anne following release of suspects

Crowd outside of the Somerset County Courthouse awaiting the release of the four men arrested for the lynching of George Armwood; the suspects had been jailed in Baltimore and returned for the court hearing in Princess Anne. Baltimore News American Collection, Special Collections, University of Maryland.

Mob Law on Delmarva

Sam Jones Tried and Acquitted
On New Year's Eve, little over two months after the Armwood lynching, a woman was found murdered at her home and Sam Jones was arrested for the crime. In February of 1934, Jones was acquitted of the charge. In the courtroom, *The Baltimore Sun* reports, "there was only a slight rustle among the spectators in the courtroom as the decision was announced." (*See page 255 for more detail about this case.*)

Chapter 7. The Ku Klux Klan

It was not the intent of this book to research the local Ku Klux Klan, but their activity appears in some of the newspapers located while researching the 1923 cases. There was a bit of surprise – not a surprise that there were members of the Ku Klux Klan on the Eastern Shore, but a surprise at the descriptions in the local newspapers. It seemed necessary to include this 1923 activity as identified, but I did not review the newspapers for all other KKK activity.

The KKK on the Eastern Shore in 1923

The Crisfield Times reported on other areas of the region with its "Eastern Shore News in Brief" section and with regular feature articles. The following is a review of the paper's 1923 editions pertaining to activities of Ku Klux Klan.

February 1923 KKK activity -- Delaware

The February 17th edition of *The Crisfield Times* reports,

> According to reports, circulated freely on the streets of Seaford and Blades the Ku Klux Klan has begun active work to clean up the morals of the two towns. It is whispered that the Klan has forwarded notification to several residents that unless certain things which are said to be at the present time going on be stopped, those concerned will be removed so far apart that communication with each other will be practically impossible. These reports, coming as they do, upon the information that one of the high officials of the Klan will visit Seaford in the near future to give a public talk on the work of the organization, has caused much stir in the two towns.[27]

The March 3rd edition (Saturday) of *The Crisfield Times*,

> Merchants in Accomack and Northampton counties, on the Eastern Shore of Virginia, are said to be joining the Ku Klux Klan. There's a reason. Should a colored debtor not pay accounts when due, after being asked to come across, he is told that a man in white hood and robe will call in the night of the first change of the moon. He pays.[28]

The same issue reports on a Ku Klux Klan speaker at a meeting held in Crisfield.

> Declaring that the Ku Klux Klan was founded and operating on the principles of One hundred per cent Americanism, the supremacy of the white race, the separation of church and state, and the protection of

---

[27] *The Crisfield Times*, "Eastern Shore News in Brief," Feb. 17, 1923
[28] *The Crisfield Times*, "Eastern Shore News in Brief," Mar. 3, 1923

> American womanhood, Dr. J.H. Hawkins of Atlanta, Ga., a national lecturer of the Klan, spoke to a record-breaking crowd in Crisfield last Sunday afternoon [February 27].
>
> The meeting was originally advertised to be held in the lodge room of the Ward building, but the gathering soon reached such large proportions that long before the hour appointed it became apparent that the lodge room would not accommodate even a small part of the crowd. The Lyric theatre was then secured, and the audience crowded the auditorium, filling the aisles, the stage, all standing room in the rear of the building, the street entrance and the sidewalks in front of the building. It was undoubtedly the largest crowd that ever assembled at a public meeting in Crisfield, its numbers being estimated as between 2000 and 2500 persons. Many women were in the audience and gave enthusiastic attention to the speaker.
>
> Dr. Hawkins, who is a lecturer of national note, was accompanied on the platform by Rev. J. L. Johnson, pastor of Immanuel M. E. church, and Rev. Chas. M. Elderdice, pastor of Mt. Pleasant M. P. Church. Rev. Elderdice introduced the speaker to the Crisfield audience.
>
> A gifted orator, master of his subject, and with an audience in a receptive mood for an explanation of the Klan doctrines, Dr. Hawkins delivered one of the most effective lectures ever heard in Crisfield. ...
>
> The applause of the audience shook the building time and again as the lecturer made a telling point, and at the close of the lecture several hundred persons who desired to become members of the Klan asked for membership blanks and stated their intention to enroll. It is understood that the application blanks have been filled out and mailed to the Klan headquarters in Baltimore for acceptance, and that Crisfield will have a Klan of several hundred members as a result.[29]

March 1923 KKK activity – Maryland and Virginia

The March 3rd issue of *The Crisfield Times* reports,

> Merchants in Accomack and Northampton counties, on the Eastern Shore of Virginia, are said to be joining the Ku Klux Klan. There's a reason. Should a colored debtor not pay accounts when due, after being asked to come across, he is told that a man in white hood and robe will call in the night of the first change of the moon. He pays.[30]

Hawkins spoke again, in Princess Anne, as reported by March 24th edition of *The Crisfield Times*.

> Three thousand residents of Somerset County filled the court house green and the street in front of the court house in Princess Anne last Sunday afternoon, and were thrilled for more than two hours by Dr. J. H. Hawkins of Atlanta, Ga., who delivered a forceful lecture on the Ku Klux

---

[29] *The Crisfield Times*, "K.K.K. Representative Speaks to Big Audience at Meeting in Crisfield," Mar. 3, 1923
[30] *The Crisfield Times*, Crisfield, MD, "Eastern Shore News in Brief," Mar. 3, 1923

Chapter 7. The Ku Klux Klan

Klan and Americanism. Citizens from all parts of the county were in the large throng which cheered the speaker at different points in his discourse. [March 18]

The meeting had been advertised to be held in the Auditorium, which has a seating capacity of about 500. Long before the time appointed for the lecture, it became apparent that the Auditorium would not hold but a small portion of the crowd, and it was therefore decided to hold an open-air meeting. Many prominent citizens were on the court house plaza with the visitor, who was introduced by Rev. W. F. Dawson, pastor of Antioch M. E. Church of Princess Anne. .....

This is Dr. Hawkins' second appearance on the platform in Somerset, he having addressed a mammoth gathering in Crisfield a few weeks ago, which resulted in the organization of a large Klan in this city.[31]

April 1923 KKK activity -- Maryland

The April 9th edition of *The Daily Banner* reports local activity in Dorchester County.

About fifteen members of Choptank Klan No. 5 entered the tabernacle, where Mrs. [Helen] Jackson was holding a meeting, last night about a quarter after nine o'clock and marched up the aisle while the large crowd present sang two verses of "America." The members of the Klan were in full regalia and at the conclusion of the singing one of their number, said to be the Exalted Cyclops, stepped forward and presented Mrs. Jackson with a purse of $75.00, handing her at the same time a letter which stated that the membership of Choptank Klan thoroughly endorsed her utterances.[32]

The article printed the contents of that letter.

The April 14th edition of *The Crisfield Times* shows the Crisfield Klan organized quickly.

Members of the Ku Klux Klan from many sections of the Eastern Shore came to Crisfield last Sunday, and with Klansmen from Crisfield and other sections of Somerset, attended divine worship at the Baptist Temple. Dr. Bob Killgore preached a special sermon to the Klan, using the "invisible empire" as the basis for one of the strongest sermons he has ever delivered to a Crisfield congregation. [April 8]

With hundreds of spectators lining the streets adjacent to the Baptist temple, seventy visiting Klansmen, in full regalia, marched from the center of the city to the house of worship. It was the first time that members of the order had appeared on the streets in their uniforms, and their appearance created considerable interest. The Klansmen marched

---

[31] *The Crisfield Times*, "Big Klan Meeting at Princess Anne, Three Thousand Countians Hear National Speaker, Dr. Hawkins' Address Thrills Big Audience," Mar. 24, 1923
[32] *The Daily Banner*, Cambridge, Md., "Masked Klansmen Appear At Meeting," Apr. 9, 1923

in double file, two abreast, their flowing uniforms and hoods concealing their identity from the spectators, and making a most impressive scene.

At the church more than 1600 persons crowded in, while fully 500 more were turned away because of the lack of standing room. The gathering was undoubtedly the largest religious gathering ever seen in Crisfield.[33]

The article further describes the minister's sermon. And Dr. Hawkins was reported to be scheduled to speak in Deal Island in Somerset County.[34]

The meeting at Deals Island is understood to have as its purpose the perfecting of a Klan in that community. Klans have already been organized in Crisfield, Princess Anne and Marion, and the organization is growing in membership and strength throughout the county. The Deals Island Klan will be the fourth K. K. K. organization in the county.[34]

May 1923 KKK activity –Maryland and Delaware

The May 5th edition of *The Daily Banner* reports on Ku Klux Klan activity in Cambridge.

Choptank Klan No. 5, Knights of the Ku Klux Klan, as the result of a proclamation issued on the 25th day of April, at Atlanta, Ga., by the Imperial Wizard, H. W. Evans, will hold a special service of praise and thanksgiving in the Spring Valley tomorrow, Sunday, night at 9.15 o'clock, permission having been obtained from the authorities to hold this meeting. The meeting is held at this hour so that it will not conflict with the services of any of the churches. Most of the ministers are expected to be present and will participate in the event, which is intended as a token of thanksgiving over the fact that the Klan has been saved from destruction by internal dissension.[35]

The May 19th edition of *The Crisfield Times* reports on Ku Klux Klan activity in Georgetown, Delaware.

Members of the Georgetown Ku Klux Klan have presented a flag to the Georgetown High School, and have requested that it be raised every clear day during the school term until worn out. Another will be presented, it is said, as soon as the present one is worn out. The organization has a large membership in the central part of Sussex County.[36]

---

[33] *The Crisfield Times*, "Preaches to Klan; Record Attendance, Members of K.K.K. March To Church In Body, Baptist Temple Filled; Hundreds Turned Away," Apr. 14, 1923
[34] *The Crisfield Times*, "Address on Klan at Deals Island, To Perfect 4th Organization In County There, Dr. Hawkins to Speak at Open Air Meeting," May 12, 1923
[35] *The Daily Banner*, Cambridge, MD, "Ku Klux to Hold an Open Meeting, Permission Obtained To Hold Service Of Praise And Thanksgiving In Spring Valley Tomorrow Night At 9.15 O'clock, Ministers To Participate And Offer Prayer," May 5, 1923
[36] *The Crisfield Times*, "Eastern Shore News in Brief," May 19, 1923

Chapter 7. The Ku Klux Klan

The same edition reports on plans for a big Ku Klux Klan meeting in Sharptown, in Wicomico County, Maryland.

> Thousands of Klansmen and other interested spectators from all parts of the Eastern Shore will be attracted to Sharptown Wednesday night, May 30 when the different organizations of the K.K.K. on the Peninsula will unite in a big open air meeting which is termed a Naturalization. It is understood that there are 30 or more Klans on the Eastern Shore peninsula, and each organization will send a large delegation, while many others who are not members of the order, will swell the crowd.
>
> Overlooking the town of Sharptown is a large ten-acre field which has been secured for the meeting and where a big class of incoming candidates will be received. A fiery cross, forty-foot high, will blaze from the hilltop and will be seen for a distance of many miles...
>
> The different Klans of the Eastern Shore have been invited to send large delegations in robe, to the meeting, and it is understood that fully 1000 robed Klansmen are expected to be present. Plans have been made to have present Dr. J. H. Hawkins, National representative of the Ku Klux Klan, Dr. Bob Killgore of Crisfield, and other Klan leaders in Maryland; and Klansmen are understood to be hopeful that a representative of the national organization, from Atlanta, Ga., may also attend....[37]

Hawkins, an organizer of the Ku Klux Klan spoke to crowds throughout areas of the Eastern Shore during 1923, encouraging increased membership and formations of chapters, during a resurgence of the Klan which would peak in activity during the 1920s.

A May 20th Deal Island meeting of the Ku Klux Klan was announced in May 12th edition of *The Crisfield Times*.

> An open air meeting at which several thousand people from the surrounding territory and all sections of Somerset County are expected to attend, will be held at Deals Island on Sunday afternoon, May 20th, when Dr. J. H. Hawkins of Atlanta, Ga., nationally known as an able platform orator, will deliver an address on the principles and purposes of the Ku Klux Klan.
>
> Dr. Hawkins is the national organizer of the Klan, and is regarded throughout the country as one of the foremost platform orators of America Eloquent, logical and convincing, the message he brings always impresses his audience deeply. With the K. K. K., as his subject he is at his best, and is one of the most effective public speakers who has ever entered the Eastern Shore.
>
> The meeting at Deals Island is understood to have its purpose the perfecting of a Klan in that community. Klans have already been

---

[37] The Crisfield Times, "Plan Big Meetings for 'Shore Klans, Members of K.K.K. to Gather in Sharptown, To Have Initiations at Open Air Meeting," May 19, 1923

> organized in Crisfield, Princess Anne and Marion, and the organization is growing in membership and strength throughout the county. The Deals Island Klan will be the fourth K. K. K. organization in the county.
>
> At the recent meetings in Crisfield and Princess Anne, Dr. Hawkins spoke to record-breaking audiences, and made a deep impression on both occasions. He is an entertaining speaker, and able to present his subject to his audience in most entertaining manner.[38]

The May 26, 1923 edition of *The Daily Banner*, Cambridge, Maryland also announced the May 30th event scheduled for Sharptown. According to the announcement, "The towns organized, according to reports, are Cambridge, Hurlock, East New Market, Easton, St. Michaels, Salisbury, Delmar, Sharptown, Mardela, Princess Anne, Snow Hill, Pocomoke City, Marion, Berlin, Ocean City, and 'also every town of any size on the Eastern Shore of Virginia and on Tangier Island.'"[39]

June 1923 KKK activity –Maryland

Denton and Chestertown, Maryland, were mentioned in the June 23rd edition of *The Crisfield Times*.

> W. H. Anderson of Denton, organizer of the Ku Klux Klan for the Eastern Shore of Maryland asked the County Commissioners of Kent County, on Tuesday, for permission to use the Court House yard in Chestertown for a Sunday meeting of the Klan to be organized there. The Board declined to give permission on the ground that they have refused for some years past the use of the grounds for public meetings, lawn fetes, etc., and that they do not feel that they could make any exception in this case. Asked as to the strength of the Klan Mr. Anderson said that there were members from practically every section of the county.[40]

July 1923 KKK activity –Maryland

The July 6th edition of *The Daily Banner* reported on the Ku Klux Klan and its participation in Cambridge's Fourth of July celebration which attracted thousands of visitors. The newspaper reported the Klan's activity and that members participating in the local parade. Representatives from clans of Delaware, and the Eastern Shore of Maryland and Virginia were in attendance. The article further reports the following.

> The clans met at the Tabernacle, where food was served by the ladies of the Baptist Church. About half past seven the order formed in marching order and paraded through the main streets of the town. The

---

[38] *The Crisfield Times*, "Address on Klan at Deals Island, To Perfect 4th Organization In County There," May 12, 1923
[39] *The Daily Banner*, Cambridge, MD, "Ku Klux to Have Big Initiation, Induction At Sharptown, Md., Will Be Public," May 26, 1923
[40] *The Crisfield Times*, "Eastern Shore News in Brief," Jun. 23, 1923

Chapter 7. The Ku Klux Klan

parade was led by Sheriff Ira Y. Wheatley and Chief of Police Daniel Brannock. The Knights of the Ku Klux Klan followed close behind, dressed in the full regalia of the order. The officers of the organization were mounted on horses and preceded the seventy five or more members, who followed behind on foot. There were two floats, one with a mounted clansman and the fiery cross, and a little red school house, which bore the inscription, "One Flag, One Country, One School." The other float carried nearly fifty hooded ladies of the Mistic Den, a supplementary order of the Ku Klux Klan.

The parade terminated at the Fair Grounds where the ceremonies were held. An even hundred new members were initiated into the order, after which Dr. J. H. Hawkins gave an address to the Knights. The members of the clans showed their appreciation for Dr. Hawkins' efforts by presenting to him a seven passenger Studebaker sedan.

Only eighty members of the Organization were present due to the storm, which kept many of the out-of-town clansmen away. Preparation had been made for one thousand members, but even in the absence of so many clansmen the ceremonies were very complete.[41]

The July 16th edition of *The Daily Banner* describes Klan activity at Easton.

Another organization of the Knights of the Ku Klux Klan took place at Easton Friday night, when members from different klans on the Eastern Shore of Maryland met and held one of the largest naturalization meetings ever held in this vicinity.

Until the organization of this Klan, there was no order representing the Ku Klux Klan in Talbot County. The naturalization was held just outside of the town on the road leading to Cambridge, and within easy walking distance. All who wished could witness the ceremonies. At nine o'clock the klans assembled and set fire to the forty foot fiery cross that was provided for the occasion. As the fiery cross blazed out its red flames the symbol of red blooded Americanism, the representatives and prospective members of the Ku Klux Klan, formed a circle around the altar, that had been placed in front of the cross. The degree team, from Cambridge, conferred the initiation upon the candidates, who numbered nearly three hundred persons.

Directly after the ceremonies, the members paraded through the main streets of the town. The parade was participated in by nearly five hundred members, who were robed in the full regalia of the Ku Klux Klan. Some of the ladies of the Mystic Den were among those who took part in the parade. The parade was over half mile long and terminated at the initiation grounds, where the Klans were disbanded.[42]

---

[41] *The Daily Banner*, Cambridge, MD, "Ku Klux Klan Holds Big Meeting, An Even Hundred New Members Initiated. Gathering of Clans From Del-Mar-Va Peninsula," Jul. 6, 1923
[42] *The Daily Banner*, Cambridge, MD, "Klan Organizes at Easton," Jul. 16, 1923

Mob Law on Delmarva

September 1923 KKK activity – Delaware

In September, *The Crisfield Times* reported on Ku Klux Klan activity in New Castle, Delaware.

> A mob of more than 1000 men broke up an initiation of the Ku Klux Klan on a farm near New Castle, Del., recently, and as a result a man and a 17-year-old youth are in hospitals. A big class of men were being initiated into the order when they were fired upon from a nearby field.[43]

January 1924 KKK activity – Delmar

The *Marylander and Herald* of January 19, 1924, reports on Hawkins' visit to Delmar, Delaware, with a curious debate.

> Delmar, Del., Jan. 16th – The Methodist Protestant Church, this city, was packed to the doors and the vestibule crowded last Sunday evening to hear a debate between Rev. E. H. Jones, pastor of the church, and Dr. J. H. Hawkins, Imperial Representative of the Knights of the Ku Klux Klan for Delaware.
>
> Dr. Jones took as his subject, "The Evils of the Klan," and proceeded to give the side as presented by the enemies of the Klan, and in his usually forceful manner, he presented the opposition argument as presented by the city press and other enemies of this powerful organization.
>
> When he had completed, Dr. Hawkins arose in the audience and proceeded to answer this critics, and gave the real principles and ideals of the Klan in a manner that could be understood by his audience.
>
> About sixty members of the Delmar Klan were present at the service in full regalia, and after the services they marched to their hall, where they were again addressed by Dr. Hawkins.
>
> The Delmar Klan is one of the best and strongest organizations in Delaware. Its membership of well over one hundred is composed of the leading citizens of Delmar, and the organization has taken a prominent part in helping the poor and needy of Delmar since its organization. During the holidays many baskets of food were distributed to the needy cases in that section by this Klan.[44]

For a time during 1924, the *Marylander and Herald* of Princess Anne devoted their entire second pages to KKK news and advertisements. Most of the articles were from national sources, with occasional local articles. Most of the ads were national ads, selling KKK music, an example of "Ku Klux Blues Fox Trot," and assorted keepsake items such as the "Kluxer Knifty Knife," a pocket knife, an ornament for the radiator car in the shape of a cross "made of aluminum highly polished with ruby

---

[43] *The Crisfield Times*, "Eastern Shore News in Brief," Sep. 15, 1923
[44] *Marylander and Herald*, "Klansmen Attend Church in Body," Jan. 19, 1924

Chapter 7. The Ku Klux Klan

glass face," and a novelty hooded rubber inflated doll called the "Klean Kut Kid."

Figure 17 Ku Klux Klan newspaper articles and advertisements

Portion of the full page of the *Marylander and Herald*, Princess Anne, Maryland, of Jan. 26, 1924, devoted to news and advertisements of the Ku Klux Klan.

This period involved a flurry of Klan activity following the revival of the Klan around 1915, about the time of the inflammatory popular movie *The Birth of a Nation*. Anti-Semitism surrounding the Leo Frank case and continued racism fueled by the film led William J. Simmons, a recruiter for men's fraternal societies, to initiate the revival. As described by the *Georgia Encyclopedia*,

> Restricting the group's membership to white American-born Protestant men, Simmons designed the notorious hooded uniform, composed an elaborate ritual for the secret order, and secured an official charter from the state of Georgia. On Thanksgiving evening in 1915, Simmons and sixteen other members of the new order, several of whom also belonged to the Knights of Mary Phagan, ascended Stone Mountain, ignited a flaming cross, and proclaimed the rebirth of the Knights of the Ku Klux Klan (Lay 2005).

The early 1920s saw new leadership with a focus on extending the Klan's political powers. This revival reached its peak in the early or mid-1920s, reportedly attracting an estimated 5 million members but the number would reduce significantly by the early 1930s.

Mob Law on Delmarva

The peak of the Klan revival during the 1920s could also have been affected by racial tensions as black soldiers returned from World War I, the fervor embodied by Red Summer of 1919. This period is discussed in greater detail in Chapter 12, Wilmington Riots of 1919.

Chapter 8. The Outside World Looks In

Outside news media depicted the Eastern Shore in an unflattering light when cases were reported, creating predictable local responses.

The Baltimore Afro-American newspaper covered some of the Eastern Shore cases. In 1921, the newspaper included the following headline involving the Stephen Long case of Worcester County.

THE PUTRID EASTERN SHORE

Figure 18 "The Putrid Eastern Shore"

Headline from *The Baltimore Afro-American* newspaper, dated December 2, 1921, reporting the conviction of John Pilchard.

The Stephen Long case is not a case of mob law but it was a sensational story in 1921. The outrage expressed by *The Baltimore Afro-American* was written about the sentencing of John Pilchard, the white man convicted of murdering Long, the prominent and respected supervisor of the segregated Worcester County schools. Pilchard was sentenced to three years for the murder, a pronouncement that solicited the *Afro's* angry headline. Warranted or not, the reaction was printed at a time when the conviction of a white man for the murder of a black man was a rarity.

Stephen Long was murdered in public and in front of his daughter on September 13, 1921. The case is detailed in Hammett Worthington-Smith's *Stephen Long (1865 – 1921) The Man An Educator.* (1994). It was widely believed that Long's assailants were "seeking a reprisal" for Long's removal of two black orphans assigned to the Pilchard family farm from the Boys' Village of Cheltenham located in Prince Georges County, Maryland. Cheltenham, a reform school for young black males, was known to have assigned youth to local farmers.

John Pilchard and William Pilchard confronted Long. John Pilchard stabbed Long to death with a pocket knife on September 13th, in front of Noah Gunby's bicycle shop near Fourth and Linden Streets.

John Pilchard was arrested and *The Baltimore Sun* of October 24, 1921 reported that John Pilchard would, "be the first white man ever tried in the Worcester county Circuit Court for killing a negro under an indictment of first degree murder."[45]

John Pilchard was found guilty, convicted of manslaughter, and sentenced to three years in the House of Correction. The conviction and sentencing was widely criticized, particularly by *The Baltimore Afro-American*, as evidenced in the newspaper's commentary in the December 2nd issue, with the heading "The Putrid Eastern Shore."[46]

In January of 1923, Governor Ritchie pardoned Pilchard, according to *The Baltimore Sun* of January 12, 1923, which also reported on rumored special privileges given to Pilchard during his incarceration. [47]

Three days after the December 4, 1931 lynching of Matthew Williams in Salisbury, H. L. Mencken evoked the image of the Ku Klux Klan in his article and headline, and strongly rebuked the people and two newspapers of the lower Maryland Eastern Shore, including *The Salisbury Times*, which reprinted Mencken's article, and introduced it with, "We submit his ravings to your consideration."[48]

The Eastern Shore Kultur

Figure 19 "The Eastern Shore Kultur" by H. L. Mencken

Headline reprinted in the Salisbury Times December 8, 1931 of the H. L. Mencken article originally printed in *The Baltimore Evening Sun* on December 7, 1931 in response to the lynching of Matthew Williams in Salisbury.

Thus began the Mencken war.

Mencken's first article was accompanied by a sketch of the lynching by the Sunpapers' cartoonist Edmund Duffy. The cartoon was entitled "Maryland, My Maryland."[49] According to author Marion Elizabeth Rodgers (2006),

> Editors from the Worcester Democrat of Pocomoke City, Maryland accused Mencken and Duffy of being "jealous" because they had not gotten to "enjoy" the lynching.

---

[45] *The Baltimore, Sun*, "To Face Court Today For Death Of Negro, John Pilchard, Stockton, Worcester County, Accused Of Killing Colored School Head," Oct. 24, 1921
[46] *The Baltimore Afro-American*, "The Putrid Eastern Shore," Dec. 2, 1921
[47] *The Baltimore Sun*, "Pilchard, Murderer, Pardoned," Jan. 12, 1923
[48] *The Salisbury Times*, Salisbury, MD, "The Eastern Shore Kultur," by H. L. Mencken, Dec. 8, 1931, reprinted from *The Baltimore Evening Sun* of Dec. 7, 1931
[49] The official state anthem of Maryland

Chapter 8. The Outside World Looks In

Figure 20 "Maryland, My Maryland" lynching cartoon, 1931

Cartoon by Edmund Duffy, which accompanied the editorial by H. L. Mencken following the 1931 Salisbury lynching of Matthew Williams.

Mencken responded with his article entitled "They serve very well." In it, as described by Rodgers,

> ...He proposed the shore be detached from Maryland and joined to Delaware and Virginia to form a new state to be called "Delmarva."
>
> Within 48 hours of Mencken's column being published, thousands of dollars' worth of orders from Baltimore's retailers were cancelled by cities along the Eastern Shore. As the 1931 Christmas season approached, residents who regularly shopped in Baltimore now began going to Wilmington and Philadelphia.
>
> Alarmed, members of the Baltimore Association of Commerce, including the Western Newspaper Union, bought advertisements in Baltimore and shore papers appealing for good will. "Please do not judge the people of Baltimore by what appears in the Baltimore Sun," one read....
>
> The Sunpapers' office was besieged with complaints. Subscriptions were cancelled. Store that sold copies of the newspaper were forced to

> stop, on threat of boycott. Copies of the Sunpapers were thrown on the streets and burned before they could be placed on sale. Two circulation trucks were ambushed, their papers thrown away, and their drivers beaten. Reporters who went to Salisbury to cover the story were threatened with violence. According to Mencken, one of the photographers, Robert F. Knieche, "was saved from rough handling, and maybe even murder, only by escaping in an airship."
>
> Talk of revenge went on for weeks. The editor of the Easton Journal advised Mencken not to set foot on the Eastern Shore "for the next 20 years. In Salisbury, they'd rather lynch you." He warned that Mencken's toes, and perhaps his ears, might be taken as souvenirs...

The newspaper would go on to report lynchings, notably the next Eastern Shore lynching, two years later in Princess Anne. Continued Rodgers,

> "A curious feature of the whole uproar was that public opinion in Baltimore seemed to be predominantly on the side of the lynchers," recalled Mencken. "I got more threatening letters from city people than from the simians of the lower Shore itself."

Editorials aside, reporters of newspapers serve as watchdogs.

The Baltimore Afro-American covered the state execution of Euel Lee, which occurred only days after the October 1933 lynching of George Armwood in Princess Anne. Lee narrowly avoided being lynched in October of 1931 at the time of his arrest. During his three years of trials and appeals, Eastern Shoremen expressed their anger, some even brought up Lee's name during the Armwood lynching. That time period spanned at least two lynching events on the lower Eastern Shore; and throughout that time, reports of the Lee case frequently filled the local newspapers. Clarence Mitchell, then a reporter for *The Baltimore Afro-American*, reported on the execution of Euel Lee at the state penitentiary in Baltimore, and in an article with the headline "Crowd Outside Makes Merry As Lee Dies," Mitchell described some of the crowd.

> Only here and there comments dropped about Euel Lee, while the recent lynching of George Armwood figured largely in the current conversation. "Well," said an Irishman who was chewing on some unknown substance, "they sure did that fellow up bad the other day down at Princess Anne." His companion answered, "Not half as bad as--" and as an AFRO reporter moved a little closer, he failed to finish the statement.[50]

Newspapers reporting on lynchings often reported on the assumed guilt of the victim, guilt which had not been legally established. Newspaper

---

[50] *The Baltimore Afro-American*, Baltimore, MD, "Crowd Outside Makes Merry As Lee Dies," Nov. 4, 1933

Chapter 8. The Outside World Looks In

reporters were present during and/or following mob actions. A reporter for *The Philadelphia Inquirer* reported on the aftermath of the killing of George White who was burned at the stake.

> Wilmington, Del., June 23 -- On a freshly-ploughed field, beaten by thousands of feet into asphalt smoothness, a thin scum of ashes marks the funeral pyre of George White, the negro murderer of Helen S. Bishop, who met death at the stake early this morning....
>
> Everywhere throughout the city the one topic of conversation today was the lynching. Men were found who did not hesitate to say that they took a hand in the affair. Others look up to them as heroes. Minor officials of the Commonwealth of Delaware express satisfaction over the result.[51]

A January 1900 issue of the African American newspaper *The Richmond Planet* of Richmond, Virginia includes it's yearly listing of lynchings for the period of January 5, 1897 to January 5, 1898, including three Maryland lynchings, in Clarksville, Annapolis, and Salisbury.

---

[51] *The Philadelphia Inquirer*, Philadelphia, PA, "Delaware Calmly Views Death at Stake," Jun. 24, 1903

Mob Law on Delmarva

Figure 21 Listing of 1897 Lynchings

Portion of the listing of lynchings from January 5, 1897 to January 5, 1898, printed in the January 13, 1900 issue of *The Richmond Planet*

Chapter 9. More to Learn, Mysteries to Solve

Most cases leave the reader with more questions than answers.

For instance, how was it that Luther Moore was made to spend a year on a road gang in Augusta County after his arrest and prior to being tried in 1924 for attempted murder near Temperanceville, Virginia on the Eastern Shore? And was this a regular practice on parts of the Eastern Shore?

And whatever happened to Frank Furbey, who was convicted in April of 1923 and began serving life imprisonment, while yet another man, a white man named Philip Zill, was arrested for the crime for which Furbey was convicted? Was Zill ever brought to trial? Did Furbey continue to serve his sentence?

What happened to the two men – Lemuel Showers and a man known as Hildred --arrested in 1907 in connection to events which led to the apprehension and lynching of James Reed in Crisfield, Maryland?

How did the 1914 death of Benjamin Goslee of Wicomico County affect his family, and just who were his family, and how did he lead his life up until the day Joseph Darby poured oil onto him and set him on fire?

What were the full circumstances surrounding the murder of Millington, Maryland white physician Dr. J. Heighe Hill which ultimately led to the execution of four black men and commuted sentences of four others?

Onancock, Virginia, experienced a so-named riot and related violence in 1907. But Pocomoke, Maryland, was also affected by the Onancock events due to tense feelings and circumstances by which "several negroes were badly bruised and beaten" as they attempted to reach camp meeting grounds. What happened to them, who were they, and how were their lives affected in addition to those of Onancock?

How did the 1921 murder of black school superintendent Stephen Long in Pocomoke, Maryland, affect the community? Is the rumor correct that Long was murdered as a result of actions he took to ensure an education for two black youth hired out to white farmers? And if so, how prevalent was this hiring out practice on the Eastern Shore during that time period?

How did the 1908 violence unleashed in Rehoboth and Lewes, Delaware, affect the people who experienced the rioting? Who was the black man "beaten into insensibility" and the others who were "picked up bodily and thrown from Horn's pier"? Who was the elderly man who "took refuge in the Hotel Townsend," escaping as soldiers "were proceeding to carry out a threat to beat down the doors and lynch him"?

Who was the unidentified black man found beaten to death the day after Matthew Williams was lynched in 1931 on the courthouse grounds of Salisbury, Maryland? He was identified as unknown on the death certificate and he was buried in the town's Potter's Field. How did his death affect his family?

What were the unreported details of the so-called riot in Laurel, Delaware in 1911, described in newspapers in a manner resembling the wild west?

Why were there an unusually high number of reported riots in Delaware compared to other parts of the Eastern Shore? Was it simply that others did not get reported? Were they connected with other prominent incidents of violence? How were they documented in local newspapers and in urban newspapers outside of the area?

And who were the brave men of Centreville, Maryland, who in 1894 stepped up on more than one occasion to ensure that the prisoner William Jackson was not lynched? Jackson was later that year convicted and executed, but who "assembled about the jail in large numbers, armed with clubs and other weapons with which to defend Jackson from lynchers"?

There are many more such examples; the above are only a few of the questions you may have when viewing the material.

There are tales of extraordinary efforts made by law enforcement taking circuitous routes to transport prisoners to Baltimore for safe keeping and avoid roving mobs. But then there were implications of complicity or looking away when lynchings or near-lynchings were expected.

Beyond the newspapers, individuals, the witnesses, have written their accounts, risking dangerous incrimination, family or community resentments, and ostracism. There are people who will not talk openly, in ways that might identify them, but wish to tell their memories or the stories of their family members.

Chapter 9. More to Learn, Mysteries to Solve

What were the responses and repercussions for those from the black community who resisted the violence? And what of those who spoke out?

After the May 1898 lynching of Garfield King in Salisbury, Maryland, a local committee formed and their lengthy condemnation of the lynching was printed in the June 4, 1898 edition of the *Salisbury Advertiser*, including,

> "We believe in public office as a public trust. That trust is betrayed when the functions of that office cease to be effective. Where was the sheriff of Wicomico county when Garfield King was lynched? What resistance did the jailer make? We demand in the name of God and humanity an explanation."[52]

> "We believe in public office as a public trust. That trust is betrayed when the functions of that office cease to be effective. Where was the sheriff of Wicomico county when Garfield King was lynched? What resistance did the jailer make? We demand in the name of God and humanity an explanation.'"
>
> *June 4, 1898*
> *Salisbury Advertiser*
>
> From a committee composed of members of Salisbury's black community, including Solomon T. Huston, A.R. Shockley, F.N. Butler, James O. Pinkett

What happened to the people arrested for which no information was located; were they sentenced, convicted, or did they flee successfully? What is provided here represents only a relatively small percentage of questions, for there are questions, mysteries, which have not been located or included. So while reading the accounts, think of the questions, the missing facts, the effects on people. And for the victims of violence, regardless of the circumstances, who were they, what were their lives like? Imagining or wondering won't give us a clearer picture, but it will emphasize how much we don't know.

---

[52] *Salisbury Advertiser*, Salisbury, MD, "Condemnation Resolution," Jun. 4, 1898

Chapter 10. The Race Riot Cases

The term "race riot" has been overused and sometimes erroneously used, but it will be used here, for no other reason than to describe cases of violence not specifically highlighting one or two individuals accused, lynched, or convicted and executed for crimes. Some of the so-called riots are well known by local citizens still living. Other riots were identified only by information located in newspapers, but the less well-known cases were included, hinting at the fear and intimidation that might have been present at the time. There may have been similar incidents in other locations yet, further compilation and research about these incidents are needed.

The following are incidents reported in newspapers as riots or race riots, but racial incidents of intimidation were not limited to or reported as riots, and a few of these are included.

Cape Charles Violence, 1887

Historian Brooks Miles Barnes referenced earlier examples of racial violence in his article on the 1907 Onancock riots on the Virginia Eastern Shore. The *Peninsula Enterprise* of December 10, 1887 reported that the city council held a special meeting to discuss the possibility of obtaining military equipment and arms.

> The council are determined to spare neither money nor means to crush out all such lawlessness as has occurred at times for the past few months. It has been not only a source of great annoyance, but has caused the citizens much uneasiness, as they feel that life or property are greatly endangered. The council also offered a reward for the arrest and conviction of the party who so seriously injured a deputy sergeant in the affray on Friday night last. ....

> A fatal affray occurred here on Friday night of last week which resulted in the shooting of one Dick Wilson, colored, in the abdomen, who has since died of the wound. The facts in the case were as follows: The town sergeant in attempting to break up a disorderly crowd assembled in front of Parson's restaurant, arrested two negroes who were engaged in a fight and called to his assistance Mr. McCubbin a merchant of the place. In taking the negroes to the lockup some two hundred yards distant, the sergeant and his assistant were followed by the crowd of negroes who first threatened to rescue the negroes and one of them finally struck McCubben [sic] with a brick, knocking him senseless. – The sergeant went to the assistance of McCubben and in the affray shot as he supposed the man whom he thought had struck McCubben, but

Chapter 10. The Race Riot Cases

> which proved to be afterwards one of the negroes which he had had in custody. The citizens of Cape Charles generally agree that the sergeant was justified in using his pistol. McCubben was seriously injured and fears are entertained that his wound will prove fatal. The Commonwealth's attorney of Northampton will investigate the matter, witnesses having been summoned for that purpose.[53]

Wachapreague Riot of 1899

Brooks Miles Barnes referred to the Wachapreague riot in his article on the 1907 Onancock riots on the Virginia Eastern Shore. The *Peninsula Enterprise* of February 4, 1899 reports among the Wachapreague neighborhood news.

> A small race-war broke out on our streets on Saturday last and was renewed on Monday morning. A drunken shucker named Sheppard assaulted Capt. Levin Richardson without just provocation, and was promptly knocked down. Another negro shucker who interfered was summarily dealt with by the whites and the difficulty was thought to be at an end. But on Monday morning a negro named Pete Dunton renewed the difficulty. Clubs, base ball bats and other handy weapons were speedily brought into play and the would be rioters promptly suppressed. Wachapreague is entirely without an officer of the law, and steps will be taken to preserve the peace until the next Spring election.[54]

Onancock, Regulators 1890

The *Peninsula Enterprise* of January 18, 1890 reports on Onancock.

> A band of white men, styling themselves "regulators," on Saturday last notified one Joe Finney, colored, recently released from the county jail, and of rather unsavory repute, that his departure from this neighborhood would be in accordance with "the eternal fitness of things," and that unless he left the town by 6 p. m. on Saturday he would be summarily dealt with. Finney accepted their advice without remonstrance. One Dan Bagwell, colored, was similarly dealt with last week.[55]

---

[53] *Peninsula Enterprise*, Accomac, Virginia, "Local News, Cape Charles City," Dec. 10, 1887
[54] *Peninsula Enterprise*, Accomac, Virginia, "Neighborhood Notes, Wachapreague," Feb. 4, 1899
[55] *Peninsula Enterprise*, Accomac, Virginia, "Neighborhood Notes, Onancock," Jan. 18, 1890

Mob Law on Delmarva

Wilmington Riot of 1903

Rioting occurred following the June 22, 1903 lynching of George White.

The Baltimore Sun edition of June 26, 1903 includes,

> Wilmington, Del., June 25 – A race riot began here shortly after 9 o'clock tonight in which about 400 negroes participated. It is now probably that the National Guard will be called out to preserve the order. About 200 shots were fired between whites and blacks, resulting in one unknown negro being killed and the following persons being wounded:
>
> Police Sergeant McDermott, pistol wound in scalp; only slightly injured.
>
> Patrolman Green, slight pistol wound over right eye; injuries not serious.
>
> William Cramer, colored, badly wounded in stomach.
>
> James A. Mercer, colored, pistol wound in scalp; seriously wounded.
>
> Two negro leaders, Moore and Joseph A. Shockley, were arrested with inciting a riot. The early evening crowds of negro men and boys began to parade the principal thoroughfares. Some were singing and shouting, and all used boisterous language.

The article goes on to state that the black man found dead, thought dead during the rioting, was as yet unidentified and thought to have been killed "by a man of his own race during a free fight in a colored settlement known as 'The Shoe.'" The article also reports on whites being "enflamed" by stories of acts alleged to be retaliation by blacks, including poisoning of cows belonging to the Ferris Industrial School, the superintendent of which was the father of the woman assumed murdered by George White.[56]

---

[56] *The Baltimore Sun*, "Negroes in Riot, Mob of 400 Parade Streets of Wilmington and Beat White Men," Jun. 26, 1903

Chapter 10. The Race Riot Cases

Camden Riot of 1904

The Delaware Pilot reports,

> Camden, Aug. 25. Last Saturday was registration day here and such a day and evening will long be remembered by the citizens, especially by the town bailiff.
>
> In the evening the business part of the town, particularly around the hotel, represented a maelstrom of disorder. The streets were so lined with drunken, impudent negroes that it was next to impossible to get through the throng and the air was filled with oaths and insults.
>
> Several fights were in progress during the evening and a simple drunk was the virtue of the night.
>
> Bailiff Hinsley was the only bailiff on duty that evening and he couldn't begin to handle the crowd.
>
> At one time a disorderly darkey was arrested, but before the lock-up was reached a half hundred angry, threatening negroes surrounded the bailiff and amid shouts, threats and curses the prisoner was pulled from the officers and hustled out of town. Fullman is his name and a warrant is now out for his arrest.... [t]here is a prediction going the rounds that there will be a race riot in this town before many disorderly Saturday nights have passed.[57]

The article further describes Saturday nights being full of "negroes and rough white crowds," creating a "hotbed of rowdyism, driving away store customers and giving to visitors a low opinion of the town's management."

> Wyoming, the home of Delaware's chief executive and less than a mile from here, is getting a taste of the disorder that emanates in Camden.

---

[57] *The Delaware Pilot*, Lewes, DE, "Race Riot Predicted," Aug. 27, 1904

Mob Law on Delmarva

Southern Delaware Riots of 1905

Newspaper accounts describe various racial riot incidents in both Philadelphia and in southern Delaware in the summer of 1905. The reported Delaware violence identified here occurred in Townsend, Greenwood and Kenton.

Townsend, Delaware

In the June 28, 1905 issue, *The Baltimore Sun* reports various racial riot incidents in Philadelphia and in southern Delaware.

> Philadelphia, June 27 – A special dispatch to the North American from Townsend, Del. referring to the race riots already noted in The Sun, contains the following:

> Southern Delaware has been thrown into a state of Excitement during the last few days by race riots between the whites and the negroes. More than 15 persons have been wounded, among whom are two police officers, who were shot while attempting to quell the disturbances.

> The blacks have openly declared that on next Saturday night they will take possession of the town of Greenwood and will have revenge for the severe beating they received at the hands of townsfolks last Saturday.

> The riots have grown out of talk of asking the State Legislature to enact a dis-franchisement law, which would prevent negroes who can neither read nor write from voting. Similar laws have been enacted in Maryland and other nearby Southern States, and, fearing that they would be barred from the polls, the negroes are forcing the issue.

> Excepting one family in each of the harassed towns, including this place, Greenwood, Bridgeville and Seaford, all negroes have been driven out and the whites are arming themselves for future clashes.

> Those negroes who have been allowed to remain are those who have lived in the respective towns for years and have behaved satisfactorily. No others are allowed to return, and as the negroes are cognizant of this fact they probably will not come singly, but in a body and well armed.

> The all-night riot which occurred here last Saturday night was the bloodiest that has occurred so far. Five men were shot and a dozen beaten.

"Not until every negro had fled the town was quiet restored, and it came near being resumed Sunday when several of the negroes appeared in town for medical attention, but cooler heads prevented further trouble. No one was killed."

July 1, 1905
The State Register

Chapter 10. The Race Riot Cases

> The melee was instigated by three negroes at Main and Commerce streets, the two prominent thoroughfares of the city. At the time the streets were crowded with men, women and children, it being the height of the Saturday night shopping hour. The black trio pounced upon a white man who was advocating or, at least, speaking in favor of more stringent election laws.
>
> This attracted a number of others to the scene, and when Bailiff Powell arrived a few minutes later a small riot was in progress. He separated the two factions, when one of the negroes struck him on the face, stunning him.
>
> The other two negroes then joined in the fight, and, to save himself, the officer drew his revolver and fired at them. At least one of the negroes was struck and he fell to the pavement.[58]

The dispatch in the article reports an attacks on officer Powell and others, with gunfire between blacks and whites in Townsend. Following the incidents, Attorney General Robert E. Richards dispatched detectives to make arrests. The article further reports,

> As far as can be learned the only negroes who were shot in the riots were Walter Hopkins, who was wounded in the leg, and another named Caulk, who was wounded in the hand.

The article reports there having been incidents at Bridgeville and Seaford, without describing specifics.

Greenwood, Delaware

The July 1, 1905 issue *of The State Register* of Laurel, Delaware reports the following.

> Probably the worst race riot between whites and blacks which ever happened in Sussex county took place in Greenwood Saturday night, in which 200 whites and half as many blacks took part.
>
> The trouble began over a half-witted white man being terribly beaten by three negroes. The news of the fight soon spread among the whites and an uprising ensued. Two hundred whites began to rid the town of negroes. Every negro found, man or woman was run out of the town and several pitched battles took place. Truck patches near town were badly damaged in the struggle.
>
> The porch of one house was nearly torn down by the fighters. A dozen negroes were caught one at a time near town, beaten into insensibility by the angry mob and left for dead in the fields.

---

[58] *The Baltimore Sun*, "Race Riots in Delaware; Whites and Negroes are Arming for Conflict; Bloody Fighting Expected; War Grew Out of Agitation in Favor of a Disfranchising Amendment – Blacks Driven Out," Jun. 28, 1905

The fighting continued until early Sunday morning. Not until every negro had fled the town was quiet restored, and it came near being resumed Sunday when several of the negroes appeared in town for medical attention, but cooler heads prevented further trouble. No one was killed.[59]

Townsend, Delaware

The same article describes rioting in Townsend.

> Disorderly negroes took possession of Townsend late Saturday night and a furious fight followed, in which the town bailiff and several other men were badly injured. Clayton Powell, the bailiff, attempted to stop two negroes from fighting. A gang of the roughs set upon him, seized his own pistol, shot him in the leg and beat him insensible. John Parvis and several other men went to Powell's aid, and Parvis was also knocked unconscious. A general exchange of pistol shots followed in which two negroes, named Calk and Hopkins were wounded.
>
> After Parvis had been knocked unconscious several negroes wanted to shoot him, when one remarked: "What's the use; he's dead anyway," and the negroes departed.[59]

Kenton, Delaware

The July 8, 1905 issue *of The State Register* of Laurel, Delaware reports the following,

> Manifesting astonishing defiance of the law worthy of the wild west tactics, two negroes living just outside of Kenton Saturday afternoon shot Magistrate Francis Johns and Constable William Wallace. The constable had been ordered by Magistrate Johns to carry out a writ of the court, but the assailants defied courts, officers and all laws and opened fire viciously upon the two representatives of the law.
>
> About noon while Frank Attix, a prosperous young farmer, was driving from Smyrna to his farm near Blanco he was accosted by two colored men who asked for a ride. Both had been drinking and Attix refused them. The negroes then jumped on the wagon. Both attacked Attix, one of them striking him over the head with a club. Attix finally escaped and hurried to Kenton where he swore out warrants for the negroes, whom he had identified as Philip Shepperd and Howard Honey. Justice of the Peace Frank Amos Johns and Constable Wallace drove to the home of a negro named Bob Pryor where the two had been located.
>
> As soon as they approached the house Shepherd and Honey opened fire on the officers hitting them both. Wallace was shot in the breast by a pistol ball and Squire Johns had his face riddled by shot from a shotgun. The officers retreated, but heard Pryor tell the others to "kill the damned whites" as they hurried away.

---

[59] *The State Register*, Laurel, DE, "Turbulent Negro Toughs Terrorize Citizens in Town of Greenwood and at Townsend," July1, 1905

Chapter 10. The Race Riot Cases

Constable Wallace at first started to serve his warrants alone, but was advised on all sides not to attempt it single handed, and returned to consult the magistrate as the best way to bring the men without bloodshed. Magistrate Johns, who had just returned from luncheon, suggested that perhaps he might drive out with the constable and see whether the men were intending to resist arrest, or would come peaceable upon seeing the magistrate.

Hardly had the representatives of the law reached the house however, when both men opened fire and a bullet hit the magistrate in the head and the constable in the face.

The men were left helpless by their assailants until resistance arrived from Kenton, together with several passersby and the wounded officers were removed to Kenton for immediate attention.

Shepherd and Honey meanwhile escaped from the house and after placing Pryor under guard the armed posse started on the trail of the two negroes.

Meantime Sheriff Edward Baker of Dover, cooperating with two State Detectives, was accomplishing some quick results. Sheriff Baker organized two posse, one headed by himself and State Detectives James P. Ratledge, and another by Deputy Sheriff John W. Foreaker and State Detective J. H. Hawkins, and behind fast horses the officers sped to Kenton, a distance of twelve miles, reaching there by 5 o'clock.

The negroes escaped but were pursued by an armed posse. Robert Pryor, colored, who is said to have aided the men to escape, has been arrested and held in $2,000 bail for a further hearing and is now in jail.

Detective Ratledge, who is still on the scent, has detailed descriptions of the men and is sending them broadcast. If they are not captured Governor Lea is expected to issue an offer of a reward for their arrests.[60]

---

[60] *The State Register*, Laurel, DE, "Officers Defied by Vicious Negroes; Two Constables Wounded in Attempt to Arrest Malefactors," Jul. 8, 1905

Mob Law on Delmarva

Southern Delaware Riots of 1906

Newspapers also reported on violence in lower Delaware, specifically the Seaford and Laurel areas.

The Baltimore Sun headline of its August 19th article was "Race Riot Threatens, Strange Negroes Being Run Out of Seaford, Del."

> "White residents are parading streets and every strange negro is being run out of town."
>
> August 19, 1906
> The Baltimore Sun

As a result of the influx of negroes here from Maryland and Virginia a race riot is brewing tonight. White residents are parading streets and every strange negro is being run out of town.

The trouble started over a strange negro striking a white boy. The people becoming alarmed formed into a small army and began running and beating negroes not known here wherever found. John Walker was caught and beaten into insensibility. Joseph Selby, another negro, was knocked down with a plank and kicked into the street.

The lockup is filled and a temporary jail has been provided to lock up more negroes.

It was evident as early as 6 o'clock this evening that there would be trouble, and the Town Council immediately put on an extra force of policemen, but this did not stop the turbulent negroes.

William Trussell, a traveling man from Cumberland, Md., was attacked by the blacks and had to fight his way out. As a result he broke a finger and was injured internally.

Linden L. Short, a young man, was also attacked and badly beaten by the negroes.

Merchants are compelled to close their stores, fearing onslaughts from enraged colored men.

To add to the confusion the electric lights went out about 9 o'clock. Pistol shots were heard in all directions and razors and knives were seen glittering in every negro's hand. Great apprehension of more serious consequences prevails.[61]

The Baltimore Sun August 22nd article reports more rioting.

> Seaford, Del., Aug. 21 – Another outbreak occurred here early this morning, when a gang of 20 or 30 negroes attacked the homes of

---

[61] *The Baltimore Sun*, "Race Riot Threatens—Strange Negroes Being Run Out of Seaford, Del.," Aug.. 19, 1906

Chapter 10. The Race Riot Cases

William Prettyman, James Thomas and William Loveall and demanded admission. Being refused, they riddled the front doors with bullets, afterward breaking into the houses. All the occupants escaped unhurt, although several bullets passed through their clothing. They were compelled to seek shelter in cornfields until this morning, when the trouble was reported to the police.

Since Saturday night's riot hundreds of strange negroes have come to town and white persons have to walk out of their way. This evening one negro, James Neary, of Norfolk, demanded $5 change from a merchant, and, not getting it, abused him. Upon being arrested, two revolvers, two razors and a blackjack were found on his person.

The present pro tem of the Town Council, Stansbury E. Parson, it is said, made the statement that the negroes should carry weapons to protect themselves. As a result one merchant has sold every firearm he had in stock. The Chief of Police, Arthur Marvel, has resigned and the town is without protection.

The canning factories employ several hundred negro women to skin tomatoes, and, with their knives, they march up the aisles, not giving the white women room to pass.

The situation is serious. The Town Council will be compelled to put on a large force of policemen to avert serious trouble Saturday night, when the negroes are paid off.[62]

The Baltimore Sun August 27th article reports,

Wilmington, Del., Aug. 26 – Conferences were held in the principal towns in lower Delaware last night to devise means to stop the race riots that have been occurring regularly, particularly Saturday nights. The State authorities will co-operate with the authorities of the towns. There were no serious outbreaks last night. The disturbances have been caused principally at Laurel and Seaford by negroes from Maryland, Virginia and the Carolinas and disorderly whites going into town from nearby farms and becoming intoxicated.[63]

---

[62] *The Baltimore Sun*, "Seaford Negroes Shoot; Riddle Doors of Houses, But Occupants Escape; Town Official Says 'Arm!'; On This Advice Blacks Buy Up The Supply Of Pistols – Whites Walk Out of Way On Streets," Aug. 22, 1906
[63] *The Baltimore Sun*, "To Prevent Delaware Riots; Authorities of Towns Take Steps To Regulate Negroes," Aug. 27, 1906

Mob Law on Delmarva

Onancock Race Riot of 1907

Brooks Miles Barnes details the events of the Onancock riots in Accomack County, Virginia, during the summer of 1907 (1984).

> "Fifty negro families have been ordered by the whites to leave Onancock by or before 9 A. M. Monday under threats of serious trouble. An old minister, finding this notice on his door on returning from church, immediately vacated. …. Uzzle and Burton are still at large, and it is likely lynchings will follow if they are caught."
>
> August 12, 1907
> The Baltimore Sun

The riot was triggered by a debt owed by Sylvanus Conquest, a young black clerk in the store owned by black businessman Samuel L. Burton, to white Onancock livery owner John M. Fosque. Burton was described as "a handsome, well-dressed, and articulate six-footer." He had taught in the Accomack County public schools and was the owner of a store in the segregated area of Onancock. Burton "enjoyed the reputation of a shrewd businessman, owned some real estate, and was thought to be moderately wealthy. He served as head of the black Masons and Odd Fellows and as an officer of the black agricultural fair association." Barnes attributes some contributing factors for the events to the local labor shortage and activity of blacks to set their labor costs and to limit their spending to black-owned businesses.

The incidents began on Friday, August 9, 1907, when Constable Tankard "Tank" G. Kellam arrived at Burton's store, where Sylvanus Conquest worked as a clerk, to retrieve the horse and buggy for which Conquest was accused of being delinquent in the rental fees from white livery owner John M. Fosque. Kellam and Conquest argued, with Conquest claiming that the horse belonged to Burton. Burton joined the argument, a crowd of blacks gathered, and Kellam left the store.

Burton paid Conquest's debt, but Conquest was charged with resisting arrest. Conquest was brought before the Mayor, and Burton testified as a witness. Barnes records, "When he [Burton] finished testifying, he was told to leave the stand but moved too slowly for Constable Kellam who jerked the chair from under him." Conquest was found guilty and fined fifty dollars.

Chapter 10. The Race Riot Cases

As a result of what was felt to be a light sentencing for Conquest and because of Kellam's experience at Burton's store, a message was sent to the black community informing them of a curfew in the white neighborhood for that Saturday night, "instructing those who planned to shop in the white neighborhood on Saturday to do so but to leave by 8:30 P. M."

On that Saturday evening, James D. Uzzle entered the white section of Onancock on his way to the post office. In Barnes' article, Uzzle, "a well-educated, small man of around thirty-five, shared with Burton the leadership of Onancock's black community. Uzzle doubled as principal of the black public school in Onancock and as editor of the *Peninsula Times*." On his way to the post office, four or five white men taunted him for being in town and attacked him, knocking him to the ground and battering him, Uzzle reportedly pulled a gun and fired, hitting the son of a white merchant, who suffered a minor wound to the leg.

The incident triggered activity in the white community, with rumors that blacks planned to burn and riot the town. A white resident sent word to Samuel Burton urging him to leave town for their safety. Burton and Conquest closed the store and reportedly hid in the woods.

That same evening, a horse and buggy left downtown Onancock for the rail station at Tasley, driven by a black man, Braden Short, accompanied by three white men, delivering the mail. Reportedly, while passing Burton's store on the way out of town towards Tasley, there was an exchange of gunfire, reported as an "ambush" of the vehicle by the black resident John Topping, who was fired upon during the incident and was attended to by Onancock's black physician, Dr. I. Moon. The circumstances as reported were murky, but Burton and Conquest were accused of orchestrating the ambush.

A mob, reportedly led by the constable, Tank Kellam, surrounded Burton's store, and fired into the store. Unable to locate Burton and Conquest, some of the mob terrorized the black neighborhood. Burton's store and Uzzle's printing shop were burned to the ground.

All of this occurred over a weekend, and by Sunday morning, a town committee reported a list of the names of eight blacks accused as troublemakers and a threat to the community, including Dr. Moon and the pastor of the African Methodist Episcopal church. The minister was ordered to leave town; Dr. Moon was permitted to remain, thanks to recommendations of two white physicians.

Mob Law on Delmarva

The Baltimore Sun of August 12th reports,

> Fifty negro families have been ordered by the whites to leave Onancock by or before 9 A. M. Monday under threats of serious trouble. An old minister, finding this notice on his door on returning from church, immediately vacated. …. Uzzle and Burton are still at large, and it is likely lynchings will follow if they are caught.[64]

That day the town council met, forming resolutions to seek assistance from Governor Claude A. Swanson, and for an injunction against the blacks from holding their fair held annually in nearby Tasley, Virginia.

Governor Swanson decided the circumstances dire enough to visit Onancock himself, arriving by boat at Onancock on Monday. Swanson ordered a detachment of fifty soldiers from Norfolk to the area until the end of the Tasley fair which was scheduled for August 27th. Tensions calmed over the next few days to the point that the injunction resolution was rescinded, but some incidents continued, including firing by whites upon black residents in nearby Onley and threats of lynching. Governor Swanson was persuaded to continue the militia presence until the end of the fair.

Among the incidents involved, James D. Uzzle was run out of town.

The following excerpt is from Barnes' article.

> Despite the evident prosperity, race relations in Onancock in the summer of 1907 were strained, and judging from the Eastern Shore's recent history, the ensuing riot should not have been a great surprise. In the late 1860s, gangs of whites terrorized freedmen in upper Accomack County, the peninsula's only recorded lynching took place in the lower part of the county, and two minor riots occurred at Accomac Court House. After the end of Reconstruction in 1869, racial strife subsided but did not disappear. In 1887 at Cape Charles City in lower Northampton County, a white town sergeant was seriously injured and a black man in his custody killed when a crowd of blacks attempted to prevent the prisoner's incarceration. Three years later, a band of Onancock white men, calling themselves "regulators," ran a couple of black petty criminals out of town, and in 1899, "a small race-war" broke out in the streets of Wachapreague on the Accomack County seaside. An application of "clubs, base ball bats and other handy weapons" settled the issue in favor of the Wachapreague whites.

---

[64] *The Baltimore Sun*, "Burn Negroes' Houses, Onancock Citizens Destroy Newspaper Office and Store, Blacks Ordered Out of Town," Aug. 12, 1907

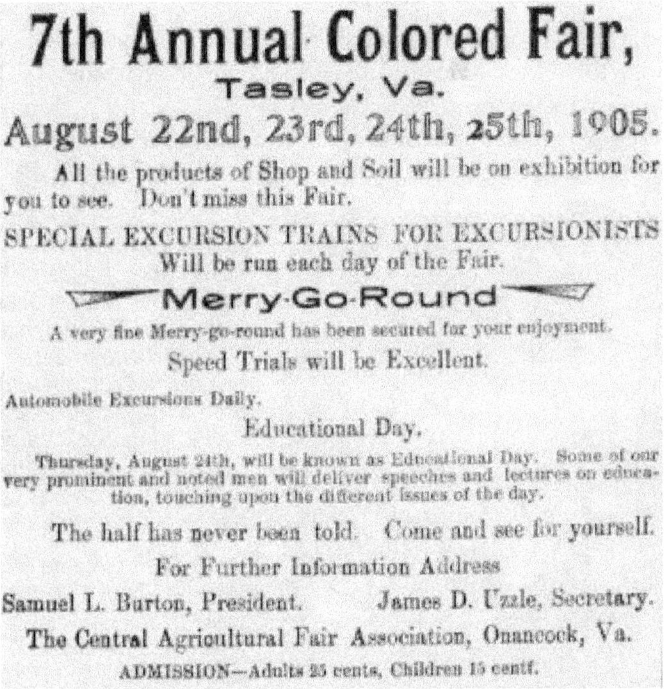

Chapter 10. The Race Riot Cases

7th Annual Colored Fair,
Tasley, Va.
August 22nd, 23rd, 24th, 25th, 1905.

All the products of Shop and Soil will be on exhibition for you to see. Don't miss this Fair.

SPECIAL EXCURSION TRAINS FOR EXCURSIONISTS
Will be run each day of the Fair.

Merry-Go-Round
A very fine Merry-go-round has been secured for your enjoyment.
Speed Trials will be Excellent.
Automobile Excursions Daily.

Educational Day.
Thursday, August 24th, will be known as Educational Day. Some of our very prominent and noted men will deliver speeches and lectures on education, touching upon the different issues of the day.

The half has never been told. Come and see for yourself.

For Further Information Address

Samuel L. Burton, President.   James D. Uzzle, Secretary.
The Central Agricultural Fair Association, Onancock, Va.
ADMISSION—Adults 25 cents, Children 15 cents.

Figure 22 Advertisement for the Tasley Fair, Tasley, Virginia
Advertisement from the 1905 *Peninsula Enterprise*.

A Sylvanius Conquest was listed in the 1910 U.S. Census in Hampton, Virginia, age 25, listed as a boarder, one of three boarders at the William S. Addison household. He is listed as single and a barrel maker. He appears in a directory in 1912 (on Ancestry.com) at Newport News, Virginia, with his occupation identified as cooper. A U.S. World War I draft registration card dated June 5, 1917, was located for Conquest, which identifies him as born July 26, 1888, residence in Hampton, Virginia, married with a five-year-old child, occupation cooper, and born in Accomack County, Virginia.

Mob Law on Delmarva

Pocomoke City, Maryland 1907

The events that unfolded in Onancock also affected Pocomoke, Maryland, a town located just north of the Virginia State line. *The Baltimore Sun* of August 13th reports, "Pocomoke City, Md., Aug. 12 – Intense excitement prevailed in Pocomoke City on Saturday night when news of the Onancock race riot was received...."

> *"A lynching has never occurred in Pocomoke City, but such has gradually become the temper among a certain element of the whites that only a very slight matter would fan the spark of race hatred to a blaze and cause a race war of no small proportions."*
>
> *August 13, 1907*
> *The Baltimore Sun*

Trouble began brewing at 10 P. M. when orders were received from Cape Charles by Robert W. Copper, station agent at the New York, Philadelphia and Norfolk Railroad depot that a special train be prepared to start at once from Pocomoke City to Onancock, carrying officers and reinforcements to aid the whites in a struggle with the blacks then in progress. ....

Later advices came from Virginia about 11 P. M., stating that several negroes had been killed, and the blacks were under control, so the special was not run. The crowd at the station, however, seemed loath to disperse, after hearing this later news and appeared bent on wreaking vengeance on any of the blacks who should happen to come across their path.

A large negro camp meeting opened, early Saturday evening on Hall's Hill, about a mile outside the corporate limits, on the Snow Hill and Stockton road, and several hundred blacks were due to arrive at the depot on the northbound train arriving here shortly before midnight. The mob at once determined to prevent these from landing at the point of the gun, but a few cooler heads prevented serious trouble by meeting the negroes on their arrival and directing them by an out-of-the-way and circuitous route to the camp grounds. Before all the blacks could get fairly started on their way a number of the whites rushed in, blows were struck and several negroes were badly bruised and beaten, while pistol shots fired rapidly in succession could be heard all over the town, making it appear almost as if pandemonium had broken loose. The shots, however as afterward transpired, were all in the air, and no one was seriously injured. ....

Pocomoke City has a wide reputation throughout the Eastern Shore of Maryland and Virginia as being one of the most dangerous spots on earth for a negro whenever any race excitement is in progress, and the negroes in attendance at the camp meeting here now are thoroughly cowed and frightened. Many of them could be seen yesterday on the county roads walking to New Church and Stockton, there to take the

Chapter 10. The Race Riot Cases

first train for safer territory. The religious services at the camp grounds, which were advertised to continue all through the week, will very likely come to an abrupt close today, as the blacks, while looking forward to this annual meeting as the largest and most enjoyable event of the year, have concluded that discretion is the better part of valor, and that Pocomoke City is getting to be an unsafe spot for any number of blacks to congregate in.

A lynching has never occurred in Pocomoke City, but such has gradually become the temper among a certain element of the whites that only a very slight matter would fan the spark of race hatred to a blaze and cause a race war of no small proportions. The resident negroes of the city fully realize this, and unless under the influence of liquor or aggravated by blacks from other places, keep exceedingly quiet and well behaved.[65]

---

[65] *The Baltimore Sun*, "Excitement in Pocomoke, News Of Trouble In Onancock Makes Bad Feeling Toward Negroes," Aug. 13, 1907

Mob Law on Delmarva

Rehoboth, Delaware Riot 1908

The Baltimore Sun described rioting between white soldiers from Camp Hill and black vacationers in the Rehoboth area, where both whites and blacks were injured during the summer of 1908. The incidents occurred during the resort excursions, the segregated use of the beaches allowed only at certain times of the year.

The August 1, 1908 issue of *The Baltimore Sun* includes the following.

> *"One aged man took refuge in the Hotel Townsend. He escaped by a rear door just as the soldiers with a battering ram were proceeding to carry out a threat to beat down the doors and lynch him."*
>
> *August 1, 1908*
> *The Baltimore Sun*

Lewes, Del., July 31 – A riot occurred between the soldiers of Camp Hall and colored excursionists at Rehoboth last night, in which one soldier's skull was crushed and several others were injured, while a number of colored men were badly beaten.

Charles Ferguson, private of Company H, First Regiment, Delaware National Guard, of New Castle, whose skull was crushed, is in a critical condition. William Knox, a colored waiter, is badly bruised and injured internally. Several other negroes were secretly carried to their homes. The provost guard was called out to quell the riot, and many soldiers received slight wounds. Governor Lea has authorized 15 warrants for members of Company H.

Yesterday was Governor's Day at the soldiers' encampment. Thousands of visitors came in on the special excursions and the beach was crowded. At night in the bustle on the boardwalk one of the soldiers of Company H was jostled by a colored woman and accidentally trod on her foot. The man and the girl began to shower the soldier with vile epithets, and the storm broke. The man threw a brick and crushed the skull of the soldier.

The militiamen were so incensed at the attack that a hunt was started for the brick thrower. Citizens joined and a general riot started.

A negro was beaten into insensibility, several of them were picked up bodily and thrown from Horn's pier overboard. The colored people were badly frightened, and fled from the beach. Many of them had clothes torn from their backs.

Members of Company H went to Camp Hall, armed themselves with ball cartridges and started on the warpath in real earnest.

Chapter 10. The Race Riot Cases

One aged man took refuge in the Hotel Townsend. He escaped by a rear door just as the soldiers with a battering ram were proceeding to carry out a threat to beat down the doors and lynch him.

A detail of the troops who had remained quiet was sent out to arrest the riotous guardsmen. A clash ensued, in which a number were slightly injured.

It was not until the Governor had sent a detail of 50 men on the trail of the colored man who had started the trouble that the men were appeased.[66]

Wilmington Riots of 1910

Riots occurred nationwide during the summer of 1910, following the famous victory of boxer Jack Johnson. Newspapers reported on outbursts throughout the country, including Wilmington, Delaware, in July of 1910.

The Baltimore Sun July 5, 1910 article includes the following.

> *"White, the negro, was rescued by the police, and then the whites tried to lynch him. The police finally landed the man in the police station."*
>
> *July 5, 1910*
> The Baltimore Sun

The victory of Johnson over Jeffries was the cause of a race riot in Wilmington tonight. A number of the participants were wounded. An attempt was made by angry whites to lynch a negro after he had been arrested and an apartment house occupied by negroes was bombarded with stones. The crowd numbered 5,000. The police responded to a riot call and finally dispersed the mob.

The injured include Michael Brown, a white man, who started the trouble by arguing the outcome of the prize fight with a negro. He was seriously hurt about the head and also cut with a razor. Several others whose names the police could not obtain were also injured.

The affray started at Fourth and Church streets. A mob of whites chased a gang of negroes. One of the latter, Benjamin White, fled for his life into a negro apartment house known as Jones flats. The whites began bombarding this place with missiles of all kinds. The negroes responded similarly, injuring several whites.

---

[66] *The Baltimore Sun*, "Soldiers in Race Riot; Rehoboth Scene of Battle Between Guardsmen and Negroes; Thrown Brick Starts Fight; Soldier Treads on Woman's Foot and Gets a Crushed Skull – Governor Lea Has to Take Action," Aug. 1, 1908

Mob Law on Delmarva

The police threatened to kill some of the participants before they could be subdued.

White, the negro, was rescued by the police, and then the whites tried to lynch him. The police finally landed the man in the police station.[67]

Laurel, Delaware Race Riot of 1911

Newspaper accounts detail violence in areas of Laurel and Seaford, Delaware, in the spring of 1911.

The following is an excerpt from the April 3rd issue of *The Baltimore Sun*.

Laurel, Del., April 2 – One white man is dead and several other residents of Laurel are carrying wounds as a result of a race riot which occurred here late last night and early this morning. From 11 o'clock last night until 4 o'clock this morning the best people of Laurel were terror-stricken. Women and children, and even men, crowded into downtown stores, which offered shelter from the blacks and the storm of bullets, and remained huddled together until after daybreak, when the warfare ceased because the blacks were afraid of being recognized.

Three negroes and one white man have been arrested and committed for court without bail. The jury of inquest, which will sift the whole affair, is to meet tomorrow, and by that time the authorities expect to have four other prisoners in jail awaiting trial on the charge of shooting up the town.[68]

From the April 5, 1911 issue of *The Baltimore Sun*,

> "Shrewdness of the local authorities probably saved Robert Whitney, the negro accused of slaying Olin Stockley in the race riot here Saturday night, from being lynched by a mob of vengeful white people."
>
> April 5, 1911
> The Baltimore Sun

Laurel, Del., April 4 – Shrewdness of the local authorities probably saved Robert Whitney, the negro accused of slaying Olin Stockley in the race riot here Saturday night, from being lynched by a mob of vengeful white people. After the testimony of Mrs. Mollie Wright, the white woman who declared she saw Whitney fire the fatal shot, had been taken by the coroner's jury the negro was taken out the back door of the magistrate's office and hustled off to jail. Later, it is said, a mob

---

[67] *The Baltimore Sun*, "Razors in Wilmington," Jul. 5, 1910
[68] *The Baltimore Sun*, "One Dead in Riot. Many Other White Men Injured In Race War At Laurel, Del." Apr. 3, 1911

Chapter 10. The Race Riot Cases

of angry men went to the town prison intending to lynch him, and only the trick of the officers prevented the negro from being killed.

State Detective Frederick A. Walls and other officers engaged in running down the rioters arrested two negro roadsters this afternoon, who were suspected of being the ones who shot at James T. Wilson as he was driving to Delmar last night, but the two proved a clear alibi and were released on the condition that they leave town immediately.

A report from the Salisbury hospital says that George Hudson, another white victim of the riot, is gradually weakening after the amputation of his legs, and there is no hope of his recovery. A previous unofficial report was to the effect that he was dead.

The funeral of young Stockley was held in the Methodist Episcopal Church this afternoon. He was buried in the Odd Fellows' Cemetery. There was a large crowd in attendance.

Authorities in charge of investigations being made in the cases of Stockley and Hudson declare that both men were willfully murdered by vengeful negroes, as neither of them participated in the trouble, and believe the whole trouble arose from racial antipathy evinced by colored inhabitants of Laurel. The accused men will not face trial for disorderly conduct or inciting to riot, but will be brought to answer the charges of murder.[69]

The *Salisbury Advertiser* of April 8th reports, with the headlines "Rioting in Laurel, Del., Two Men Lose Their Life, White Men Arrested as Leaders."

Trouble broke out in Laurel, Del., on Saturday night between what seemed to be a body of white and a body of colored men, though later reports would indicate the colored men were led by the white men. In the hail of shot, two white men lost their lives. The first to succumb to his injuries was Otto Stockley, 18 years old. He was shot during the beginning of the attack, but did not die until late Sunday afternoon in the Peninsula General Hospital, at Salisbury, where he was taken for treatment.

The riot occurred on the Main Street of Laurel about ten o'clock when a crowd of colored men, mad with liquor, marched down the streets shooting right and left. George Hudson, a farmer fifty years of age, of Bethel, who was brought to the Hospital here, died on Wednesday.

The officials detailed in arresting those responsible for the trouble changed their course of investigations on Wednesday and arrested Edgar Walls, Roland Beauchamp and Charles Rogers, three white men, whom they believe were the leaders of the colored men.

At first everyone was willing to think the colored men entirely responsible for the outbreak and threatened to lynch the first one who appeared in the white section, but since the arrest of the white boys indignation toward the colored folk has diminished and officials declare

---

[69] *The Baltimore Sun*, "Officers Saved Negro, Took Him Through Back door Away From Mob, Angry Men Wanted Whitney," Apr. 5, 1911

Mob Law on Delmarva

it will be useless to retain the extra officers, as disorder has subsided.
...

The three white men are held to await the verdict of the jury. The strongest evidence is against Walls, as several prominent citizens are ready to swear that the young man made remarks after the riot that would implicate him. Walls denies the charge and also the report that he confessed to the shooting when questioned by the chief of police. Hudson was wounded just as he was getting into his carriage to go to his home at Bethel. His friends and citizens of Laurel are stung to fury over his death, and if Walls is held by the Coroner's jury an attempt may be made to lynch him. Hudson was shot in the legs and died following the amputation of both.

At Georgetown indictments were returned by Sussex County Grand Jury against George Williams, alias "Slim Jim," charging the illegal sale of liquor, and John Collins, pointing a pistol. These men were arrested last Sunday following the riot. It is believed that the Grand Jury will take up the cases of the other prisoners later.

The others injured are John Thompson, shot in the legs while he was shaving a patron in his barber shop, struck with several buckshot; George Cannon, residing near Laurel, struck with several buckshot; James Spicer, shot in the ear, and Edgar Quillen, shot in the side.[70]

---

[70] *Salisbury Advertiser*, Salisbury, MD, "Rioting in Laurel, Del., Two Men Lose Their Life, White Men Arrested As Leaders," Apr. 8, 1911

Chapter 10. The Race Riot Cases

Seaford, Delaware Race Riot of 1911

The following article from the *Gettysburg Times*, dated May 6, 1911,

> *"In the company of officers the colored men were led out of town, with hundreds of the young men at their heels, vowing vengeance."*
>
> May 6, 1911
> Gettysburg Times

Seaford, Del., May 8 – A repetition of the recent fatal race riot at Laurel, Del., was avoided here by the arrival of police, constables and a dozen men sworn in as special [officers], who dispersed an angered mob, which threatened to attack the colored residents of the town and drive them out.

The trouble started as hundreds of persons, mostly women and children, were leaving Wright's Auditorium. Several colored men took places on an opposite corner and as the women came up, either stepped in front of them or elbowed them off the sidewalk into the street.

Leonard Hatfield resented these tactics and rebuked others of the colored men, who became insolent and told him that they would do as they pleased. Hatfield knocked one of the colored men, Harry Blockson, down with a blow of his fist. Other colored men took up the fight and Hatfield knocked another one down, this time with a stone. The blow rendered the colored man unconscious.

Small boys on the street, seeing the fracas, immediately started to run every colored man seen out of the town. They cried: "Race riot," "Get your guns," "Kill them," "They can't do in Seaford as they did in Laurel," and other phrases, calculated to stir up trouble.

Women screamed, and for a time grave trouble appeared imminent, but the police arrived and arrested the colored men and Hatfield. All were taken before Mayor John P. Dulaney and fined $5 each.

Hatfield objected to paying the fine, declaring that he was protecting the white women, and the mob demanded that the fine be remitted and the colored men held for court. The fines were paid later.

In the company of officers the colored men were led out of town, with hundreds of the young men at their heels, vowing vengeance. It was not until late in the morning that quiet was restored and at several times it was feared that rioting would break out with a concerted attack on the colored section of the town.[71]

---

[71] *Gettysburg Times*, "Police Prevent a Race Riot; Whites and Negroes Clash at Seaford, Del.; Women were insulted; Colored Men Pushed them into the Street and Fight which Followed Soon Drew a Mob," May 6, 1911

Crisfield, Maryland Riot of 1912

October, 1912, Crisfield, Maryland

The Baltimore Sun reports on a race riot in Crisfield.

> Crisfield, Md., Oct. 18 – In a race riot which called out Sheriff Tull and Deputy Townsend the first week at Blake's general store, in the Quindacqua neighborhood, Capt. Washington Taylor, a white man, was badly cut up with a pair of brass knuckles by some one who attached him in the dark.
>
> The trouble started over a bicycle belonging to a white boy which a colored boy took. The Sheriff and deputy each reached the scene in about 30 minutes after the hurry call and arrested Harry Spence, colored, as the culprit to await the action of the grand jury. There has also been a shooting affair in town in the colored quarter and race trouble at Tangier Island.[72]

Delmar Riot of 1914

January 27, 1914, Delmar, Wicomico County, Maryland (& Sussex County, Delaware)

Newspapers reported on violence occurring in the border town of Delmar in Wicomico County, Maryland and Sussex County, Delaware, in the first months of 1914.

The Wicomico News includes the following in the January 29, 1914 edition.

> Tuesday night a telephone message was received by the sheriff's office from Delmar saying a race war was on there and asking the sheriff to come with his men to take charge of the order in the town. Sheriff Brady with his deputies rushed to Delmar in two automobiles but on arriving found that the call had been premature. The authorities in Delmar said a negro had passed an insulting remark to a white woman and had then started to run. Within a few minutes the town was all excitement but the affair soon quieted down and when our officers arrived there was no need of their services.[73]

The Baltimore Sun of January 28, 1914 reports on a riot involving efforts to locate and arrest Howard Jackson for assault on a white woman.

---

[72] *The Baltimore Sun*, "Race Troubles in Somerset—Whites and Negroes Clash; Capt. Washington Taylor Wounded," Oct. 18, 1912
[73] *The Wicomico News*, Salisbury, MD, "Trouble At Delmar," Jan. 29, 1914

Chapter 10. The Race Riot Cases

Salisbury, Md., Jan. 27 – Sheriff William Brady and his deputy, Ephraim Benson, were summoned to Delmar, on the Maryland and Delaware boundary, tonight to quell a race riot.

The trouble is said to have arisen over the effort of the railroad men to find a negro, Howard Jackson, who is said to have attempted several days ago an assault upon Mrs. George Green, the mother of a railroad man. Efforts to keep the attack quiet proved unsuccessful. A mob was formed to search for the alleged offender.

> *"The negroes were driven from their homes and ordered to leave the town. It is said not a negro family in town was left undisturbed."*
>
> January 28, 1914
> The Baltimore Sun

The homes of the negroes on the Maryland side of Delmar were visited and when the whites tried to enter the houses they were met with resistance. According to information received here a pitched battle ensued, in which a number of shots were fired and clubs and stones freely used. So far as is known no one was seriously hurt, but a number are said to have received cuts and bruises.

The negroes were driven from their homes and ordered to leave the town. It is said not a negro family in town was left undisturbed.

Unable to control the mob and fearing bloodshed, the calmer among the whites telephoned to Sheriff Brady asking him to come armed. He hastily collected a number of deputies and left with them for the scene in three automobiles, heavily armed. Their arrival had a quieting effect upon the mob and some of the negroes returned to their homes.

The officers remained on the scene overnight to prevent a further outbreak, which was threatened.[74]

---

[74] *The Baltimore Sun*, "Race Riot in Delmar—Guns and Clubs Freely Used In Battle Between Whites and Blacks," Jan. 28, 1914

Seaford, Delaware Riot of 1915

May 1, 1915, Seaford, Sussex County, Maryland

The Baltimore Sun reported on violence in Seaford, Delaware, where a fight resulted in injuries to a minister and others. Two black men were arrested and threats of lynching were reported.

According to *The Baltimore Sun* of May 2, 1915,

> "Holmes Nicholson, son of the Rev. John L. Nicholson, of the Methodist Protestant Conference, was cut about the face and hands and is supposed to be in a dying condition as the result of a race riot between negroes and white men of this town late tonight."
>
> May 2, 1915
> The Baltimore Sun

Holmes Nicholson, son of the Rev. John L. Nicholson, of the Methodist Protestant Conference, was cut about the face and hands and is supposed to be in a dying condition as the result of a race riot between negroes and white men of this town late tonight.

The trouble started in front of Wright's Auditorium when a negro threw a whisky bottle among a crowd of men. He was chased to the colored section of town, where a fight ensued for several minutes. When Officer Wright arrived at the scene Nicholson's throat was severely cut and the jugular vein thought to be severed, while Thomas Johnson was severely cut in the face and body. Nicholson was brought down town, but at a late hour had not had the services of a doctor.

Two negroes thought to have done the cutting are in the local jail, where on the outside a crowd of white men threatened to break open the jail and lynch them. A telephone message was sent to the Sheriff at Georgetown. The main street of the town was crowded with excited people. Nicholson, who is the worst one hurt, is a popular young man of this town and his friends are threatening to do vengeance. The stabbing was done in front of the house of Mayor Walter B. Robinson.[75]

---

[75] *The Baltimore Sun*, "Race Riot in Delaware—Son of Minister Stabbed—Another Man Cut—Threats of Lynching Heard," May 2, 1915

Chapter 10. The Race Riot Cases

Wilmington, Delaware Race Riot of 1915

The only reason this case is included here is because of one newspaper account located referring to a "race riot" in Wilmington, though the account refers specifically to Joseph Johnson. The information is described here.

The Baltimore Sun of October 23, 1915 reports the following.

> *"Only the timely arrival of a police squad saved Joseph Johnson, a negro, from injury at the hands of a mob of whites."*
>
> October 23, 1915
> The Baltimore Sun

Wilmington, Del., Oct. 22 – A race riot developed in East Fourth street this afternoon, following trouble over the payment of 15 cents for a key to a Yale lock. Only the timely arrival of a police squad saved Joseph Johnson, a negro, from injury at the hands of a mob of whites. Johnson later was fined $20 and costs in the City Court.

The negro ordered a key from Harry Pogoet, who has a hardware store, but when Johnson called for it today he did not want to pay Pogoet for making it. Johnson grabbed the key from Pogoet's hand and started out, but Mrs. Pogoet seized him. He picked up a hammer and struck her. Pogoet grappled with the negro, and a crowd collected. The negro reached the street, and again he attacked Mrs. Pogoet, knocking her down and kicking her repeatedly.

The crowd was preparing to handle the negro roughly when the police arrived.[76]

---

[76] *The Baltimore Sun*, "Race Riot Over 15 Cents; Negro Refuses to Pay for Key and Attacks Woman," Oct. 23, 1915

Middletown, Delaware Race Riot of 1915

The Baltimore Sun of November 15, 1915 reports on rioting in Delaware.

> "This is the second riot that has occurred here recently."
>
> November 15, 1915
> The Baltimore Sun

Middletown, Del., Nov. 14 – Samuel Gunning, 22 years old, of this town, was shot and probably fatally injured in a race riot that occurred here late last night. The bullet passed through Gunning's overcoat, coat, sweater, vest and two shirts and entered the body just below the breast. It lodged in his back, below the shoulder blade. The wounded man was rushed to Dr. Edward M. Vaughn's office and the bullet removed. He was then taken to the Delaware Hospital, where his condition is said to be critical.

The riot started when Policeman Ruffle arrested a negro for carrying concealed weapons. Other blacks gathered and charged the officer, using bricks, revolvers and razors. In the fight Chief of Police Harry H. Milvand was slashed about the face and body. His coat was cut to threads. Policeman Hamburg also was badly injured. Ruffle was hit by a blackjack and dazed.

In the exchange of shots Gunning was wounded.

Two negroes were arrested and are now awaiting trial. A revolver, taken from one of the prisoners, showed that the trigger had been pulled four times but only one cartridge was exploded. The bullet taken from Gunning's back is of the same caliber as those in the pistol.

This is the second riot that has occurred here recently.[77]

---

[77] *The Baltimore Sun*, "Shot in Race Riot, Negroes Attack Middletown (Del.) Police Injuring Three Of Them And Bystander," Nov. 15, 1915

Chapter 10. The Race Riot Cases

Wilmington, Delaware Riots of 1919

The year 1919 is known for its "Red Summer," a period of nationwide surges of violence and murders characterized as riots. Books on the subject of the Red Summer describe year-long violence. Wilmington's year-end violence has been described in books. Some researchers attribute some of the violence to the return of African Americans who served in World War I.

The Baltimore Sun includes the following on November 13, 1919.

> *"Meanwhile the negroes alleged to have been implicated in the shooting of the two policemen were taken from the jail in which they had been placed and sent to Philadelphia under heavy guard, because of fear by the police that an attempt might be made to lynch them."*
>
> *November 13, 1919*
> *The Baltimore Sun*

Wilmington, Del., Nov. 13 – Rioting between whites and negroes broke out here tonight, following the killing of one policeman and the wounding of another by negroes whom they were questioning regarding a recent robbery.

Angered by the double shooting, bands of white[s] roamed the streets tonight. A clash occurred when 300 suddenly came upon four negroes. Both sides opened fire and Bannel Field, a negro, fell, with a wound in the head from which he is expected to recover.

The whites then closed in on the other negroes, who were saved only by the prompt arrival of 15 policemen. The patrolmen used their clubs freely, while the three negroes, breaking away, fled. Later police reserves w[e]re ordered to patrol the negro quarters and break up any gatherings.

Meanwhile the negroes alleged to have been implicated in the shooting of the two policemen were taken from the jail in which they had been placed and sent to Philadelphia under heavy guard, because of fear by the police that an attempt might be made to lynch them.[78]

The blog *Historical Amnesia*, posted on November 18, 2009, with the heading "90th Anniversary of Race Riot in Wilmington, Delaware," with the following article (2009).

---

[78] *The Baltimore Sun*, "Race Riot in Wilmington, Delaware Negroes Saved From White Mob By Police," Nov. 14, 1919

Mob Law on Delmarva

Ninety years ago in November, the city of Wilmington, Delaware, reverberated with racial tension. When three black men, Lemuel, James, and John Price, were arrested for killing white patrolman Tom L. Zelby (or Seebley), a white mob numbering 300 formed, roaming the streets, "seeking vengeance," according to the *New York Herald."* Accounts differ, but after a shooting incident involving Dillard or Bannel Field and Buck Hayes as targets of the mob, the hysterical crowd stormed through a predominantly black neighborhood, throwing bricks through the windows of the homes.

Centreville, Maryland Riot of 1919

The Baltimore Sun reported on violence in Centreville, Queen Anne's County, Maryland in December, describing, "Dec. 14 – Shortly before midnight last night local officers nipped in the bud what they believed was a plot uprising by a group of negroes against the white people of Centreville." The article went on to report of a judge punching a so-called insolent man, rumors of possible retaliation, or threats and fears of a racial outbreak.

The Baltimore Sun of December 15, 1919 reports,

> Centreville, Md., Dec. 14 – Shortly before midnight last night local officers nipped in the bud what they believed was a plot uprising by a group of negroes against the white people of Centreville.
>
> Five colored men were arrested and placed in jail on the charge of disorderly conduct, pending the possible institution of more serious charges against them by the State's Attorney.
>
> The trouble started after Burgess Griffin, Charles Gassoway, John Hard and William Johnson, negroes, were arraigned before Justice Robert Coursey on the charge of gunning without licenses and for not having the written consent of Register of Wills William E. Bishop, on whose farm they were hunting. When arrested they could not produce permits from the landowner, but an investigation showed that they all had obtained licenses.
>
> Justice Coursey dismissed the case against Hard, as he was an employee on the Bishop farm and was legally entitled to hunt. Griffin and Gassoway, however, were each fined $15 and costs. Gassoway paid his fine, but Griffin is alleged to have used insulting language to the justice, and Magistrate Coursey promptly administered a sentence of 30 days in jail for contempt of court.
>
> This angered Griffin so that he is alleged to have become more violent in his insults. Instantly declaring the case closed, Justice Coursey attached the negro and proceeded to administer a trouncing to him.

Chapter 10. The Race Riot Cases

After Griffin had been taken to jail reports reached Justice Coursey's office that a group of negroes were discussing means of getting revenge. Several in the group are alleged to have made remarks calculated to start racial ill feeling, and Sheriff James W. Yeates and Constables John P. Williamson and Marion C. Council dispersed the crowd and ordered them to leave instantly for their homes. Charles Griffin, Gilbert Griffin, Charles Fisher and Charles Gassoway, all negroes, were arrested on the technical charge of disturbing the peace, but it is understood that more serious charges will be instituted tomorrow.

For nearly an hour last night there was every sign that a racial outbreak would be the result of the trials earlier in the evening. It was rumored that certain negroes had threatened they would "get even" with Justice Coursey, and a crowd of whites gathered to protect the officers should any trouble start.

The officers met the situation promptly by ordering all crowds to disperse, and shortly after midnight the streets were practically cleared.

Centreville has never before had any public manifestation of ill feeling between the two races. None of the negroes arrested is a resident of Centreville, and colored citizens of the town took no part in the disturbance. Local officers are keeping a close watch to prevent any clash between the whites and blacks.

The men arrested last night all employed State Insurance Commissioner Thomas J. Keating as their Counsel.[79]

Ridgely, Maryland Violence of 1931

The Baltimore Afro-American reports on a near-riot in Ridgely, Maryland, about two weeks after the December 4, 1931 lynching of Matthew Williams in Salisbury, Maryland.

> Ridgely, Md. – This town, although 50 miles from Salisbury, Md., where a lynching took place four weeks ago, is still in the grip of anti-Negro terrorists.
>
> Residents here report that orders have been sent out to permit no colored people in town after 6 o'clock p.m.
>
> A near inter-racial riot was thwarted here two weeks ago when school children and older boys fought on their way home from school. Commissioners appealed to forestalled an effort of gangsters to drive all colored people out of stores and off the streets.[80]

---

[79] *The Baltimore Sun*, "Justice Punches Negro; Centreville Magistrate Gives Him Thrashing For Insolence; Race Riot Then Threatens; Following Summary Punishment, Gathering of Blacks in Streets is Quelled By Officers," Dec. 15, 1919
[80] *The Baltimore Afro-American*, Baltimore, MD, "Curfew at Ridgely," Jan. 9, 1932

Mob Law on Delmarva

Princess Anne, Maryland Rioting of 1934

Newspapers reported on rioting in Princess Anne, nearly a year after George Armwood was lynched in the town.

During the year following the October 1933 lynching of Armwood, Somerset County experienced several cases. In February of 1934, Sam Jones was acquitted of charges of murder of a white woman at New Years. In July of 1934, Howard McClendon was sentenced to life imprisonment for the murder of Patrolman Harry Daugherty in Crisfield.

On Wednesday, September 5, 1934, Bowland was arrested for attempted criminal assault. The September 7th edition of the *Marylander and Herald* includes the following.

> James E. Bowland, 33 year-old negro, is said to have attempted to criminally assault Mrs. Mary E. Waddy, a highly respected white woman, in the kitchen of her home in East Princess Anne, around three o'clock Wednesday afternoon. Mrs. Waddy is a widow and is 66 years old.
>
> The negro has been employed by the Waddy family as a farm hand for the past four years and Mrs. Waddy had no suspicions of his intentions when he entered the home and asked for some grease with which to grease a cultivator. Going into another room to get the grease, she was followed by the negro who crept up behind her, encircled her with his arms and threw her violently to the floor and, but for the desperate fighting and shrill screams of the woman causing neighbors to rush to her assistance, he would have undoubtedly accomplished his vile purpose.
>
> Mrs. Waddy in a highly nervous condition was rushed to the office of a Princess Anne physician and a warrant was issued for the arrest of Bowland. Deputy Sheriffs Norman and Charles Dryden left at once to search for the negro who they soon located at the home of his father about four miles from the home of Mrs. Waddy.
>
> The negro was brought to Princess Anne and given a hearing before Justice Edgar A. Jones, who held him without bond for the action of the Somerset Grand Jury, which meets here the last week in this month, and ordered that he be rushed to the Baltimore City jail to remain until called for.
>
> From the time of the attempted attack, officials and all others connected with the case preserved the utmost secrecy and the negro had been spirited out of town before the general public knew there had been any trouble. The attack was committed around 3 p.m., the warrant issued at 7, the Negro arrested at 7.30, given a hearing at 8 and lodged in the Baltimore jail by Deputy Norman Dryden at midnight.
>
> When the news got out, small crowds began to gather on the streets of the city but upon learning that the negro had been taken away several

Chapter 10. The Race Riot Cases

hours earlier, they soon dispersed and as we go to press everything is quiet and it is thought that should the negro be returned to Princess Anne, there will be no violence.[81]

A few days later, on Saturday, some rioting was reported to have occurred. *The Baltimore Afro-American* covered the rioting story, and in its September 15th coverage, the newspaper reported there were complaints expressed on the streets of recent arrests of blacks for alleged crimes against white women. With the descriptions of the cases, the newspaper describes the following.

> Another of these cases is that of James Boland [*sic*], a former Sunday school teacher, who is accused of having attempted to rape Mrs. Anna Waddy, a 65-year-old white woman, last week.
>
> According to some current rumors in the community, Boland is not guilty but he was trying to collect $118 in salary that he said was owed to him by Mrs. Waddy.

The case was removed to Dorchester County due to the change of venue requested by Bowland's appointed defense, Senator Beauchamp. On The *Baltimore Afro-American* article of September 15, 1934, reported by Clarence Mitchell, includes the following.

> Princess Anne, Md. – Flames of race antagonism that have been smoldering in Princess Anne since the lynching of George Armwood, last October, burst into fever heat on Saturday night [September 8th] when a gang of white hoodlums attacked several colored citizens.
>
> Reports circulated to the effect that the entire colored population was being driven from town on Saturday night, were denied by colored residents who would talk to AFRO reporters on Monday. Many of the terror-stricken townsfolk refused to talk for fear of reprisals.
>
> Residents were prone to dismiss the disorder as trivial, despite the report that men, women and children had been sent scurrying in all directions by the enraged whites. Varying reports give the number of whites in the mob from 200 to 500.
>
> The small force of three policemen, headed by Chief Marion Austin, was ignored as if it did not exist.
>
> The town was in a turmoil for more than an hour on Saturday night, and outside help was summoned by Sheriff Luther Daugherty as officials recalled the burning of George Armwood in the courthouse square during an outbreak last October.
>
> The Rev. R.C. Hughes, pastor of the Methodist Church in Princess Anne, declared that he had no information about such a thing, when

---

[81] *Marylander and Herald*, "Mrs. Waddy Attacked by Negro, James Bowland Attempted Criminal Assault on Widow, Age 66, in East Princess Anne," Sep. 7, 1934

interviewed by the AFRO, and his residence is not two blocks from the place where the trouble is supposed to have started.

Dr. T. H. Kiah, of the Princess Anne Academy, also denied having any knowledge of such a large number of persons engaging in a fight.

He pointed out that such reports were also circulated last year, when persons accused of lynching George Armwood were returned to Princess Anne.

A young printer, who lives at Princess Anne, stated that he saw the whole disturbance, and estimated the number of persons in the melee at approximately twenty-five.

He laughed at the story of 300 colored persons being chased from the town, and declared that there is hardly that many colored people living there.

An undertaker in the town stated that the whole disturbance never got off the main street, and not a single home was entered by persons creating the disorder.

Eye-witnesses charge that a mob, led by a white man named Stacey, attacked Roy Shields, a native of the town, and severely beat him with clubs and other weapons.

Shields was rescued from the crowd by officers, according to a witness, but his attackers were not dispersed until one of them had made a speech.

The speech is thought to have centered around recent arrests of colored men on the shore for alleged crimes against white women. ...

The trouble is supposed to have started when two colored men engaged in a fight before a new beer tavern on the town's main street.

Whites are alleged to have gathered to witness the battle, but contestants either fell or was pushed into their midst.

The two fighters were arrested but released on Monday, according to residents at Princess Anne, for lack of evidence against them.

It is charged by some who witnessed the trouble, that this officer is familiarly known as Shaggy. ....

The stories of what happened during the clean-up differ. The whites place the blame on the colored people, and the colored people charge that the whites started the fray.

The colored version is that the mobsters charged Shields, for no reason, and began beating him.

Whites assert that Shields had drawn a knife on the officer named Shaggy, and their assistance was solicited by the policeman, who was getting the worst of a tussle for possession of the weapon.

Chapter 10. The Race Riot Cases

> Another man named Wilson is alleged to have been passing in a car at the time, and the militant whites leaped to his running board, smashing him in the face. ....[82]

The following brief account was reported in the *Marylander and Herald* on September 28, 1934, in a column about the September term court in session.

> In his charge to the jury Judge Duer laid great stress on the recent disturbance in Princess Anne, in which colored people were beaten and driven from the streets of the town, and asked that it be thoroughly investigated and that the blame be placed where it belonged.[83]

November 26, 1934, James Bowland was sentenced to 20 years imprisonment.[84]

---

[82] *The Baltimore Afro-American*, "Lynching Shore Riots Princess Anne Gang Attacks Townspeople," Sep. 15, 1934
[83] *Marylander and Herald*, "September Term Court in Session," Sep. 28, 1934
[84] *Marylander and Herald*, "Bowland Gets 20 Years Sentence," Nov. 30, 1934

Mob Law on Delmarva

Chapter 11. Eastern Shore Cases

The scope of this project encompassed the period from 1870 through the 1940s. The period was selected somewhat arbitrarily but also for purposes of convenience with the expectation that newspaper searches might reveal a more consistent reporting of lynchings and near-lynchings. The period spans the era described as the Jim Crow period and a portion of the reconstruction period following the end of the Civil War.

However, certain pre-1870 cases were significant. Whenever the pre-1870 cases appeared within view, they were added, but for the period was not searched in detail. In the early 1800s, murders of slaves or freedmen were not consistently reported in newspapers, but some listed a few. In 1810, the slave Steven was executed by hanging in Dorchester County, Maryland, for "theft-stealing." Also in 1810, the slave Peregrine was executed by hanging in Queen Anne's County, Maryland, for murder. In 1822, "Jenny, a negress," was hanged in Somerset County, Maryland. In 1831, the slave Henny was executed by hanging in Dorchester County, Maryland, for murder.

Jacob Hamilton
Lynched October 1861 in Smyrna, Delaware

> *"A rope was procured, a noose was made, and when the constables made their appearance in the street with their charge, the crowd gathered around, seized him and ran him to a beech tree on the banks of a mill dam at the edge of the town."*
>
> October 15, 1861
> The Baltimore Sun

Jacob Hamilton was lynched for allegedly attacking two daughters of John Cloak, reported as a "wealthy citizen" who lived on the outskirts of Smyrna. *The Baltimore Sun* of October 15, 1861, began "A negro named Jacob Hamilton was hanged by a mob at Smyrna, Del., on Friday last" reporting on the story as related by a correspondent of the *Philadelphia Ledger*, includes the following.

[After hearing screams,] Mrs. Cloak immediately proceeded to the apartment, when she was attacked by a man who was struggling with her daughters in the dark. Mrs. Cloak added her screams to those of the girls, and Mr. C. at once hastened to her aid. He, too, was attacked and beaten in a shocking manner. While the struggle was going forward, a colored servant, who slept in an outbuilding, procured a ladder, and by placing it

> against the windowsill enabled the three ladies to escape. The intruder also got away and without being recognized. His object was evidently to violate the person of one of the young ladies.[85]

Hamilton worked on the Cloak farm and he was arrested. Allegedly there was evidence found on him; this and "other circumstances" led to Hamilton being accused.

> The prisoner was of course committed to answer the charge against him, and he was ordered to be conveyed to Dover jail, a few miles distant. Hamilton was a very powerful man, and in order to guard against his escape while on his way to prison, his arms were pinioned behind his back.
>
> While the hearing and the trying were in progress, preparations were being made outside for lynching the prisoner. A rope was procured, a noose was made, and when the constables made their appearance in the street with their charge, the crowd gathered around, seized him and ran him to a beech tree on the banks of a mill dam at the edge of the town. The rope was placed around his neck, the other end was tied to an outstretched limb of the tree, and in a few seconds the poor wretch was dangling in the air.
>
> All this took place in broad daylight, at half-past nine o'clock in the morning, in the sight of hundreds of spectators. Among the onlookers on there were probably two hundred females. No person attempted to vindicate the outraged law. Hamilton met his fate without a murmur or a struggle. While being hurried to the place of execution, he denied his guilt, but, it is said, just at the moment he was about being suspended, he confessed.
>
> The body was allowed to hang until four o'clock in the afternoon, when I was cut down, and a coroner's jury was empaneled to inquire into the manner in which the man had come to his death. After a post-mortem examination, a verdict was rendered to the effect that the deceased had died from the effects of strangulation, the result of hanging, inflicted by some person or persons unknown to the jury.

---

[85] *The Baltimore Sun*, "Lynch Law at Smyrna," Oct. 15, 1861

Chapter 11. Eastern Shore Cases

John Holden
Lynched April 1866 at Pungoteague, Virginia
A bizarre story surrounding the death of John Holden in 1866, at Pungoteague in Accomack County, Virginia.

Brooks Miles Barnes of the Eastern Shore Public Library provided information from the publication, *The Virginia Eastern Shore in the War of Secession and in the Reconstruction Period* by James Egbert Mears, 1957. (Mears 1957)** Mears had included a section "Miscellaneous Items among the Freedmen's Bureau Records, Relating to the Virginia Eastern Shore." The items included a letter quoted from George H. French, First Lieutenant and Assistant Superintendent, to Capt. A. S. Flagg, A. Q. M. and Supt. R., F. & A. L., dated April 16, 1866, from Drummondtown, Virginia.

> Capt.: -- I have the honor to make the following report in regards to the murder committed at Pungoteague, in this county, on the 12th inst.
>
> A colored man by the name of John Holden went to the house of Mr. Drummond, and finding him absent, remained until after dinner, which was given him by Mrs. Drummond. After dinner Mrs. D. went to the barn to feed the horse and was followed by Holden, who with an axe struck her on the back of the head, leaving Mrs. D. dead as he supposed. He, Holden, then returned to the house and demanded money from a colored servant which he thought was in Mrs. D's possession. The girl, refusing to give him the money, he also struck with the axe in the same manner as he did Mrs. D. He then proceeded to the garden, where there were two or three other ladies, and after following them awhile with his axe, went away, telling a colored woman that he was coming back and kill them all.
>
> A search was immediately made for Holden by the citizens, who were enraged at the act, and he was found near his house and taken to Pungoteague the same evening, and after confessing the crime, also that he murdered a colored man last fall, and he wished he could kill another white man, he was hung to a tree by the citizens and remained there until morning, when his body was taken down and placed in a church by some colored people.
>
> I knew nothing about it until about noon of the 13th. I went immediately and saw Mrs. Drummond and the colored woman, who were alive at the time with no prospect of recovery. I said nothing about arresting any one but went down as though it was my duty to do it at the time.

Mears reported that "Holden was hanged to a tree near the present entrance to St. George's Episcopal church."

William "Obie" Evans
Lynched July 1867 at Leipsic, Delaware
The lynching of Civil War veteran William E. Evans has been researched by historian Yohuru Williams for a recent article entitled "'Revenged in the Most Terrible Manner': The Lynching of African American Civil War Veteran William 'Obie' Evans" (2013-2014).

Born in Reedsville, West Virginia, Evans had been enslaved but was listed as free when he was mustered into service on April 19, 1861 (Williams 2013-2014, 35). Following the war, Evans found employment in Delaware after spending much of 1866 trying to redeem the bounty funds to which he was entitled from the war. He settled in Leipsic in the spring of 1867 to work for white farmer William Collins, also a Union veteran. In a tenuous arrangement of a loan to Evans for provisions, Evans turned over to Collins his army document guaranteeing future payment of his bounty (2013-2014, 41-44).

On the morning of July 25th Evans' body was founded hung from a willow tree, above prominent wagon wheel marks, along a public road about a mile outside of Leipsic. Newspaper descriptions reported that the night before, when Collins and his wife were absent from home, a mob of about six or eight arrived at the Collins farm, seized Evans, put him in a wagon, and left in the direction of Leipsic (Williams 2013-2014, 48-50).

Williams' article goes into greater depth about the case.

William Wilson, William Wells, Frank Rounds and George Bailey
Executed March 1869, in Princess Anne, Maryland
William Wilson, William Wells, Frank Rounds and George Bailey (some with aliases) were executed on March 5, 1869, in Princess Anne, Somerset County, for the crime of murder. The multiple executions were for the murder of Capt. Benj. F. Johnson and shipmate Henry Cannon of the schooner *Brave*.

The crimes for which they were executed involved the murder of the white captain and mate of the schooner Brave nearly a year before. The

Chapter 11. Eastern Shore Cases

four were reported to be employed on the schooner, a Crisfield vessel engaged in dredging for oysters on the Chesapeake Bay. The abandoned boat had been discovered with the two bodies. Wilson and Wells were apprehended in April 1868, in Virginia on the Eastern Shore. The two were taken to the Princess Anne jail. While awaiting trial, the men reportedly made several failed attempts to escape.

Rounds was apprehended in Baltimore. Following conviction and sentencing, Wilson and Wells were kept in the jail, awaiting the conviction and sentencing of Rounds, in order to have a joint-execution. But on November 11th, Wilson and Wells made another attempt to escape. According to *The Baltimore Sun*,

> They performed the wonderful task of filing off their irons with a brick, then burned a hole through the inner wall of the jail, which is of wood, and picked an aperture through the outer stone wall. On Sunday, 15rh of November, Wilson was again captured by two citizens in the woods belonging to one of them, who found him sitting by a fire eating parched corn, in an almost starved condition, and suffering much from a wound in the foot, which he had sustained in effecting his escape.
>
> He was at the time in such a pitiable condition that he made no resistance whatever, but quietly submitted to be heavily ironed and taken back to prison. A week later, Wells, the other fugitive, was discovered in the woods near Seaford, Sussex county, Delaware, by some citizens. He started to run, but a threat to shoot brought him to a stand, and he was also carried back to the jail at Princess Anne. Wilson, on being taken back to jail, stated that the wind was blowing very hard, and that it was raining, and the day was just breaking when he got out the last stone of the prison wall from which he escaped. He jumped out first, and got scared at a hobgoblin (an old ram) and cut his foot when he started to run. He, however, waited for Wells, and they started and struck the railroad over the Bombay Hook bridge. He reached the woods near sunrise, and obtaining matches from a darkey, built a fire, around which they stayed all day, and slept in a fodder stack next night, feeding on parched corn the while. He crossed Tony Tank railroad bridge on Thursday in the daytime and

> *"Intense excitement prevailed among those engaged in the oyster business in the section where the horrible deed was committed, and but for the strenuous resistance of the officers of the law when their arrest was made, the two now in jail here would have been swinging to the limbs of the nearest tree."*
>
> *April 17, 1868*
> *The Baltimore Sun*

Mob Law on Delmarva

passed through Salisbury that night, through Main street, while the band was playing, and Wells left him in that town. [86]

The Baltimore Sun of April 17, 1868 reports,

> Wm. Wilson and William Wells, the two negro men lately committed to jail at Drummondtown, Va., have been brought to Princess Anne, Md., and lodged in jail there. They are charged with the murder of Capt. Benjamin Johnson and Henry Cannon, (not Pritchett, as heretofore stated) of the schooner Brave, on the Annamessix [sic] river near Shark's Point, Somerset county.

The two other suspects were being located at the time of the article, which also described the following quoted from the Princess Anne newspaper, *The Princess Anne True Marylander.*

> Intense excitement prevailed among those engaged in the oyster business in the section where the horrible deed was committed, and but for the strenuous resistance of the officers of the law when their arrest was made, the two now in jail here would have been swinging to the limbs of the nearest tree.[87]

The four suspects were arrested, convicted and sentenced to death. The March 6, 1869, edition of *The Baltimore Sun* includes,

> Princess Anne, Somerset County, March 5, 1869 – The execution of William Wilson, Wm. Wells, Frank Rounds, and George Bailey, the four colored men tried in this county and convicted of the murder of Capt. Benj. F. Johnson, of the schooner Brave, and Henry Cannon, the mate of the same vessel, took place here to-day. The men had, since their sentence, been constantly attended by ministers of various denominations, and fully confessed the crime.
>
> At one P.M. the four prisoners in their shrouds, were brought on the schaffold [sic] by Sheriff Miles, in the presence of about five thousand spectators. They were very solemn, save Bailey, who appeared smiling.
>
> Their ministers Messrs. Healton and Carroll, sung a hymn, in which the condemned joined The Rev. A.C. Healton then read several passages of scripture and offered an eloquent prayer, in which they joined with audible groans.
>
> The prisoners then, all in turn, addressed the crowd, confessing their guilt, and warning the hearers not to imitate them in their conduct. They also thanked those who had had charge of them for their treatment. Bailey said his true name was George C. Bryan.

---

[86] *The Baltimore Sun*, "The Schooner Brave Tragedy, Execution of Four Colored Men at Princess Anne, Somerset county, Maryland–Terrible Scene on the Gallows," Mar. 6, 1869
[87] *The Baltimore Sun*, "The Late Tragedy on the Eastern Shore," Apr. 17, 1868

Chapter 11. Eastern Shore Cases

> The rope and black caps were then adjusted. The sheriff shook hands with them, ad for a few seconds they were left, and the drop fell precisely at forty minutes past one o'clock.
>
> Rounds, Wells and Bailey died almost instantly, but Wilson struggled and groaned fearfully, and getting his hands and legs free, while yet hanging by the neck, caught hold of Rounds, then of his own rope, and drawing himself up, got on the scaffold again. The jailer ascended, tightened the noose again, and pushed the wretched man off, jerking the rope violently as he fell. The culprit continued to struggle for five minutes, some of the crowd yelling "that's right, you ought to suffer." The execution occupied 45 minutes. Towards the last four or five thousand spectators were present.

The March 6th article gives details of their crimes, which occurred the year before in March of 1868, and of their capture. The schooner had been found with the two bodies. Wilson and Wells were apprehended in Virginia on the Eastern Shore. Rounds and Bailey (as he was known then) were apprehended in Baltimore. The birth places and ages were provided in the article.

> Frank Rounds was born in Birche county, North Carolina, and was the slave of Right W. Wond, 27 years old. George Bailey was born in Talbot county, Md., was the slave of Ninian Pinkney, and 21 years of age. Charles W. Denby, alias Charles W. Wilson, was born in Baltimore, lived with Mrs. Jane Humphreys, and aged about 20 years. Lindsey C. Wells, alias William Wells, was born in Buckingham county, Va., was the slave of R.G. Morris, Richmond, and 21 years of age.

The Princess Anne jail was the site of an execution of four men. As researched by Sherrilyn A. Ifill for her book "On the Courthouse Lawn," their executions occurred at the gallows erected next to the jail in Princess Anne. (Ifill 2007)

In the January 6, 1887 edition of *The Baltimore Sun*, the newspaper reports on the case of James Stevens, executed in Somerset County. That edition the newspaper described previous executions in Somerset County.

> There have been thirteen executions in Somerset county during the past ninety years. The last was that of Hiram Fooks, which took place on the 12th of July, 1878. The crime of which he was convicted was the murder of Jack Taylor, colored, which occurred in Fairmount, in October, 1887. Fooks was hanged at the almshouse, about four miles from Princess Anne. On the 5th of March, 1869, four colored men, Rounds, Baily, Wilson and Wells, were hanged in Princess Anne for the murder of Benjamin F. Johnson and Henry F. Connor on board the schooner Beave, in Kage's straits, in March, 1868. The execution of Stevens will be the second hanging in the history of the county for the crime for which he will suffer death, another colored man named Morris having

been executed in 1863 for committing a felonious assault upon Mrs. Moore, a white lady residing at that time in Brinkley's district. The first execution in the county occurred in 1797. Jenny, a negress, was hanged in 1822, and this is the only instance of the execution of a woman. The following other executions complete the thirteen within the limits of the county during the period of ninety years: John Gowanus, in 1858; Alfred Dashiell, in 1858, and "Ned." Davis and "Bob." Jones, in 1863. All these executions were publicly conducted, but under a recent act of the Legislature the execution of Stevens will be conducted in as private a manner as possible.[88]

Unidentified Man

Arrested November 1870 in Queen Anne's County, Maryland

An unidentified man was reported as arrested in November of 1870, for a crime on Kent Island, Queen Anne's County, Maryland. A black man was identified for an alleged "outrage" of one of two daughters of Mr. H.C. Legg of Queen Anne's County.

The Baltimore Sun reports on the arrest of a man not identified in the November 18, 1870 article.

> "There is considerable excitement and some talk of lynching him."
>
> November 18, 1870
> The Baltimore Sun

Yesterday evening, (Tuesday) as the two daughters of Mr. H. C. Legg, Kent Island, Queen Anne's county, Md., were returning from school, they were overtaken by a negro who knocked the eldest one down and attempted to outrage her. The youngest one fled, and, by her cries, alarmed her father, who came to the rescue, but could not catch the negro. At the time when the *Steamer Urbana* left it could not be ascertained whether the negro accomplished his purpose. The negro was arrested today. There is considerable excitement and some talk of lynching him.[89]

---

[88] *The Baltimore Sun*, "Reading the Death-Warrant," Jan. 6, 1887
[89] *The Baltimore Sun*, "Correspondence of the Baltimore Sun," Nov. 18, 1870

Chapter 11. Eastern Shore Cases

John Jones
Lynched July 1872 in Cecil County, Maryland
On July 29, 1872, in Elkton, Cecil County, Maryland, John Jones was lynched for alleged crime of arson and attempted murder. *The Baltimore Sun* first reported the lynching of John Jones in the August 1, 1872 edition of the newspaper. The article begins,

> *"John Jones was taken to a tree near the road, and being already manacled, had a rope tied around his neck and then by sheer force was drawn up so that his feet did not touch the ground, and then left to strangle to death. What became of the other two negroes no one knows."*
>
> August 1, 1872
> The Baltimore Sun

Elkton, Cecil county, July 30, 1872. On Sunday night last, 28th, the house of a Mr. Griffith, in Kent county, was burnt down under such circumstances as seemed to warrant the belief that it was done by an incendiary. A negro by the name of John Jones was suspected of having done the act, as the day before when discharged by Mr. Griffith he used threatening language to him and went away. Not only was the act a premeditated one, but it seemed evident that the villain determined to make sure that the house should not be saved, for around the pump was found piles of burning material for its destruction. The house was totally destroyed, and Mr. Griffith, with his family, barely escaped. The negro John Jones and his son, with another negro, were suspected of having done the act and were apprehended and had a hearing before a magistrate, who ordered them to be sent to the Elkton jail for a further hearing. During the examination, or a little while after, the son of John Jones confessed that his father did the deed; that he and himself went together, fixed the material, and then he ran, leaving his father to touch the material off, his father threatening him that if he told on him he would shoot him. A very strong feeling was aroused by the deliberate act of the three negroes, and so while being conveyed to Elkton, on Monday night about ten o'clock, while the wagon containing the party, under the charge of a constable, was passing through the woods about six miles below Elkton, it was surrounded by a party of ten or twenty men disguised, and the negroes were taken from the wagon, and the man John Jones was taken to a tree near the road, and being already manacled, had a rope tied around his neck and then by sheer force was drawn up so that his feet did not touch the ground, and then left to strangle to death. What became of the other two negroes no one knows. It is surmised that they were taken into the woods and shot, or they were allowed to escape. The pantaloons leg and pocketbook of one of them was found the next morning, which gives rise to the belief that they were also made way with, and one lost that portion of his clothes in his efforts to get away. A powerful feeling exists among the people to find out who the parties were who took the law thus in their own hands, though everyone thinks that hanging was what the negro deserved for committing such a devilish piece of revenge on a sleeping man and family.[90]

The Baltimore Sun article of August 2, 1870 includes the following,

> A brief account was given yesterday by a correspondent of The Sun of the lynching of a colored man, near Elkton, Cecil county, Md., who was charged with having set fire to the house of Mr. Griffith, in Kent County. The following additional particulars of the affair have been obtained by a reporter sent to investigate the manner:
>
> The house burned down belonged to Mr. Walter S. Griffith, living the "Head of Sassafras" river, which divides Cecil and Kent counties, situated about fifteen miles from Chesapeake City, on the line of the Chesapeake Canal. The house occupied by Mr. Griffith was a frame building, three stories in height, containing about ten rooms, and was valued at about $3,000. It was located on a farm about 200 acres, cultivated principally as a fruit farm, and the owner had in his employ a number of colored laborers. Among them was one, a mulatto, of stout build, average intelligence, but accredited with a violent temper, named John Jones, who had been discharged some time since by Mr. Griffith. Jones had occupied, together with his wife and stepson, aged 14 years, a tenant house on the farm, and on Saturday last, in response to an order from Mr. Griffith, vacated the premises, but in doing so gave expression to threats, it is alleged, of "getting even with him" (Griffith).
>
> On Sunday night Mr. Griffith was aroused from his slumbers by the smell of fire, and on arising found the house in flames. He succeeded, with a narrow escape, in saving himself, wife, an aunt and nephew from the flames, he being compelled to jump from a second story window whilst attempting to save some property. The family fled to the house of a neighbors, and the dwelling, as also a smoke-house near it, were totally consumed. Various conjectures were indulged in as to the perpetrators of the arson, as it was plainly evident that the building had been set on fire.
>
> On the same night the stepson of Jones, whilst in Warwick, a town in Cecil county, about six miles away, made acknowledgments which justified the arrest of father and son on Monday and they were arraigned before Justice William S. Ball, of Warwick. In the examination the boy confessed that his father, himself, and a colored man named Green, employed by a Mr. Lynch, living in Delaware, had been to a social entertainment among the colored people, about three miles below Griffith's farm, and about ten o'clock on Sunday night, as they were passing the house of Mr. Griffith, his father halted, entered the barn, procured a bundle of straw, placed it beneath the porch, and set fire to the house.
>
> The boy testified that his father threatened to shoot him and the man Green if they became informants in the case, and the three beat a hasty retreat. Upon this testimony, verified by the man Green, Justice Bell

---

[90] *The Baltimore Sun*, "Incendiarism and Lynch Law in Cecil County, Md.," Aug. 1, 1872

Chapter 11. Eastern Shore Cases

committed the two men and the boy to jail to await trial, and a young man named James Merritt, a farmer living in the neighborhood, was detailed to convey the prisoners to the jail at Elkton, located about fourteen miles away. Mr. Merritt left Warwick about 8 o'clock P.M. for Elkton in a one-horse wagon, with the colored man Jones, handcuffed and the other two named, in the wagon, being held as witnesses.

About 9 ½ P.M. Merritt reached Elkton, bareheaded, his horses in a foam, and he greatly excited, declaring that he had been attacked on the road by a gang of men and his prisoners rescued. At an early hour on Tuesday morning, Sheriff Thomas, of Cecil, started, in company with Merritt, to the spot described by him where the attack had been made, and in a woods, about fifty yards from the roadside, near the fruit farm of Mr. John Price and distant about seven miles from Elkton, was found the body of the colored man Jones hanging to a tree, a small hickory tree, about a foot in diameter, the rope about his neck having been drawn over a limb about ten feet from the ground, and the body drawn up, barely clearing the ground. After hanging the man the perpetrators of the outrage had outrage had bound the rope about his body and tied him fast to the tree.

The remains were taken down, and Justice G. F. Cressfield, of Chesapeake City, was summoned to hold an inquest. A single witness examined was the young man Merritt, he being the only person seeming to have any knowledge of the affair. He testified that he left Warwick with the prisoners between seven and eight o'clock, and had passed along the road about seven miles, when in going by the woods opposite Price's farm, the horse attached to his wagon was seized by a man in the road, and in an instant several men surrounded the wagon, one firing a shot at him. He returned the fire emptying a six-barreled revolver, but with what result he did not know. The prisoners were taken from the wagon, the man Jones being carried to the woods. His companions started to run, and witness, fearing for his own life, put whip to his horse and hastened on to Elkton. He saw no vehicles on the road except a wagon with two men, near Back Creek Mills, distant some nine miles from Elkton, and could not distinguish the occupants; don't know whether the attacking parties were citizens of the neighborhood or not.[91]

The August 5th edition of *The Baltimore Sun* reports,

Since the occurrence the authorities of Cecil county have been unremitting in their efforts to ferret out and bring to justice the perpetrators as also to capture the escaped companions of Jones, but have failed in discovering the whereabouts of either.[92]

---

[91] *The Baltimore Sun*, "The Recent Lynching in Cecil County; Burning of Mr. Griffith's House—Hanging of the Alleged Perpetrator—Particulars of the Affair, etc.," Aug. 2, 1872
[92] *The Baltimore Sun*, "The Cecil County Lynching Case," Aug. 5, 1872

Mob Law on Delmarva

Ernest Smith

Executed August 1874 in Talbot County, Maryland

Ernest Smith (17 years-old) was convicted of rape in April of a white woman, Kate Bartlett of the same age. He was sentenced and executed by hanging in Easton on August 7, 1874.

> "....it is alleged that at the time of the trial of Smith a party was formed to take the prisoner from the sheriff on the way from the court house and lynch the criminal, but the plot miscarried."
>
> August 7, 1874
> The Baltimore Sun

The Baltimore Sun reported fears of trouble for the scheduled execution. The sheriff requested precautionary military guard assistance for the day of the execution, by gallows.[93]

It seems to be apprehended that the execution of the colored man Ernest Smith, at Easton, Talbot county, Md., which takes place to day, may be attended by trouble, and to preserve the peace and maintain the law two companies of the Sixth Regiment, Colonel Clarence Peters commanding, left the city last night under orders to serve as a guard and assist the sheriff in the discharge of his duty. ..... The jail yard is said to be so small that the execution could not take place within the walls conveniently. He will therefore be hanged about fifty feet in the rear of the prison.

The article continues,

> The crime of Smith, and the subsequent alleged murder of Mrs. Whitman by Wheeler and Hines, two other colored men, with the additional circumstance of the alleged attempt of a colored man named Benson to outrage a lady, have conspired to arouse a great deal of indignation in Talbot county. Indeed it is alleged that at the time of the trial of Smith a party was formed to take the prisoner from the sheriff on the way from the court house and lynch the criminal, but the plot miscarried.

Smith was described in August 8, 1874 edition of *The Baltimore Sun*, reporting on the execution.

> Smith would have been 18 years next November. He was of a very dark copper color, with a head that in shape reminded one somewhat of that of the original of the species according to Darwin. He was about five

---

[93] *The Baltimore Sun*, "The Talbot County Execution—Fears of a Rescue from the Gallows—Detail of Military from Baltimore—Two Companies of the Sixth Regiment in the Field," Aug. 7, 1874

Chapter 11. Eastern Shore Cases

feet, three or four inches in height and looked to be of medium stoutness and strength.[94]

The article describes the crime for which Smith was convicted.

> He was raised near Trappe, a village in this county, not far from where the crime was committed. It was about 10 o'clock on Sunday morning on the 19th of April last, Miss Bartlett, whose parents are respectable country people in humble life, had started from home to walk to a married sisters, and was on the public road at a point skirted by woods when Smith met her. She resisted with all her might, screaming so as to be heard by several persons who were at a considerable distance, until he smothered her cries by cramming his hat in her mouth. Just after he had perpetrated the crime a neighbor on his way to church was seen up the road and Smith fled. He went to Trappe, changed his clothes and was at a colored church when he was arrested an hour [or] two afterwards. She proceeded to her sister's and unfolded to her, amid tears and sobs, the horrible story of the outrage. They together, then went to their mother's who at once sent to Trappe to have Smith arrested.

Smith was executed at noon from the gallows erected at the Easton jail. *The Baltimore Sun* of August 8, 1874 includes,

> There was an immense collection of people at the scene of the execution, mostly from the country round about Easton, which is the county town of Talbot county, and a handsome place of about 2,200 population. As early as eight o'clock this morning the stream of people from the country began to circulate through the streets leading towards the center of the town, where the court house and, near it, the jail are located. They came in all sorts of vehicles – buggies, rockaways, light and heavy wagons, horse carts, ox carts, on horseback and on foot. By eleven o'clock the main street and the streets running into it, into which the country roads of each side of the town lead, were as populous as the busiest thoroughfares of a great city. Of course both races, of which the population is composed here, were represented, though it was remarked that many colored persons kept away. They were of both sexes, though there was but a small proportion of women compared with the other sex. There was a large sprinkling of boys in the crowd, but not many, though some, small girls.

> The scaffold was the same on which Fred Lawrence, a colored man, who killed his wife in Easton, was executed in 1871, and on which McCotter, who killed his father-in-law, Tinsley, in Dorchester county, was executed at Cambridge last March. Mr. Wm. D. Roberts, the builder, superintended its erection each time.

---

[94] *The Baltimore Sun*, "The Gallows in Talbot County; Hanging of Ernest Smith, Colored, at Easton – Apprehensions of a Rescue Unfounded – History of the Case – Scenes and Incidents," Aug. 8, 1874

Mob Law on Delmarva

George Wheeler and George Hines
Wheeler executed March 1875 in Talbot County, Maryland; Hines sentenced to prison

The Tuesday July 21, 1874, edition of *The Baltimore Sun* reported the murder of Mrs. Margaret Whitman on the previous Saturday night, July 18 in Talbot County.

> "When Wheeler and his accomplice were arrested the excited people at Long Woods clamored for their immediate execution, and had it not been for the wise counsel of Hedge Thompson they would have carried their desire into execution, a rope then being in possession of the capturing party"
>
> July 21, 1874
> The Baltimore Sun

Easton, Md., July 20 – A brutal murder was committed near Long Woods, Talbot county, Saturday night. A negro man, George Wheeler, assisted, it is alleged, by another named Wm. Hines, murdered a white woman, Margaret Whitman, by knocking her brains out with a piece of buggy shaft. He also knocked down her husband, nearly killing him. The following particulars have been obtained: Between 10 and 11 o'clock on Saturday night Mrs. Whitman and her husband, who lived on the farm of Dr. Neal, near Long Woods, Chapel district, were returning to their home from the store of Thomas Rouen, who is also constable at Long Woods. When about two hundred yards from the store Mrs. Whitman heard persons running, and looking back she saw Wheeler and Wm. Hines, both colored men, approaching at a rapid rate. Wheeler carried in his hand a piece of carriage shaft, and upon coming up with Mr. Whitman he struck him over the head with the piece of shaft, felling him to the ground and rendering him insensible. Upon returning to consciousness Mr. Whitman retraced his steps to the store of Mr. Rouen, and stated what had happened. Constable Rouen, with a number of men immediately, started down the road, and upon reaching the place found the dead body of Mrs. Whitman lying by the roadside, her skull having been horribly crushed.

Whitman knowing who his assailants were, so stated to the party with him, and a search for the colored men was begun. On Sunday morning Wheeler was found lying behind the barn of Dr. Neal, but when he saw the men coming towards him he attempted to run away, but was caught after having run a few yards. It was then discovered that he had cut his throat very badly, but failed to sever the jugular. Upon being questioned as to the murder of Mrs. Whitman, he confessed that he had committed the crime, aided by the man Hines, who was also arrested during the morning. The gash in the throat of Wheeler was sewed up by Dr. Neal, and in a short time thereafter the murderers were conducted to the jail at Easton. When Wheeler and his accomplice were arrested the excited people at Long Woods clamored for their immediate execution, and had

Chapter 11. Eastern Shore Cases

it not been for the wise counsel of Hedge Thompson they would have carried their desire into execution, a rope then being in possession of the capturing party. Wheeler stubbornly refused to give the reasons which induced him to murder Mrs. Whitman, but it is believed that he was prompted to the act on account of a slight quarrel which he had with his victim a few days ago, Wheeler at that time being employed upon the farm of Dr. Neal.[95]

The July 22 edition of *The Baltimore Sun* reported on an account by a correspondent at Oxford in Talbot County, describing revenge as a motive for the attack on Mrs. Whitman by Wheeler. The account states that both Mrs. Whitman and George Wheeler had been employed by Dr. Neal. Whitman had reported that Wheeler was not sick, as he had claimed for not working that day.[96]

Wheeler and Hines were tried and convicted in November.[97] On March 12, 1875, George Wheeler was executed at a gallows erected on a vacant lot about a mile from Easton, witnessed by a mostly black crowd. In preparation for the execution, Wheeler was visited that day by friends and the Rev. Martin Webb.

The Baltimore Sun March 13th edition describes the execution by hanging,

> ...on the scaffold erected about half a mile from Easton, in public view, on a vacant lot. He met his fate unflinchingly. There was a vast crowd of colored people collected by the occurrence, but there were few white persons as spectators. This was the third execution, all of colored men, which has taken place in this county within the past three years, and the more there are, it would seem, the larger the crowds that gather. The day was a bright and lovely spring day, and the streets of the town were filled with people before noon, many colored women taking advantage of the gathering to reap a harvest by the sale of fried fish and other food at tables in front of the market house.
>
> ...They then walked forth from the cell, the prisoner attended by the sheriff and deputy Fiddemon, the clergyman, colored men, and others followed. Going down the stairs to the wagon the colored men sang a hymn. Rev. Mr. Newnam told Wheeler to try to keep quiet and not make so much noise as Lawrence, who was the colored man hanged at Easton two years before. He could not be restrained though, and the singing was kept up by the colored men nearly all the way to the gallows, Wheeler joining in most of it, sometimes looking upward to the skies, but never apparently observing the great crowd about and around him in road and field....[98]

---

[95] *The Baltimore Sun*, "Brutal Murder in Talbot County, Maryland; A Woman Killed and Her Husband Seriously Beaten By Negroes," Jul. 21, 1874
[96] *The Baltimore Sun*, "The Murder in Talbot County," Jul. 22, 1874
[97] *The Baltimore Sun*, "Convicted of Murder in the First Degree," Nov. 27, 1874
[98] *The Baltimore Sun*, "Execution of George Wheeler at Easton," Mar. 13, 1875

Mob Law on Delmarva

After the hanging, the body was taken "to Potter's field, about a half mile on the other side of Easton, where the body was buried. His mother, who lives in Centreville, had written for permission to take charge of it, but yesterday morning she had to send word to the sheriff that she was unable to get any one to go to Easton for the purpose, and in consequence it was buried as stated."

The Baltimore Sun of March 11, 1875 reports that Hines was "sent to the penitentiary for aiding and abetting in the murder."[99]

---

[99] *The Baltimore Sun*, "Two Executions of Colored Men for the Murder of White Women – Hangings at Belair and Easton," Mar. 11, 1875

Chapter 11. Eastern Shore Cases

Jenkins Showell
Executed August 1876 in Worcester County, Maryland
The August 12, 1876 edition of *The Baltimore Sun* reported on the execution of Jenkins Showell at the gallows at the Worcester county almshouse grounds, "for committing outrage upon Margaret Purnell, colored, aged 50 years, and also upon Mrs. Sally Mary Hadder, a young married white woman, November 26, 1875."[100]

The crimes of Showell, about 25-years-old, are described in the August 11, 1876 edition of *The Baltimore Sun*.

> The crimes for which Showell is to pay the death penalty were committed November 26, 1875. His first victim was Margaret Purnell, colored, upwards of fifty years of age, whom he met or waylaid on a path through the woods, whom he violated and robbed of what money she had. From this act of rapine he went direct to the house of Mrs. Sally Mary Hadder, a young married woman, whose husband was away at work. The house is situated about three miles from the town of Berlin, in this county, on the road to the Trappe. Finding no one but the lady in the house, Showell, who had a knife in his hand, asked for some fruit and tobacco, which were refused. He then demanded money, threatening to kill Mrs. Hadder unless it were given him. Becoming greatly alarmed she drew out her pocketbook and handed it to the robber, who on seeing that it contained only a few copper coins, cast it down and made an aggravated assault upon Mrs. Hadder, throwing her on her own bed, which was in the room of the small dwelling, and overpowering her resistance accomplished his purpose. The victim was very roughly treated and pregnant at the time, and wholly unable to meet the brutish force of her assailant. The two deeds of violence were committed within less than two hours. …
>
> Showell was captured the same night at his mother's house, whither he had fled for refuge, and in the storm that prevailed was conveyed to Berlin lockup and kept a day until he could

> *"Showell was captured the same night at his mother's house, whither he had fled for refuge, and in the storm that prevailed was conveyed to Berlin lockup and kept a day until he could be brought to the county jail at Snow Hill, where he was secure from the indignant threats of lynching, which were with difficulty repressed by calmer and more law-abiding citizens."*
>
> *August 11, 1876*
> *-- The Baltimore Sun*

---

[100] *The Baltimore Sun*, "The Gallows in Maryland. Execution of Jenkins Showell—His Last Hours—Scene at the Gibbet—Speech of the Doomed Man—A Quick Death," Aug. 12, 1876

> be brought to the county jail at Snow Hill, where he was secure from the indignant threats of lynching, which were with difficulty repressed by calmer and more law-abiding citizens.[101]

The Baltimore Sun also includes,

> In answer to questions he admitted that before going to the Maryland penitentiary he had outraged a white woman in Delaware, for which he was arrested and held some months in Georgetown jail. It was suggested the wrong man had been caught for that offense, and Showell quickly replied, 'No, they had the right man, but the evidence was not sufficient to convict me.' This, he added, was his first crime. The principal witness in this case, it is understood, would not testify to the wrong done her on account of the publicity of the court-room, and so the culprit escaped from Delaware justice."

The August 12th edition of *The Baltimore Sun* gives an account of Showell's last days. The day before the execution he was visited by many people, both black and white.

> The prisoner appeared to be a cleanly fellow, with dark brown complexion, woolly hair and beard, large and fierce black eyes, firm chin, strong jaws, good teeth, straight nose, altogether a good looking man of apparently thirty years of age, though he says he was a boy when emancipated, and is now not over twenty-five years old. He is about five feet ten inches high, and weighs about 160 pounds.

> The condemned man passed a restless night, occupied chiefly in singing and praying. His breakfast was very light, and he seemed nervous and excited. His spiritual adviser, Samuel G. Waters, of the Colored M.E. Church, calmed him as much as possible, and by ten o'clock he was all ready for the law to do its work, having professed conversion and to being ready for death. The sounds of the prisoner's singing, accompanied by the clinking of his irons, were heard outside the prison until morning. Early in the forenoon his aunt visited him to say farewell.

> By eleven o'clock Snow Hill was full of people, and the execution grounds presented the scene of a great bush meeting, with the scaffold as the central object. Ox carts loaded down with whole families, and many wagon loads of watermelons, contributed to give this feature to the scene presented. The scaffold was in a clear spot of about an acre in the midst of a thick pine grove, the larger trees of which were full of men as thick as blackbirds. It is estimated that fully two thousand people were present at one o'clock when the execution was set to take place, a large proportion of them women, including as many whites as blacks. A number of the whites were very young girls. During the forenoon it rained heavily, when the ox carts were tilted and the occupants got

---

[101] *The Baltimore Sun*, "The Gallows To-Day. Jenkins Showell, Colored, to be Hanged for an Outrageous Crime—History of the Case—The Doomed Man's Antecedents," Aug. 11, 1876

Chapter 11. Eastern Shore Cases

under them for shelter. Before noon, however, it cleared off beautifully, and the woods looked fresh and green.

The condemned man robed in black, which came down to his feet, which were encased in carpet slippers, was brought from the jail at fifteen minutes to twelve o'clock. His hands were pinioned with a white cord, and he was escorted by a guard of fifteen men armed with shot guns. He was assisted into a carryall and rode on the back seat with Mr. Waters. As he appeared at the prison door he shouted in a voice husky from shouting, "all right! I'm going home to go to glory." He continuously shouted these words for three miles on the road to the gallows, which was thronged with people who joined in the long procession, and behaved very orderly indeed.

At five minutes to one o'clock Showell, assisted by the colored minister, ascended the scaffold. Perfect quiet prevailed among the large concourse of people, who had come from all parts of the country to witness the death scene. Sheriff Dewitt Clinton Fooks and his deputy, E.J. Pruitt, also ascended with the prisoner. Charles Johnson and two other colored men to whom the prisoner wished to say good-bye were called to the platform and exchanged a few words with him.[102]

Showell gave a lengthy religious speech, followed by jumping and shouting although his voice was failing from all the shouting. Rev. Theo. A.H. O'Brien of the M.E. Church gave a lengthy prayer, and a hymn was sung by the ministers and prisoner assembled on the gallows. Then Sheriff Fooks cut the cord of the trap, executing Showell. The body was buried on the almshouse property.

---

[102] *The Baltimore Sun*, "Execution of Jenkins Showell – His Last Hours – Scene at the Gibbet – Speech of the Doomed Man – A Quick Death," Aug. 12, 1876

Samuel Chambers and George Collins
Executed March 1878 in Delaware

Historian Yohuru Williams refers to the time period of 1860 to 1880 during which the state of Delaware executed seventeen men for various criminal offenses including the crimes of rape and murder. (2005, 299-300). Of those executed for the crime of rape, fourteen were black. Williams describes two of the cases.

> *"It is evident that the Negro has no rights in Delaware which a white Governor is bound to respect."*
>
> -- Philadelphia Times

The most sensational of these cases occurred in 1887 when two black field hands, Samuel Chambers and George Collins, were arrested for the rape of a white woman and assault on her husband. The victims, a pair of vagabonds from Philadelphia, claimed that the laborers had lured them into a field under the pretense of helping them find work when they suddenly assaulted the husband and took turns sexually assaulting his wife. After a near-lynching of one of the suspects, the men were tried, convicted and sentenced to die.

Shortly after their conviction, the husband, Peter Smith wrote a letter in which he admitted that he and the woman were not married and that she was a Philadelphia prostitute who had agreed to have relations with the two field hands in exchange for money. He further admitted that it was the woman who had struck him on the head when he protested the arrangement. When the field hands refused to pay the agreed upon fees, after the deed was done, the pair fabricated the story in retribution. Prompted by Smith's story, a group of prominent Wilmington citizens gathered to try to win a reprieve for the two men. They even found the woman, Kate O'Toole, who, while not fully admitting her perjury in court, also wrote a letter asking the governor to pardon the men. On March 18, State Secretary of State Ignatius C. Grubb delivered the governor's final report and decision regarding the Middletown outrage. Citing his inability to interfere with the courts, Governor John Price Cochran refused to commute their sentences and the two men met their deaths on the gallows on March 22, 1878. In response to the governor's decision not to intervene, the editor of the *Philadelphia Times* observed, "It is evident that the Negro has no rights in Delaware which a white Governor is bound to respect." "The lessons taught by yesterday's tragedy," responded the *Wilmington Every Evening*, "is not what the *Times* attempts to sum up in the above sentence, but rather that the meanest and poorest woman who lives in or comes to our State shall be safe from such outrages committed by these men."

Chapter 11. Eastern Shore Cases

William Neal

Acquitted and Released for 1880 crime in Delaware
William Neal was indicted for the crime of rape of Margaret E. Gosser. In 1881 the case was remanded on appeal to the Supreme Court for re-trial, where Neal was acquitted and released.

The case became a significant Supreme Court case for its effect on jury selection. The following are a few references about the case. The two by Yohuru Williams refer to the George White lynching in Delaware but refer to the Neal case.

> "Roots of My Peers: Neal v. Delaware and Its Effect on Jury Selection in America," *San Francisco Law Review*, Vol. 5, pp. 111-118 1995), Edward A. Gibson

> "Permission to Hate, Delaware, Lynching, and the Culture of Violence in America," Yohuru R. Williams, Delaware State University, *Journal of Black Studies*, September 2001

> "A Tragedy with a Happy Ending? The Lynching of George White in History and Memory," *Pennsylvania History*, Vol. 72, No. 3 (Summer 2005), pp. 292-304, Penn State University Press, by Yohuru Williams

The case description by Edward A. Gibson in the 1995 San Francisco Law Review is interesting in that Gibson suspected he had a family connection with Neal, as his maternal cousin. Neal, described by Gibson as a "self-made minister who could not read or write," was arrested and indicted on charges of first-degree rape of Margaret E. Gosser, a white woman living in Black Bird Hundred. Neal's court-appointed attorney later became a United States Senator and United States Attorney. (Gibson 1995, 111).

Neal's attorney failed to get a change of venue petitioned on the basis of jury selection, and before an all-white jury, on August 27, 1880 Neal was convicted and sentenced to be hung. Higgins filed a writ of error to the U.S. Supreme Court, and according to Gibson, Justice John M. Harland delivered the opinion of the court which reversed the Delaware Court and voided Neal's conviction. Neal's retrial was held on December 2, 1881. The retrial ended in acquittal. According to Gibson, Neal "was taken in a covered wagon to the state line dividing Delaware and Maryland because of the fear of his being attacked."

Neal's case would be cited in later Supreme Court cases.

Williams wrote (2005, 300),

> Undaunted by their inability to save Chambers and Collins, two years later many of the same persons involved themselves in the case of William Neal, a black field hand accused of the rape of a white housewife near Smyrna, Delaware. Despite considerable lynching talk, Neal's life was saved by a quick thinking sheriff who lodged him in a nearby hotel for safekeeping. After a brief trial Neal was sentenced to death. Although the persons who championed his cause were nonpartisan, the defense became most associated with a Wilmington lawyer and Republican named Anthony Higgins. It was primarily his idea to challenge Neal's conviction on the basis of the lack of representation of blacks on juries. The argument was fairly simple, that no black man had ever served on a jury was prima facie evidence of the state's attempts to undercut the Fifteenth Amendment since jury rolls were drawn directly from the pools of eligible voters. The idea was also to kill two birds with one stone, as a ruling on juries would inevitably assist voting rights for blacks. It worked and in 1881 the case was remanded to Delaware for retrial. This time with a solidly Republican jury William Neal was acquitted and released.

Williams wrote that the Supreme Court case offered optimism for change because of its important legal precedent but that it would take decades for the ruling to be enforced with any consistency.

James Redden
Executed August 1882 in Delaware
The Baltimore Sun reported that Redden was executed by hanging for criminal assault on a 13-year-old girl, presumably white, although her race was not identified. The article reports the following.

> James Redden, who was also known previous to his arrest as 'Jim Loat,' was a full-blooded negro, about 21 years old and slightly under the medium stature. His face was beardless and somewhat stupid and sullen in its habitual expression. He had lived around Odessa, in the central part of this county, most all his life, and had earned a reputation for general good-for-nothingness and an ugly disposition. Besides some petty offenses, he was charged with having, some two years ago, decoyed a drunken tramp into the woods, robbed him and beaten him in a dangerous manner.
>
> On Thursday, Feb. 23, of the present year, Redden entered the house of Henry Purse, a tenant of the late Bishop Scott, one and a half miles below Odessa, during the absence of Purse and his wife, who had gone out to their daily labor, leaving the house in charge of their daughter Sallie and her baby sister were the only inmates. The negro asked the little girl for something to eat, which she prepared and set before him.

Chapter 11. Eastern Shore Cases

Having eaten, he lingered in the house for three hours, and during that time forcibly outraged Sallie, who resisted with all her feeble strength. Redden was arrested in Odessa on the evening of the following day, and with some difficulty gotten out of town and lodged in New Castle jail on Saturday morning. Threats of lynching were made, public feeling being intensified by the memory of the Neal case, but the crowd lacked a leader.[103]

George Lake
Executed June 1883 in Dorchester County, Maryland
Executed for criminal assault of a white woman. George Lake was convicted and executed by hanging in Cambridge.

> "Great excitement was aroused by the act, and but for the efforts of Justice Woodland, Lake would have been handled roughly."
>
> April 21, 1883
> The Democrat News

Under the title "Ravage Most Foul!!!," the April 21, 1883 edition of *The Democrat & News* of Cambridge reported the crime and Lake's arrest, additionally stating, "Monday morning a writ was issued by Justice Woodland and placed in the hands of Constable T. H. Vickers, who arrested Lake on Monday evening and turned him over to the authorities in Cambridge on Tuesday. Great excitement was aroused by the act, and but for the efforts of Justice Woodland, Lake would have been handled roughly."[104]

The June 30, 1883 edition of *The Democrat & News* of Cambridge reported the execution. The gallows were erected outside of the Orphan's Courtroom window, on the south east side of the courthouse and surrounded by an enclosure. The account provided considerable detail of Lake's last hours. Before the black cap was placed on him for the hanging, Lake asked where he would be buried, indicating his wish to be buried with his sister.[105]

The Baltimore Sun of June 30, 1883, reports the following.

---

[103] *The Baltimore Sun*, "Execution of James Redden—History of His Crime," Aug. 26, 1882
[104] *The Democrat & News*, Cambridge, Maryland, "Ravage Most Foul!!!" Apr. 21, 1883
[105] *The Democrat & News*, Cambridge, Maryland, "The Execution of Geo. Lake on the Scaffold; Appearance of the Prisoner; Lake's Last Words," Jun. 30, 1883

Mob Law on Delmarva

> CAMBRIDGE, Md., June 29 --George Lake, colored, convicted at the April term of the Circuit Court of Dorchester County of criminal assault upon Mrs. Clara Simmons, of Hooper's Island, in this county, atoned for his crime on the gallows today. During his imprisonment he manifested little or no concern about his impending doom, seeming perfectly callous and unconcerned up to the beginning of the present week, when his spiritual advisers noticed that he had at least begun to realize his situation. He was removed from his cell at the deputy sheriff's residence to the courthouse about 2 o'clock this morning, where he remained until the hour for the execution…. He was attended during the last religious services, and also upon the scaffold, by Revs. Sturgis, Monroe and Collett.[106]

The Baltimore Sun June 30th article describes the crime for which he was convicted.

> The assault on Mrs. Simmons was committed on Sunday night, the 15th of April. Her husband and daughter were absent at church. She was at home with her little child, who was asleep. She was in her bedroom and was asleep in a chair, when she became conscious of something over her face. She awoke and felt a shawl over her head. She thought at first it was her husband, but in attempting to pull off the shawl a rough hand caught hers and she knew it was not her husband. She made another effort to pull off the shawl, and saw that the hand was that of a black man. She struggled harder and got off the shawl, and saw it was George Lake. She called him by name and asked him what he was doing in her room. He got the shawl over her mouth and eyes again, and after a protracted struggle she was overpowered.
>
> Lake was living about half a mile from her house, and was familiar with it, having been in the employ of her husband. Lake was arrested and fully identified. The crime created universal indignation, and threats of lynching were made, but wiser counsels prevailed. On the 27th of April Lake was tried, convicted and sentenced in the Circuit Court at this place.
>
> After being sentenced Lake broke jail at night and succeeded in getting several miles away before his absence was discovered, but scores of people turned out and scoured the surrounding country for him, and he was caught the next day and brought back to his old quarters.[106]

---

[106] *The Baltimore Sun*, "Execution of George Lake—Mrs. Simmons's Assailant Hanged at Cambridge—His Last Hours," June 30, 1883

Chapter 11. Eastern Shore Cases

Frederick Cephas
Executed August 1884 in Dorchester County, Maryland

Frederick Cephas was executed by hanging at the gallows at the Cambridge jail, sentenced for the murder of a white woman, Mrs. Celia Murphy (sometimes named Mrs. Celia Bush in newspaper accounts) in Williamsburg, Dorchester County, on April 7th. The woman was found with her throat cut.

The following are excerpts from the May 6, 1884 account from *The Baltimore Sun* about the beginnings of the trial.

> Cambridge, Md., May 5 – The trial of Frederick, alias "Bug" Cephas, colored for the murder of Mrs. Celia Murphy, better known by her maiden name of Celia Bush, near Williamsburg, Dorchester county on the 7th of April last, was commenced here this morning before Judges Wilson and Goldsborough. The courtroom was crowded, and great interest was manifested, many ladies being present. ….
>
> State's Attorney Henry made a brief opening statement, in which he characterized the murder as one of the wickedest and most atrocious crimes that had ever been committed in Dorchester county. The evidence would show that an innocent old woman, who enjoyed the respect and confidence of all who knew her, had been brutally beaten and murdered; her house had been robbed, and it was evident that the only motive for the murder was the hellish lust for money. …
>
> Mr. S. T. Milbourne replied for the defense. He agreed with Mr. Henry that the crime was one of the most horrible o record; but the jury must be thoroughly satisfied of the prisoner's guilt before convicting him. The accused was poor and friendless, and had no one to look to for sympathy and help. His only reliance was in the impartiality of the jury. ….[107]

Witnesses found her home broken into, robbed, and Mrs. Murphy missing. The testimony described the discovery of the body and pieces of the sapling believed to have been used to kill Mrs. Murphy. The location was "in the direct line of flight through the woods from the scene of the murder to Cephas' house." Others testified seeing Cephas fleeing on the Saturday following the murder. Lizzie Jenkins, a black woman known to be living with Cephas, testified that Cephas and a neighbor, Sam McGlotten, had had a conversation about money in Mrs. Henry's home, and testified to bloodstains on Cephas' clothing.

> Cornelius Murphy, the divorced husband of Miss Bush, arrived here this afternoon. He states that he was at least twenty miles away from the scene of the murder when it is supposed to have occurred, and that not-

---

[107] *The Baltimore Sun*, "The Murder of Celia Bush, Bug Cephas on Trial – The Prisoner Gets Sick in Court," May 6, 1884.

> withstanding the bad relations which existed between himself and his former wife, no one can regret more than he does her untimely and horrible fate. Her conduct in refusing to refund him money he had paid for her, he ascribed to a great extent to the advice of others, who he says, possessed an influence over inimical to himself. He claims to have advanced her altogether more than one thousand dollars. It is thought by lawyers here that he will be able to secure a share of the property.

In June of 1884, the trial concluded and Cephas was found guilty and sentenced to be executed. A new witness, John Pearson, testified to hearing Cephas discuss the location of money in Mrs. Murphy's home, and other incriminating statements.[108]

Cephas was executed at the gallows in Cambridge on August 1, 1884.[109] [110]

> At twelve o'clock Cephas emerged from the side entrance of the jail. The sheriff and guards walked in the lead, Cephas and his colored spiritual advisers, Rev. W.H. Thomas and Charles H. Young, on either side, and a strong guard in the rear. The march was from the jail to the entrance of and through the courthouse to a high window with the sash removed, through which the sheriff, Cephas and his spiritual advisers passed by steps to the gallows, singing "Jesus Lover of My Soul." Cephas joined lustily in the singing, and walked firmly and boldly upon the gallows. His manner was firmer than that of those who accompanied him. Upon reaching the scaffold Rev. Mr. Young delivered an appropriate prayer, during which the slightest muscular twitch about the mouth was noticed in Cephas. At the end of the prayer he responded firmly, "Amen."

After the hanging, Cephas' uncle, Major Stanley, and a neighbor, Levin Cannon, took the body to be buried 'near Crotcher's Ferry, on the land formerly belonging to Jacob Wilson, where Cephas's father lies buried."

Charles Williams
Executed January 1886 in Dorchester County, Maryland
Williams, threatened with a lynching, was arrested, convicted and executed by hanging in Cambridge for the crime of assault of a white woman in the Hoopers Island district of Dorchester County.

---

[108] *The Democrat and News*, Cambridge, Marylad, "The Gallows to be Again Erected in Dorchester County, The Trial and Conviction of Cephas for the Killing of Mrs. Murphy," Jun. 14, 1884
[109] *The Baltimore Sun*, "Bug Cephas Hanged; Meeting His Fate with Great Coolness—His Last Words on the Scaffold," Aug. 2, 1884
[110] *The Democrat and News*, Cambridge, Maryland, "The Gallows Again! Executionn of Fred Cephas; He Walks Boldly to his Death; His Appearance andLlast Words; Cut Down in 20 Minutes; A Criminal That Was Convicted by 'Soap,'" Aug. 5, 1884

Chapter 11. Eastern Shore Cases

The Baltimore Sun of May 18, 1885 reported that Charles Williams was arrested for assault along a road on a white woman, Mrs. George S. Keene of Meekins Neck in the Hoopers Island District. He was apprehended at Powell's Mills and taken to Church Creek for identification. The article includes,

> He was raised in Lake's district, Dorchester County, by Capt. Thomas Andrews, and during the past winter was employed as a hand on Capt. James Willing's oyster-boat *Pilot*. Threats of lynching were freely indulged in Cambridge on Saturday night, but no disorder has so far occurred.[111]

On January 8, 1886, Williams was executed in Cambridge. *The Baltimore Sun* reported,

> Cambridge, Md., Jan. 8 -- Charles Williams, the colored assailant of Mrs. Eliza J. Keene, of Dorchester county, in May last, was hanged here at 11:20 a.m. today. The execution of the death penalty is seldom accompanied by so much hardiness and obduracy and such utter destitution of good feeling. During all the months since the commission of his crime Williams has exhibited no gleam of pity for his victim and no evidence of his contrition. Even yesterday, the day before his execution, he disavowed all faith with the foulest blasphemy. He was sullen, vindictive, and persisted in charging the witnesses with perjury and the court, the jury and the officers of justice with a conspiracy to send him to the scaffold. His spiritual advisers, Revs. M.H. Thomas and Charles H. Young, remained with him until 11 o'clock last night, singing, praying, and exhorting him. About 11 o'clock Rev. J.E. Bryan, pastor of the M.E. Church of Cambridge, also visited him, but he had settled himself to sleep, and declined to be disturbed. He slept well until 6 o'clock this morning, when he got up and ate a hearty breakfast of beefsteak and ham and eggs, saying at its conclusion; "Well, I have had a good breakfast, I suppose I shall eat my dinner in hell."
>
> At 11:05 he walked, with Sheriff Martin on one side and Special Deputy Gustavus Parks on the other, to the scaffold, preceded by Rev. W.H. Thomas and James H. Young, colored. His arms were bound together at the elbows. He was neatly dressed in black. He laughed and talked with the officers as he went along, and but for the cords one would have supposed he was going to some pleasant meeting. He was taken through the courthouse and passed through a window to the platform of the scaffold. He coolly took hold of the dangling rope and said to the spectators, "What do you think of that, gentlemen?" and seeing an acquaintance, he called out, "Capt. Dean, this is a nice place to bring a man to. This is the first gallows I ever saw, and I never thought to die on the gallows."

---

[111] *The Baltimore Sun*, "Brutally Assaulted—A Dorchester County Lady Waylaid by a Colored Man," May 18, 1885

He then made a rambling speech, in which he said he was convicted by a set of liars; that he was going to stand a new trial today, when he would not be judged by liars, etc. At this moment his eyes lighted upon a citizen among the spectators in whose boat he had worked as a dredger and towards whom he evidently felt great bitterness. He broke out; "Yes. Captain, you are standing there to see me hung, and you ought to be here on the scaffold instead of me. I could tell things you would not like to hear," etc. A spectator then addressed to him the following question; "Williams, you have only a few minutes more to live. Tell us, are you guilty or innocent of the crime charged against you?"

He replied, "I am innocent." As the black cap was about to be placed over his face his curiosity was excited, and he asked, "What is this?" In the course of his remarks he said it would be well if other persons here had as much nerve as he had. He shook hands with the sheriff and Deputy Parks and his spiritual advisers, and while standing with the tips of his fingers in his pockets, the sheriff suddenly chopped the spring rope, and the body shot down with great velocity.

The pulse ceased to beat in seven minutes, and the body was let down in twenty-one minutes, and Williams was pronounced dead by the attendant physicians. Death resulted from strangulation.

Williams's mother and sisters have not visited him for several weeks, and he declined to see them during his last moments. His body was taken in charge by Undertaker Willis, and was buried this afternoon at the county alms-house. There was a comparatively small gathering of people at the execution.

Williams was about twenty years old, five feet nine inches in height, and powerfully built, with a chestnut complexion, receding forehead and thick lips. He was raised in Lake's district, Dorchester County, by Capt. Thomas Andrews and during the winter of 1885 was employed as a hand on an oyster boat.[112]

---

[112] *The Baltimore Sun*, "Charles Williams Hanged for Assaulting a Woman – Unrepentant to the Last," Jan. 9, 1886

Chapter 11. Eastern Shore Cases

James Stevens, alias Sewell Wright
Executed February 25, 1887, in Somerset County, Maryland

James Stevens was convicted and executed by hanging in the jail yard in Princess Anne, Maryland, for the crime of assaulting a white woman. *The Baltimore Sun* article of Oct. 15, 1886 includes a description of the alleged crime.

> Princess Anne, Md., Oct. 14 – Among other indictments found by the grand jury of Somerset county so far is one against Jas. Stevens, alias Sewell Wright, colored, for committing a felonious assault upon Mrs. Mary Trehearn, an aged widow lady of Dublin, on the night of the 11th of July last. Mrs. Trehearn, who in a few days will have passed the age of fourscore years, for several years past has resided at her home in Dublin district wholly by herself. During this time she has been quite feeble in health. On the night in question she had retired, and about ten o'clock was awakened by some one entering her room (which is on the lower floor) by means of the window. The light which she had left dimly burning in the room before going to bed was extinguished by the intruder. Hearing an unusual noise in the room, she arose and struck a match to see what was the matter, but no sooner had she done so than the match was blown out and she was thrown forcibly upon the bed. The old lady resisted the fierce attack as long as her feeble strength allowed, but was overpowered by her assailant. The following morning Mrs. Trehearn visited her neighbors and made known to them her fearful experience of the previous night, and informed them that she had marked her assailant with the imprint of her fingernails in the struggle beneath his eye. A party immediately started in pursuit, and finding fresh tracks near the door, traced them from the scene of the assault about a mile distant, to the home of James Stevens. Not finding him at home they continued the search, following the tracks until they reached a house, where Stevens was found. He was immediately arrested, and an examination was made, which revealed the scratch under the eye, as described by the old lady. He was carried before a justice of the peace, who, after a preliminary hearing, committed him to jail to await the action of the grand jury.
>
> The prisoner is a large, muscular colored man, about thirty-five years of age. The case will come up for trial in a few days.[113]

The Baltimore Sun reported that on Oct. 22, 1886, Stevens, alias Sewell Wright, was sentenced to death, for the assault on Mrs. Mary Trebearn, 80 years old.[114] Stevens was hung on Feb. 25, 1887 in the jail yard. "He ate a hearty breakfast about twenty minutes after seven; it was prepared at the Washington Hotel, and was taken to him by Deputy Sheriff Slemons. It consisted of beefsteak, ham and eggs, buckwheat cakes, Maryland biscuits

---

[113] *The Baltimore Sun*, "Indicted for a Serious Assault," Oct. 15, 1886
[114] *The Baltimore Sun*, "Sentenced To Death. James Stevens, Colored, Condemned for Felonious Assault in Somerset County," Oct. 23, 1886

and coffee." He was given a new suit of clothes and taken out of the jail to the scaffold, "which stood within an enclosure near the jail, so constructed as to hide the scene from the public." He was accompanied by "Rev. Dr. Henry B. Marlin of the P.E. Church, his spiritual adviser, Mr. W.C. Hardy, of counsel for the prisoner, and deputies Slemons and Davy." A multi-racial crowd of 300 stood by.[115]

Alexander Moses

Arrested August 1887, Queen Anne's and Caroline Counties, Maryland

Alexander Moses was jailed in Denton for an alleged assault on a white woman and there were reported threats of lynching. The outcome is yet undetermined.

The August 18, 1887 issue of *The Baltimore Sun* reports,

> "The affair has caused some excitement, and there were threats of lynching."
>
> August 18, 1887
> The Baltimore Sun

Alexander Moses, a colored youth 23 years old, was today lodged in Denton jail by Constable R. Kemp Williams, charged with having attempted a criminal assault on Mrs. Henrietta Doty, wife of Ephraim Doty, a farmer, living near Greensboro, Caroline County. The offense was committed at ten o'clock this morning. Mrs. Doty was in the back yard, washing, when the negro crept up from behind and dealt her a blow on the back of the head with a stout club, inflicting an ugly though not serious wound. Mrs. Doty ran toward the kitchen door. Her assailant tried to detain her, but she eluded his grasp, gained the inside and bolted the door. She then got her husband's pistol and opened fire upon the negro, who beat a hasty retreat and escaped uninjured. Mrs. Doty gave the alarm, and several neighbors began a hunt for Moses, who lives with a German named Simon, on an adjoining farm. He was arrested as he was about to go to the field for his afternoon's work. He was taken to Mrs. Doty's house and was identified by that lady as her assailant. He was then taken by Sheriff Curry before Justice Christian, at Greensboro, who committed him to jail. He will be given a hearing tomorrow.

THE SUN correspondent visited Moses at the jail this afternoon. He stoutly denies the assault, and declares that he does not know Mrs.

---

[115] *The Baltimore Sun*, "James Stevens Hung," Feb. 26, 1887

Chapter 11. Eastern Shore Cases

Doty, and was never at the house until taken there by his captors today. He has been in this vicinity only a few months, having come from near Dover, Del. He is of small stature, and has a repulsive countenance. Mrs. Doty is about 30 years old, and has three small children. Her husband owns the small farm on which they live, but is away for much of the time. He is employed on the dredging machine that is deepening the river between Denton and Greensboro. The affair has caused some excitement, and there were threats of lynching.[116]

George Smith, alias William Black

Sentenced March 1889 to prison for crime in Cecil County, Maryland

George Smith was convicted to sixteen years in the penitentiary for the assault of a 13-year-old white girl. His arrest also generated talk of lynching.

The Baltimore Sun of January 12, 1889 reports the arrest of George Smith.

> *"He was captured there last night by a crowd of excited and indignant farmers. It is said that there was much talking of lynching. Wiser counsels prevailed, however, and Smith was taken to the home of Constable Lee, where he was kept last night and brought to jail this morning."*
>
> *January 12, 1889*
> *The Baltimore Sun*

Constable T. Emory Lee, of Cherry Hill, Cecil county, brought to Elkton jail this morning George Smith, colored, aged 24 years, charged with committing a felonious assault on Mary Ward, the thirteen-year-old daughter of James Ward, a farmer, who lives on the farm of Taylor Reynolds, near Blue Ball, in the fourth election district of Cecil county, not far from the Pennsylvania line. The assault, it is alleged, was committed in the woods near the residence of the girl's father. Smith was committed by Justice James Spence, on the information of Mr. Reynolds. The prisoner has only been in Cecil county about a year, coming here from Harford county, where he resided near Darlington. He has worked recently for Arthur Mackie and Walter Armstrong, fourth district farmers. He was out of work at the time of the assault, but made his home with Mr. Mackie. He was captured there last night by a crowd of excited and indignant farmers. It is said that there was much talking of lynching. Wiser

---

[116] *The Baltimore Sun*, "Attempted Criminal Assault—A Plucky Maryland Woman Foils Her Colored Assailant," Aug. 18, 1887

counsels prevailed, however, and Smith was taken to the home of Constable Lee, where he was kept last night and brought to jail this morning.[117]

The article describes Smith where he was held in the Elkton jail.

> The Sun's correspondent saw him there this morning. He is a well-built man, of medium stature, dark brown in color, and has a small mustache. He denied having assaulted the girl, and says he never saw her. He walked to Kimbleville, Pa., that day, and on his way home passed the farm upon which the Wards reside. He said about sixteen men came to Mr. Mackie's house about eight o'clock last night, some on horseback and some afoot. They were mostly armed, some with guns and others with revolvers. They struck him in the face several times, knocking him down, and then tied him, hands and feet. The ropes about his feet were taken off, and he was compelled to walk to Blue Ball, a distance of several miles. He was then taken to a store, where a consultation was held by the members of the party, the purport of which he did not know. He was taken from there to the constable's house, at Cherry Hill. The assault is alleged to have taken place yesterday afternoon

In Elkton Maryland, George Smith, alias William Black, was convicted on March 27 and sentenced on March 28 to sixteen years in the penitentiary.

> George Smith, alias William Black, colored, was convicted of assaulting with felonious intent Mary L. Ward, the fourteen-year-old daughter of James F. Ward. He dragged the girl, who was on an errand, from a public road to the woods, and attempted to assault her. He was caught that night hid in a chimney. His counsel offered no defense.[118]

Magruder Fletcher

Lynched April 1889 in Accomack County, Virginia

Magruder Fletcher, about 35, was lynched in Onancock for an alleged assault of the wife of a white waterman.

The Baltimore Sun of March 12, 1889 reports the following.

> Onancock, Va., March 11 – Late last night Magruder Fletcher, a powerful young colored man, broke into the house of Mrs. Obediah McCready, about 30, in Messongo Neck, in the northern part of Accomack county, and violently assaulted her. Mrs. McCready's

---

[117] *The Baltimore Sun*, "A Young Girl Assaulted—Arrest of a Colored Man in Cecil Charged with the Crime," Jan. 12, 1889
[118] *The Baltimore Sun*, "Convictions by the Cecil Court," Mar. 28, 1889; "Prisoners Sentenced at Elkton," Mar. 29, 1889

Chapter 11. Eastern Shore Cases

husband was absent from home at the time, being engaged in catching oysters across the Chesapeake bay, and the only persons in the house besides Mrs. McCready were her two young children, aged five and three years, respectively. The colored man, who had been employed by Capt. McCready to cut wood for his wife during his absence, entered through an upstairs window. When Mrs. McCready first became aware of the negro's presence in the house he was standing by her bed with his hand on her throat. He threatened to kill her and her little children if she should scream. He assaulted Mrs. McCready four times, leaving just before daybreak.

As soon as he was gone Mrs. McCready, half dead with fear and excitement, hastened to her nearest neighbor and gave the alarm. The news spread rapidly, and a crowd soon collected and went in pursuit, determined to swing her assailant to the most convenient limb. In the meantime Justice Ambrose Kyler, being informed of the facts of the case, issued a warrant and dispatched Constable Gladding with a posse to arrest the perpetrator, who was thought to be hiding in the swamps near his home. Constable Gladding arrested Fletcher, who was hiding from his pursuers. All the surrounding country was aroused, and men were scouring the woods in every direction.

Constable Gladding managed to take his prisoner away by a circuitous route without meeting any of the would-be lynchers till he was several miles away from the scene of the occurrence, when he was met by several men who demanded that the prisoner should be surrendered to them, but as the constable and his posse showed a determination to prevent a breach of the law they were allowed to proceed. They then hastened on rapidly with the prisoner to Accomack Court House, where he was put in jail this afternoon and chained to the floor to prevent his escape. The colored man seemed greatly relieved when he was put in jail, and spoke of his narrow escape from lynching. He denies that he committed the crime, but his wife testifies that he was away from home all night, and did not return until nearly sunrise, and the accused himself has made several conflicting statements. The people in the community where the outrage was committed are greatly excited, and many persons believe that the jail will be stormed and the

> *"When about one mile away they halted, took the negro out of the cart, mutilated him and then suspended him from the limb of a pine tree, where he was allowed to hang till he was dead. They then fired a number of bullets into his body and rode away. The body was found hanging by the roadside early this morning, with a card pinned on his breast, with the following legend: 'We will protect our mothers, our wives, our sisters and our daughters. Committee.'"*
>
> *April 14, 1889*
> *The Baltimore Sun*

negro hung before morning, but the officials appear to have no apprehension of such an occurrence.[119]

Account from the April 14th edition of *The Baltimore Sun*,

> Magruder Fletcher, the negro who last Sunday night criminally assaulted Mrs. Mary E. McCready, a highly respected lady, in the northern part of Accomack county, was taken from the county jail last night and hanged by a band of masked men. Ever since the crime was committed there have been rumors of lynching in the air, but as two nights had passed since the commission of the crime without any demonstration, it was believed that the plan had been abandoned. Last night between 1 and 2 o'clock a band of 100 masked men filed into the village of Accomac Court House and proceeding to the home of Jailer Melson demanded the keys of the jail. The demand was refused, where upon they threatened to burn the jailer's house down, tear down the walls of the jail and break open the doors. Deputy Sheriff Melson, hearing about what was going on, proceeded to the jailer's house, where he found the men furious and determined to carry out their purpose of lynching the negro. They were all armed, and some of them were flourishing their pistols in the air. The deputy sheriff was seized, and some of the men entering the house, overpowered the jailer, and forced him to surrender the keys. They then proceeded to the jail, took the negro from his cell, and, placing him in a cart, moved rapidly out of the village in a northerly direction. When about one mile away they halted, took the negro out of the cart, mutilated him and then suspended him from the limb of a pine tree, where he was allowed to hang till he was dead. They then fired a number of bullets into his body and rode away. The body was found hanging by the roadside early this morning, with a card pinned on his breast, with the following legend: "We will protect our mothers, our wives, our sisters and our daughters. Committee."
>
> The place where the negro was hung is in the midst of a pine forest near Taylor Branch. Hundreds of people visited the scene of the hanging today, and many carried away branches of the tree on which the negro paid the penalty of his terrible crime.[120]

---

[119] *The Baltimore Sun*, "Threatened Lynching; The Accomac People Aroused; Assault on Capt. M'Cready's Wife; A Colored Man Arrested and Narrowly Escapes the Indignant Citizens—He Denies His Guilt," Mar. 12, 1889

[120] *The Baltimore Sun*, "A Virginia Lynching. Magruder Fletcher Hanged For A Criminal Assault On A Lady," Mar. 15, 1889

Chapter 11. Eastern Shore Cases

Asbury Green
Lynched May 1891 in Queen Anne's County, Maryland
Asbury Green was lynched in Centreville where a mob dragged him by rope from jail to an orchard and hung him from a peach tree. The lynching followed his arrest, trial, conviction, and sentencing for the assault of Mrs. Howard Tolsen on Kent Island. Green had been sentenced to twenty-one years in part because the court had held some doubt as to whether Green was the true attacker.

The following is the biographical account from the website of the Maryland Archives. [121]

> *"The corpse was seen by THE SUN correspondent as soon as it was daylight. The trail of the body dragged along the route was plainly shown on the ground all the way from the jail. The body had been evidently rushed in a hurry, as it had slewed from one side to another, leaving the trail well defined. The night was dark and cloudy, with a little rain and some lightning. These conditions were extremely favorable for accomplishing the work."*
>
> **Maryland Archives Online**

Asbury Green, an African American man, was lynched in Centreville, May 13, 1891 for the assault of Mrs. Howard Tolsen. Mrs. Tolsen was the wife of a farmer residing on Kent Island. Her husband was away on business when she claimed Green entered her home around 9:30 at night on February 28, 1891. Green was arrested the following day and placed in the county jail to await trial. An investigation was done and at the preliminary hearing Green was only charged with assault with intent to rape. Mrs. Tolsen did not want to disclose the fact that she had actually been raped by her attacker. It was not until a Grand Jury was sworn in during the month of May that all facts of the attack were made known.

Asbury Green's trial was held with Judges Robinson, Wickes and Stump presiding over the case. On the behalf of Green's defense several men testified that they could account for Green's whereabouts during the time of the assault. However, the jury was not convinced. The trial only lasted one day and Green was convicted on the charge of rape. He was sentenced to 21 years of confinement and hard labor in the state penitentiary. Many in the town were outraged that Green was not sentenced to death. The court did not sentence Green to death because they claimed there was some doubt of whether Green was the true attacker. At the end of the court proceeding there were several vague rumors that Green would be lynched.

---

[121] Maryland Archives Online

Sheriff T. B. Turner increased the number of guards in case there was an attempt to lynch Green. The Sheriff added seven more guards to the night shift. However, this did not protect Green from harm. Around one o'clock that next morning there was a call from the outside gate of the jail. When deputy sheriff Seward went out to see who the call was coming from a mob of men rushed him and demanded the keys to the jail. When he refused they threw him down and forcibly took the keys from him. The mob then entered the jail armed with guns, pistols, rifles, and axes. They commanded the guards to keep quiet. The men unlocked the cell and placed a rope around Green's neck and dragged him out of the jail.

Green was dragged 300 yard away from the jail to an orchard. The mob then hung him by the neck with a rope from a peach tree. Witnesses believed Green was half dead when the mob reached the orchard. The crowd of 150 to 250 men quickly and quietly dispersed. On Tuesday a jury of inquest was summoned and their verdict follows:

"Certain parties, feloniously, voluntarily and of malice aforethought, dragged from the county jail the said Asbury Green did kill by strangulation and dislocation of the spinal column and by hanging to a tree, said parties being to the jury unknown, and did then and there kill and murder the said Asbury Green" (Centreville Record, 16 May 1891).

The body of Asbury Green was buried that next Wednesday by the Sheriff and his deputies. African Americans in the area were outraged by the lynching. Several threats to burn down the town frightened citizens of Centreville. The citizens of Centreville claimed they were not responsible for the lynching. It was believed that the mob came from out of town. The Good Will Fire Company patrolled the town to ensure peace. Regardless of the threats no retaliation was reported.

The Baltimore Sun account of the lynching includes the following.

The prisoner was dragged from his cell by a rope around his neck – literally dragged through office and hall, porch and gate, out to the street corner, where some of the lynchers mounted horses, which seemed to be in readiness. The crowd then hurried down in the direction of the wharf. Green seemed to know his fate at once, and during the temporary halt begged piteously, but it availed nothing. When he was first taken from his cell he had also begged for mercy, but no attention was paid to the appeal. Outside the jail he was hurried down the street known as Broadway in the direction of the wharf. Several pistols or guns were fired as the crowd passed down. There was but little talking or swearing but some yelling on the way. The prisoner was dragged by the group around his neck about 628 yards down Broadway. Then a turn was made into the peach orchard of ex-Sheriff R. Hopper Smith. About twenty-four strides from the turning-in point the rope was thrown over the limb of a peach tree and the body was drawn up, leaving the victim's feet about eight inches from the ground. The corpse was seen by THE SUN correspondent as soon as it was daylight. The trail of the body dragged along the route was plainly shown on the ground all the way from the jail. The body had been evidently rushed in a hurry, as it had

Chapter 11. Eastern Shore Cases

slewed from one side to another, leaving the trail well defined. The night was dark and cloudy, with a little rain and some lightning. These conditions were extremely favorable for accomplishing the work.[122]

The Baltimore Sun article further reported that the body was removed to Kent Island for burial.

James Taylor
Lynched May 1892 in Kent County, Maryland

Taylor, aged 23, was lynched in Chestertown for allegedly raping eleven year old Nettie (Nellie) Silcox, the daughter of John Silcox of Kennedyville, Taylor's employer.[121]

> *"At this meeting a representative from the commissioners of Chestertown appeared before them and made one request in their behalf, and it was that the negro be carried to Kennedyville before being hung. This the men would not agree to, but said they would promise not to lynch him within the town limits as far as was in their power."*
>
> May 19, 1892
> The Baltimore Sun

The day before the lynching, a reporter for *The Baltimore Sun* visited the jail, but Taylor declined to discuss anything with him. The May 17th issue of the newspaper includes the following.

He is twenty-four years of age and has been working on Mr. Silcox's farm for over two years. He is of medium size and weighs about 105 [number unclear on copy of article] pounds. The feeling in Chestertown is very warm and a lynching is expected tonight. The sheriff has prepared an extra guard and will do all in his power to defend those in his keeping.[123]

The Baltimore Sun of May 19th included a May 18th account of the lynching on the 17th.

Chestertown, MD, May 18 -- …..As stated in The Sun yesterday, guards were placed about the jail and relieved every hour. Word reached Chestertown from Kennedyville that the lynchers would surely be here, and that the Chestertown people would be expected to hold the prisoner. As early as 9 o'clock they arrived and held a meeting near the

---

[122] *The Baltimore Sun*, "Asbury Green's Fate; Dragged by the Neck and Hung on a Bearing Peach Tree; A Mob's Violence in Centreville; The Colored Man Convicted of Assaulting Mrs. Howard Tolson Taken Out of Prison by Force and Disposed of – Work of a Body of Armed and Masked Men," May 13, 1891

[123] *The Baltimore Sun*, "A Little Girl Assaulted, A Colored Man Accused – Fears of Lynching in Chestertown," May 17, 1892

jail, but it was so secretly held that the crowd about the jail did not know of their arrival.

At this meeting a representative from the commissioners of Chestertown appeared before them and made one request in their behalf, and it was that the negro be carried to Kennedyville before being hung. This the men would not agree to, but said they would promise not to lynch him within the town limits as far as was in their power. A tree on the place of Mrs. E. R. Whiekes, about one mile from town, was thereupon agreed upon as the place of execution. This representative also requested the leader of the men, whom he did not know, not to riddle the man's body or mutilate it in any way. This was heartily acceded to. They stated that their object in resolving to do this thing was for the betterment of the county, the protection of wives, mothers and children, and for the protection of a poor ruined girl from the eyes of hundreds in a court-house and the questions of a paid attorney. The men composing this party seemed to be men of good standing and sound judgment, and a more nervy squadron would be hard to find.

Around the jail the crowds were gathering, and on Dugan's corner, opposite the jail, fully one hundred men were congregated.

One square further down on Main street the colored people were gathered in large numbers, but when The Sun reporter moved around among them just before the affair no complaining of any kind was heard.

In the jail all was quiet and secure. The sheriff's wife compelled him to stay by her side, and it was for a time feared that her life would be also sacrificed on the eventful night. In the front corridor Mr. John H. Greenwood was stationed. In the back corridor, into which Taylor's cell opened, stood Deputies Frank Plummer, Amos R. Kelley, Albert I. Dugan and William B. Plummer. These men said they were well prepared and did not expect any trouble.

Jim Taylor was dozing on his cot in the end cell, No. 6, when he was awakened to be apprised of the situation.

"Jim," said the questioner, "Do you know what is going on outside?"

"Yes, sir. They is gwine [going] to kill me, I reckon."

"Are you ready to die?" he was asked.

"Yes, sir, I think I am. I have belonged to the church for three years and I feel prepared to go."

"Now, Jim, tell us whether you did the crime they say you did."

"No, sir, I am an innocent man, and I am not afraid to say so even while I am expecting to meet my God in a few minutes."

He was told how awful it was to die with a lie on his lips, and he replied that he knew it. These were the last words he was heard to utter.

In the rear of the jail several masked men from this vicinity stood waiting armed to the teeth. The double gate leading from Cross street to the stable yard were wide open, while the small yard gate was in charge of

Chapter 11. Eastern Shore Cases

the watchman. The conditions were now all favorable to the lynching, and toward the jail a crowd of 500 people were seen advancing closer and closer. They drew near without any noise whatever. The yard gate was easily passed through, and the sixty armed men marched to the side door of the jail, which leads directly to the jail corridor. The leader called for a sledgehammer, and in an instant a heavy-built person stepped forward and with six good, hard blows, accompanied by an axe, the heavy door gave way, and it required but little force to set aside the several men who tried to block their way. Officer Kelley was caught by the throat and bears the marks of the man's nails. The keys were demanded, but they were not to be found. The negro was soon located and work was commenced to get at him. When the first blow was struck on the lock Officer Dugan protested, but when told that his life would be taken if he made any trouble he quietly stepped aside, and in a few moments the works of the lock fell jingling to the brick floor and several of the men entered the cell.

The rope was placed over the negro's head and then he was led through the corridor to the steps. In going down the steps he fell, but he was helped to his feet and led on out to the stable yard, where the big crowd was in waiting, and immediately the cry of "Don't go any further, do it right here," was raised, and it was found impossible to go further, for in what seemed like an instant, the man with the rope had climbed a small maple tree on Cross street, opposite the end of the jail, and there he was hanged until dead. His hands were not tied, and during the march from the jail to the tree he kept hold of the rope around his neck.

He was dead in one minute after he left the ground and had not made any movements with hands, feet or mouth. The limb on which he was hung was so low to the ground that the man's head just towered above those in the crowd. Every man in the crowd was armed, and cries of "Don't shoot" arose, and not a shot was fired. The lynchers seemed to be cool and deliberate, there was no drinking, and not a single shot was fired during the whole evening. When cries of "Don't shoot" were heard the crowds of colored people who were not far away ran, and so did many of the whites. .....

Taylor was buried at the almshouse today. The colored people are very indignant at the affair, but nothing has developed here yet. Dan Wright was committed to jail for denouncing the affair and shaking his fist in a white man's face and being generally disorderly today. [124]

The biographical information of the Maryland Archives website states that Taylor was 23 year old and originally from Pondtown, Queen Anne's County. He moved to Kennedyville, Kent County eight years before his lynching.

---

[124] *The Baltimore Sun*, "Jim Taylor Lynched; Taken from the Chestertown Jail and Hung to a Tree; A Determined Body of Citizens; Led by a Rope to Death – Jail Doors Beaten Down and the Sheriff Overpowered – Colored People Indignant – The First Lynching in Kent," May 19, 1893

Mob Law on Delmarva

At the end of *The Baltimore Sun* article in the May 19, 1892 edition, there is a short report from Wilmington, Delaware.

> Wilmington, Del., May 18 – A Clayton (Del.) special to the Every Evening says: "Little Nellie Silcox, the victim of the negro's brutality, died yesterday."

This is curious, considering the May 27, 1892 article of *The Baltimore Sun* describes the girl as "still in bed and is improving slowly. Dr. Jacobs, her attending physician, says she is not yet out of danger."[125]

The same May 27th article describes disputed reports about the crime.

> Chestertown, Md., May 26 – A special from Chestertown to Philadelphia and Wilmington papers yesterday says: "It is currently reported here and now generally believed that the negro, Jim Taylor, who was lynched here last Tuesday night for an alleged criminal assault upon Nellie Silcox, an eleven-year-old white girl, of Kennedyville, Kent county, was innocent of the crime. It is also reported that the white man, who was working for Mr. Silcox, disappeared on the day that the crime was committed and has not been seen since, and that Nellie asserts that this man committed the crime for which Jim Taylor was lynched.
>
> The citizens of Kent county authorized Justice T.S. Dodd to go to Kennedyville and take the testimony of the young girl. In her testimony she states that Jim Taylor, the colored man employed on her father's place, was her assailant. This testimony, which went into minute details of the case, was written down. The little girl goes on to say that after the assault Jim Taylor immediately left and went to the pump and then in the direction of Kennedyville. "He said to me before he left: 'You dare not tell.' My father and Samuel B. Latham were at the carriage house getting carriages. My mother was in the cellar and my little sister Elsie was in an adjoining room. I know it was Jim Taylor. He had on a blue-striped shirt and gray-striped pants."
>
> The witnesses to the above statement were John W. Silcox, James W. Hurtt, James A. Shaw and H.C. Denniger. The young white man Latham was seen at work on the premises with six others cultivating corn. Furthermore, the magistrate states that on the day after the assault Latham was seen by him on the premises in the discharge of his regular duties. Mr. J.W. Silcox's testimony as to Latham's whereabouts is to the same effect."[125]

---

[125] *The Baltimore Sun*, "The Kent Lynching; Denial of a Report by the Evidence of the Victim," May 27, 1892

Chapter 11. Eastern Shore Cases

Dr. Hill's Murder
Four executed January 1893 in Kent County, Maryland; four commuted sentences

> "When it became known that the lives of four of the prisoners had been saved by executive clemency indignation was expressed by many of the residents of Chestertown, while others, who had been instrumental in working such an end, were well pleased. The indignant ones loudly proclaimed that the four remaining murderers would be lynched, and it was even asserted that a large body of armed men from the vicinity of Kennedyville and the upper districts of the county would come to town tonight for the avowed purpose of lynching Fletcher Williams, Charles Brooks, Moses Brown and Frisby Comegys."
>
> January 12, 1893
> The Baltimore Sun

The April 29, 1892 issue of *The Baltimore Sun* reported on the murder of Dr. James Hill, white, of Millington, who died from wounds inflicted by having his throat cut and his head wounded. Several young men were arrested and held. Fears of lynchings were reported. Those held were Josh Baynard, Buck Brooks, Fletcher Williams, Perry Bradshaw, Henry Hurtt, Frizby Comegys and Charles Emory. The article included a lengthy interview of Josh Baynard by a reporter.[126]

The case was widely reported, but here is a brief summary from a few of the articles collected.

April 29, 1892, *The Baltimore Sun* – Several men held for questioning following the death of Dr. Hill: Josh Baynard, Buck Brooks, Fletcher Williams, Perry Bradshaw, Henry Hurtt, Frizby Comegys and Charles Emory.[126]

October 18, 1892, *The Baltimore Sun* – Report of the coming trial of sixteen prisoners in the Chestertown jail accused of the Dr. Hill murder.[127] The

---

[126] *The Baltimore Sun*, "Dr. Hill's Death—A Colored Boy Says He Saw Him Attacked on the Road—The Manner of Assault Described—As a Result of the Statement a Number of Colored Men Are Locked Up in Chestertown Jail – The Prison Closely Guarded Because of Fears of Lynching," Apr. 29, 1892
[127] *The Baltimore Sun*, "The Hill Murder—Opening of the October Term of the Kent County Court—Probable Presentments Today—The Sixteen Prisoners in the Chestertown Jail Accused of the Murder of Dr. Hill," Oct. 18, 1892

Mob Law on Delmarva

article included, "These men had been taken to Baltimore, as already stated, on account of the intense feeling and fears of lynching."

October 21, 1892, *The Baltimore Sun* – The sixteen held at the Chestertown jail were indicted.[128]

October 28, 1892, *The Baltimore Sun* – Eight held at the Chestertown jail are convicted, found guilty of murder in the first degree.[129] In addition to the eight convictions, one defendant was found not guilty. The newspaper reports from Judge Robinson's statement.

> "John Potts is not guilty. There is no evidence shown wherein John Potts entered into a conspiracy or took part in the murder, therefore the verdict in his case is not guilty." …

The article further reports,

> After the verdict was announced Sheriff Plumber informed the court that he understood threats had been made against the life of Potts and asked the assistance of the court in protecting Potts from lynching. Judge Robinson made a strong speech, in which he said he was pained and grieved that such a thing should be even whispered. 'The Law,' he continued, 'has been fully vindicated. The grand jury will meet again on Monday next further to investigate the murder, and if sufficient evidence is obtained to implicate Potts as an accessory before the act he will be indicted and tried.'
>
> Judge Wickers said he indorsed every word uttered by Judge Robinson. The sheriff was promised ample protection for Potts, who was remanded to the sheriff's custody until Monday. The grand jury was held until Monday. …
>
> Philip Manda, Frank Brainard [sic and identified as brother of convicted Joshua Baynard] and Walter Roe, Henry Hynson, John Harrison and Stephen Cooper, who have been held as witnesses, and some of them as probably participants in the crime, will be kept in jail until the grand jury adjourns. …

December 22, 1892, *The Baltimore Sun* – reported that the sentenced men held in Chestertown were visited by Bishop A. W. Wayman, of the AME church in Baltimore.

January 12, 1893, *The Baltimore Sun* – The Governor commuted the sentence of four of the eight convicted and ordered the four be sent to

---

[128] *The Baltimore Sun*, "Indictments in the Hill Murder Case at Chestertown," Oct. 21, 1892
[129] *The Baltimore Sun*, "Eight Are Convicted—Prisoners Pronounced Guilty of Murder in First Degree—Unusual Verdict of Court in Kent—John Potts the Only One of the Nine Colored Men Accused of Killing Dr. Hill Who Is Acquitted," Oct. 28, 1892

Chapter 11. Eastern Shore Cases

the Maryland Penitentiary under secrecy.[130] The four were Joshua Baynard, Henry Hurtt, Louis Benson and Charles S. Emory. The following is from this January 12th article.

> When it became known that the lives of four of the prisoners had been saved by executive clemency indignation was expressed by many of the residents of Chestertown, while others, who had been instrumental in working such an end, were well pleased. The indignant ones loudly proclaimed that the four remaining murderers would be lynched, and it was even asserted that a large body of armed men from the vicinity of Kennedyville and the upper districts of the county would come to town tonight for the avowed purpose of lynching Fletcher Williams, Charles Brooks, Moses Brown and Frisby Comegys. A careful canvass of those sections, however, fails to verify this report.

January 14, 1893 – *The Baltimore Sun* – Charles Brooks, Fletcher Williams, Moses Brown and Frisby Comegys were executed by hanging January 13th in the jail yard at Chestertown. According to the article, "The four murderers died stoutly maintaining their innocence." Further,

> The motive for the murder of Dr. Hill is said to have been revenge. He had declared that a colored man who died suddenly was not killed outright by some white men, as supposed by colored residents of Millington, but had died of heart disease super induced possibly by a blow. Dr. Hill was thirty-two years old, young, handsome and popular. He lives a widow and a baby girl."[131]

---

[130] *The Baltimore Sun*, "Chestertown Surprised—Many of the People Indignant While Others Were Well Pleased," Jan. 12, 18893

[131] The Baltimore Sun, "Four Men Hanged—Death Penalty Paid by the Hill Murderers at Chestertown—The Prompt Execution of the Law—Two of the Prisoners Struggle Frightfully and Die Hard—Declarations of Innocence—Some Excitement of the People, but No Disorder—Gov. Brown Commended," Jan. 14, 1893

Mob Law on Delmarva

Henry Taylor and Arthur Courtney
Executed December 1893 in Somerset County, Maryland

Henry Taylor and Arthur Courtney of Virginia were arrested and jailed at Princess Anne, Maryland, for the alleged murder of Capt. J. Frank Cooper on the boat *James V. Daiger* at Deals Island in Somerset County. In this case, newspaper descriptions were of a near lynching. The two men were held in Carter's Creek, Virginia, in Lancaster County, on the western shore of the Chesapeake for the murder of Capt. J. Frank Cooper. *The Baltimore Sun* of June 20, 1893 reports on the attempted lynching of the two prisoners.

"Hardly had Dr. Newbill stopped talking before the cry went up, 'We have him!' The vessel's hatch had been torn away and forty or more people were in the vessel's hold searching for the culprits. Courtney and Taylor tried to hide in the fore peak, where they were found. A rope was procured and placed around the neck of Courtney. The negro struggled, and Sheriff Tull jumped down the hold, opened his knife and cut the rope just as the negro was hoisted on deck."

"During all this time the shores were lined with men and women. Among the latter was the wife of the murdered man, who constantly cried out to the crowd to kill the men who had taken her husband's life."

June 20, 1893
The Baltimore Sun

Deal's Island, MD, June 19 – Sheriff Tull arrived here tonight with Arthur Courtney and Henry Taylor, the colored men charged with the murder of Capt. J. Frank Cooper, of Carter's Creek, Va. Sheriff Tull left Deal's Island Saturday night of a sailboat for Lancaster Court House, Va., where the two men were in jail. The sheriff was accompanied by Dr. Monmonier Rowe, Capt. W. D. Windsor, G. A. Goslee and a reporter of The Sun. The party left Deal's Island at midnight Saturday, and arrived at Carter's Creek at 12 o'clock on Sunday.

As soon as the sheriff and his party landed they were notified that if he had not come for the negroes they should not be taken alive. The two colored men were turned over to him and the party left Lancaster Court House at 6 o'clock Sunday evening. Along the road the news had preceded the sheriff and crowds of people congregated to see the prisoners. Before Carter's Creek was reached there were about fifty carriages and vehicles following the prisoners.

Chapter 11. Eastern Shore Cases

About a mile from the town a crowd of fifty men tried to stop the carriage, and asked that the negroes be turned over to them. Sheriff Tull stood up in the carriage, placed the whip to the horses and got to the landing ahead of the people who had congregated. He reached the shore, where a boat met him. He placed Arthur Courtney in the boat and rowed to the schooner which had brought his party over. As the sheriff pulled alongside the vessel he saw her deck swarming with people, all of whom demanded the surrender of Courtney, who the crowd declared was the instigator of the murder.

Sheriff Tull took his position on board of the vessel and pushed the prisoner down the hold. About this time one of his deputies came alongside with Taylor, the other prisoner. He was also placed down the vessel's hold.

As soon as both the prisoners were aboard some one in the crowd gave a signal and from all sides small boats approached and the men who were in them clambered over the vessel's sides until there was scarcely standing room. Sheriff Tull and his deputies took their positions on the hatches which covered the hold and to all he stated that he would defend the prisoners. He made a strong appeal not to be disturbed in taking the prisoners to Maryland for trial. The mob would not listen, but constantly called for Courtney. Sheriff Tull was seized and forcibly taken from the hatchway. The sheriff freed himself and returned to his post. Dr. Newbill, Messrs. Frank Newbill, McLee and Walter Damman, all citizens of the place, made appeals to the crowd, begging them to desist and allow the men to go. The crowd subsided, but it was for a purpose.

Hardly had Dr. Newbill stopped talking before the cry went up, "We have him!" The vessel's hatch had been torn away and forty or more people were in the vessel's hold searching for the culprits. Courtney and Taylor tried to hide in the fore peak, where they were found. A rope was procured and placed around the neck of Courtney. The negro struggled, and Sheriff Tull jumped down the hold, opened his knife and cut the rope just as the negro was hoisted on deck.

This failure made the mob more violent. They then got the rope around Courtney's leg and again began to pull him out. The sheriff once more parted the line with his knife. By this time the cooler heads surrounded the poor negro and took him into the cabin, putting him in the corner of the room, where they formed a ring around him. The crowd by this time got wild, and one man pressed forward with a stick in his hands and struck at the prisoner, but the negro dodged the blow and it was received by Dr. Newbill, who was assisting the sheriff in resisting the mob.

Henry Taylor, the other prisoner, is a native of the place, and the people did not believe that he had been a party to the crime. Efforts were made to liberate him. A proposition was made to the sheriff to liberate Taylor and he could take Courtney. This was, of course, declined. He had hardly gotten the words out of his mouth before one of the deputies saw Taylor, accompanied by a white man, attempting to get out of the forepeak. The deputy prevented the escape.

Mob Law on Delmarva

> Finally realizing that they could not get the prisoners, the people listened to the argument made by Dr. Newbill and others, and Sheriff Tull and his party were allowed to leave. The contention lasted until past midnight. During all this time the shores were lined with men and women. Among the latter was the wife of the murdered man, who constantly cried out to the crowd to kill the men who had taken her husband's life.[132]

The same article described Taylor as a native of Lancaster county, 18 years old, and "unusually large for his age." Courtney was described as a small black man, 25 years old and a native of the area near Carter's Creek.

The June 28, 1893 edition of *The Baltimore Sun* includes the following.

> *"As soon as the justice had adjourned the court the crowd broke through while others climbed over the railing, and in an instant the men were surrounded. While no violence was done the men, there were such expressions as 'You had better get ready to die" and "You should be hung to a tree.'"*
>
> *"The town has been full of rumors about lynching the men. The people complain about the expenses attending the trial being saddled on the county, as all the parties concerned were from Virginia."*
>
> June 28, 1893
> The Baltimore Sun

Princess Anne, Md., June 27 – Henry Taylor and Arthur Courtney, both colored, were given a hearing today before Justice Rider on the charge of murdering Capt. J. Frank Cooper on Sunday, June 11, on board of the bungy *James V. Daiger*, lying in the harbor at Deal's Island. The hearing was held in the courtroom, as the crowd in attendance was far too large to be accommodated in any other building in the town. The news that the hearing would take place attracted a large crowd. Every district of the county was represented, and long before the people of Princess Anne had finished their morning meal carriages, wagons and vehicles of every description began to arrive in town from the lower sections of the county. Many persons left their homes as early as 5 o'clock in order to reach the county seat before the hearing began. At 11:15 State's Attorney Henry J. Waters proceeded to the courtroom, where Justice Rider had taken his seat. Sheriff Tull, accompanied by Jailer Brocton and Constable Albert Goslee, then went to the jail and took the prisoners from the jail to the courthouse. The sheriff and his prisoners were followed by crowds of men and boys, who struggled with each other in order to catch a glimpse of the two men. When the party entered the court yard the people made

---

[132] *The Baltimore Sun*, "The Deal's Island Murders in Maryland Custody, Attempted Lynching in Virginia," Jun. 20, 1893

Chapter 11. Eastern Shore Cases

> a rush for the courtroom, and in an instant every seat was taken, while the aisles were crowded with those who were unable to get seats, and the space reserved for the members of the bar was also taken up by the crowd.[133]

The hearing adjourned, awaiting the decision of when to convene the trial.

> As soon as the justice had adjourned the court the crowd broke through while others climbed over the railing, and in an instant the men were surrounded. While no violence was done the men, there were such expressions as "You had better get ready to die" and "You should be hung to a tree" …..
>
> The town has been full of rumors about lynching the men. The people complain about the expenses attending the trial being saddled on the county, as all the parties concerned were from Virginia.[133]

Both Arthur Courtney and Henry Taylor were executed by hanging on December 15, 1893, in the jail yard in Princess Anne before a crowd of spectators estimated at probably two thousand. As reported by *The Baltimore Sun*, spectators "were packed dozens deep around the scaffold; they were perched on the fences surrounding the jail; they climbed neighboring trees and swayed on their branches in their desire to witness the proceedings; they climbed to the roofs of houses overlooking the jail, even to the roof of the jail itself, and perched themselves on chimney tops." Attempts to keep the execution from being a public event failed, when spectators threatened to storm the jail and lynch the men if they were not executed on this scheduled date.[134]

---

[133] *The Baltimore Sun*, "Taylor and Courtney Given a Hearing at Princess Anne; Committed for the Grand Jury; Testimony Before Justice Rider in Regard to the Murder of Capt. Cooper—Great Indignation Against the Prisoners – Rumors of Lynching," Jun 28, 1893
[134] *The Baltimore Sun*, "Courtney and Taylor Executed at Princess Anne; Death Caused by Strangulation," Dec. 16, 1893

William Jackson

Executed July 1894 in Queen Anne's County, Maryland

William Jackson, a farm hand, was arrested April 19, 1894, for killing George J. Leager, a farmer on the Chester River in Queen Anne's County, on April 18. Jackson was taken to Baltimore to avoid lynching. Jackson was executed on July 6, in Centreville.

The Baltimore Sun April 20, 1894 article describes the following.

> Centreville, Md., April 19 – George J. Leager, a successful farmer on Chester River, in Queen Anne's county, on the Round Top estate of W. Irving Walker, of Baltimore, was killed last night, shortly after 6 o'clock, and his fourteen-year-old stepson, Nathan B. Crossley, probably fatally shot by William Jackson, a negro farm hand on the place. The most intense feeling prevailed, and it was with difficulty that the cooler headed farmers among the large number of men who collected at the scene of the killing prevented the negro from being lynched to a tree within a few feet of the spot upon which his victim had fallen, shot to death....[135]

> *"The colored people in and around Centreville shared in the feeling that Jackson would be lynched, and they assembled about the jail in large numbers, armed with clubs and other weapons with which to defend Jackson from lynchers. Shortly after nightfall fully three hundred colored men were near the jail. About two hundred white men were also there. Reports of the intention of farmers living in the neighborhood of the murder to lynch Jackson added to the excitement, and it was decided to bring the prisoner to Baltimore."*
>
> Statement of Deputy Sheriff T. S. Roberts, April, 21, 1894
> The Baltimore Sun

The Baltimore Sun of April 21, 1894 details a fascinating description of crowds of local black citizens gathered to protect Jackson from being lynched.

> William Jackson, the colored man who is accused of the murder of George J. Leager and the attempted murder of Mr. Leager's step-son, Nathan B. Crossley, near Centreville, Wednesday, was brought to Baltimore yesterday and lodged in the city jail. The prompted action of State's Attorney Hopper and the sheriff of Queen Anne's county in removing Jackson from the Centreville jail probably averted bloodshed and loss of additional lives.

---

[135] *The Baltimore Sun*, "Bloody Tragedy on Chester River, in Queen Anne's County, A Farmer Killed By A Colored Man," Apr. 20, 1894

Chapter 11. Eastern Shore Cases

Deputy Sheriff T. S. Roberts, who brought Jackson to Baltimore, said: "Intense excitement prevails throughout the northern part of Queen Anne's county, and it was expected that a lynching party would go to Centreville Thursday night and take Jackson from the jail and hang him to the nearest tree. The colored people in and around Centreville shared in the feeling that Jackson would be lynched, and they assembled about the jail in large numbers, armed with clubs and other weapons with which to defend Jackson from lynchers. Shortly after nightfall fully three hundred colored men were near the jail. About two hundred white men were also there. Reports of the intention of farmers living in the neighborhood of the murder to lynch Jackson added to the excitement, and it was decided to bring the prisoner to Baltimore.

Preparation for departure were quietly made, and about 11 o'clock Thursday night I drove out of the jail yard in a buggy, with Jackson heavily ironed. For fear of meeting a party of lynchers a circuitous route was taken for Queenstown. On the outskirts of Centreville a party of colored en formed in line across the road and demanded of me where I was going with my prisoner. I told them I would take him to Baltimore, and after Jackson had begged them for God's sake to allow him to be taken to a place of safety they permitted us to drive away. A few miles from Centreville we met a crowd of colored men hurrying to the jail, and they had to be appeased with the same statement before we could continue our journey. We reached Queenstown at 1 o'clock in the morning. I at once summoned a posse to guard the prisoner, and kept him locked up in a room at the Chester Hotel until 10 o'clock, when we took the steamer *Emma Ford* for Baltimore...."[136]

Jackson was convicted and executed by hanging on July 6, 1894 in Centreville.[137]

---

[136] *The Baltimore Sun*, "Safe in Jail, Wm. Jackson, Colored, Who is Accused of Murder in Queen Anne's," Apr. 21, 1984
[137] *The Baltimore Sun*, Jul. 7, 1894

Isaac Kemp

Lynched June 1894 in Somerset County, Maryland

Isaac Kemp was shot in the jail at Princess Anne by a mob for allegedly killing Constable Ned Carver during a brawl at a store owned by Charles Miller in the Dublin District, about 7 miles north of Pocomoke. Kemp was a berry picker from Virginia, employed by Frank Barnes of Somerset County. Others arrested were reportedly removed to Salisbury. The Maryland Archives gives the background of the case.

> *"After a few minutes they found Kemp and shot at him three times through the grating of the door. They then proceeded downstairs in the jailer's private room and, after a thorough search, found the keys, and with a hurrah rushed upstairs, threw open the cell door and riddled the murderer's body with bullets, about fifty shots being fired. The mob then wanted to take the body with them, but after some argument they consented to leave it. They then fled down the stairs and bidding me good night, with a hurrah left the jail."*
>
> Statement of Jailer Dryden,
> June 9, 1894
> The Baltimore Sun

Isaac Kemp, a berry picker from Virginia, and employed by Frank Barnes of Somerset County, Maryland, was killed on Friday, June 8, 1894 by a mob of about 150 white men in Princess Anne, Maryland. Kemp was with a group of about a dozen blacks that had received pay for their work by Mr. Barnes when they arrived at a country store owned by Charles Miller located in the Dublin district about 7 miles north of Pocomoke City.

At around 9:00pm that evening, the group purchased whiskey, the black workers became unruly and began knocking displays over in the store. Constable Ned Carver, at the proprietor's request, asked the group to quell their destructive behavior, stating that the group could either leave of be arrested. One drunken member of the group said "We'll come as we --- please!" At this moment, a fight broke out between Isaac Kemp and Constable Carver. Pushed outside of the store, the fight continued with the addition of Mr. Frank McCready, Constable Carver's brother, coming to the aid of his brethren. As the fight escalated, Carver and McCready were beaten over the head with clubs and empty beer bottles. Battered and bloody, the two men were punished within an inch of their lives, but the fight continued, and for a moment stopped with Constable Carver and Mr. McCready nearly dead. Unsatisfied, Isaac Kemp ran over the Carver, and with a razor, cut and sliced the constable on his face and legs, killing Ned Carver.

With the store destroyed, and Carver and McCready left on the ground, the group fled the scene. Mr. C.A. Veasy attempted to clean up the two

Chapter 11. Eastern Shore Cases

men, and ran to Dr. Dashielle for medical treatment. Once the doctor got to the victims, McCready was badly hurt, but alive. As for Constable Carver, Dr. Dashielle said that there was nothing he could do to save him. Ned Carver was 32 years old and left behind one child.

Within 2 hours, 10 of the 12 men were arrested and placed in the Princess Anne jailhouse on Main St. The other 2 men apparently left the store as the men began to fight, and were picked up in Pocomoke City, arrested, and placed in jail there. Early in the morning hours of Thursday, June 7, a group of about 75 men approached the Princess Anne jail, explaining to Deputy Dryden that they had a prisoner for him to arraign (the other 75 men were placed on guard). Once the jailer opened the door, the mob rushed the doors, tricking the officer into letting them in. Officer Dryden refused to give the mob the keys to the jail cell, and the group began to use a battering ram to open the door. Forced to hand the keys over at gunpoint, Officer Dryden could do nothing but watch as the angry men found the supposed ringleader, Isaac Kemp. One of the other men, John Handy, confessed that Kemp was not only the lone person drinking, but also that he was the only one to hit Constable Carver with the bottle. Satisfied that the mob had found their guilty party, Kemp was riddled with about 50 bullets into his body, killing Carver's murderer.

Afraid that the mob would return for the other men, Officer Dryden requested a clandestine removal of the group to a jail in Salisbury, Maryland, about 15 miles north of Princess Anne. However, when the mob returned to the jail for the others and realized that they had been transferred, a request to send a train for 100 men to take them to Salisbury was denied. In Salisbury, word had gotten out that the men were there, and tensions between the whites who wished to lynch them, and the armed blacks in the town who vowed to protect the prisoners, created a problem. So another secret transfer of the 10 blacks from Virginia was made, taking them to murderers row in Baltimore City, and leaving the chaos behind on the Eastern Shore. Once tensions seemed to be under control, and the guilty parties were facing trial, Constable Ned Carver's body was buried in Rehoboth, Delaware.

The Baltimore Sun of June 9, 1894 includes the following statement by the jailer Dryden about the mob members reaching Kemp's cell.

> "After a few minutes they found Kemp and shot at him three times through the grating of the door. They then proceeded downstairs in the jailer's private room and, after a thorough search, found the keys, and with a hurrah rushed upstairs, threw open the cell door and riddled the murderer's body with bullets, about fifty shots being fired. The mob then wanted to take the body with them, but after some argument they consented to leave it. They then fled down the stairs and bidding me good night, with a hurrah left the jail." [138]

---

[138] *The Baltimore Sun*, "A Lynching Sequel to the Carver Tragedy in Somerset, Prisoner Shot Down in His Cell," Jun. 9, 1894

Mob Law on Delmarva

The Baltimore Sun further reports on the inquest at the site of Kemp's murder.

> At 10 o'clock Justice Rider held an inquest over the body of Kemp. Dr. Wainwright, who made a post-mortem, testified that there were eight wounds on the body of Kemp, any one of which was fatal. Alva N. Gibbons, who had spent the night in the jail with the sheriff, recognized one of the raiders in Samuel Webb, whose mask accidentally dropped off. Sheriff Sterling also identified Sewell Webb as one of the lynchers.

The remaining nine men accused of the Carver murder went on trial in Baltimore court beginning February 5, 1895.[139] The trial ended on February 9th with three of the prisoners convicted for murder in the second degree, two convicted of manslaughter and four acquitted, as reported in the February 11, 1895 issue of *The Baltimore Sun*.

> Those convicted of murder in the second degree are John Handy, alias John Handy Bell, George Holden and George Parker, the jury recommending Parker to mercy. Leonard Conquest and Alfred Conquest were convicted of manslaughter. The names of those acquitted are Thomas Smith, alias Theodore Thomas Smith, George Brown, John Williams and George Holman [sic].
>
> Sentence was suspended in the cases of those convicted on notice being given by their counsel of a motion for a new trial. The punishment for murder in the second degree is from five to eighteen years in the penitentiary. For manslaughter the penalty is imprisonment in the penitentiary for not more than ten years or a fine of not more than $500, or imprisonment in jail for not more than two years, or both fine and imprisonment in jail.
>
> It is said that when the jurors retired four of them were in favor of a verdict of murder in the first degree in the cases of all five of those convicted.[140]

Sentencing was pronounced on March 1, 1895.

> John Handy, alias John Handy Bell, and George Holden, who were convicted of murder in the second degree, were each sentenced to eighteen years in the penitentiary, the maximum penalty.
>
> George Parker, who was also convicted of murder in the second degree, but whom the jury recommended to mercy, was sentenced to ten years in the penitentiary.
>
> Leonard Conquest and Alfred Conquest, convicted of manslaughter, were each sentenced to eight years in the penitentiary.

---

[139] *The Baltimore Sun*, "Carver Murder Trial; Difficulty in Selecting a Jury in the Criminal Court," Feb. 6, 1895

[140] *The Baltimore Sun*, "Murder Trial Ended; Five Men Convicted and Four Acquitted of Killing Constable Carver," Feb. 11, 1895

Chapter 11. Eastern Shore Cases

In the case of Handy and Holden, the judge said, the border line between murder in the first degree and murder in the second degree seemed to have been passed. Their blows, he said, led to the death of Constable Carver, and the crime was that of savages rather than of civilized persons from the fact that the fatal blows were struck while Mr. Carver was on his knees. The judge saw no room for mercy as to them.

Besides the recommendation to mercy in Parker's case, the judge said he was doubtful whether or not Parker intended to take life, but there was no reason why the verdict of the jury should be disturbed. The sentence, the judge said, would be the maximum penalty for manslaughter.[141]

---

[141] *The Baltimore Sun*, "Murderers Sentenced; Men Who Killed Constable Carver in Somerset Sent to the Penitentiary," Mar. 2, 1895

Mob Law on Delmarva

Taylor Rowlett and Richard Everitt
Arrested September 1896 in Cecil County, Maryland

Taylor Rowlett, a 22 year-old laborer from Marion Station, Virginia, was arrested for the September 24, 1896 assault of Mrs. Maggie Foundes, 28, wife of John Foundes of Leeds, Cecil County. Another suspect, Richard Everitt, was also questioned. Both seemed to have adequate alibis.

The Baltimore Sun reports on September 25th,

"The excitement in Elkton last night when it was learned that Taylor Rowlette, a negro twenty-two years of age, hailing from Marion Station, Va., had been arrested at Chesapeake City on suspicion, was something great. The streets were lined with people and some talk of lynching was to be heard."

September 26, 1896
The Baltimore Sun

Sheriff Mackey has arrived at the jail with Taylor Rowlett, a colored man, of twenty-two years, who gives Mebrion [sic] Station, Va., as his residence. The authorities used every precaution to keep the fact hidden from the excited people, but was unable to do so, as fully 200 people had assembled at the jail and were eager to get a glimpse of the supposed fiend. Sheriff Mackey and State's Attorney Evans questioned the prisoner closely, but are of the opinion that the prisoner arrested at Chesapeake City is not the man wanted. [142]

The following day, *The Baltimore Sun* September 26th reported,

> The excitement in Elkton last night when it was learned that Taylor Rowlette, a negro twenty-two years of age, hailing from Marion Station, Va., had been arrested at Chesapeake City on suspicion, was something great. The streets were lined with people and some talk of lynching was to be heard. State's Attorney William S. Evans, to guard against any outbreak that might occur, telephoned Sheriff Mackey to be on the lookout. It was after 10 o'clock when the sheriff brought the negro from the buggy and marched him into the jail. Several hundred people had congregated in and around the prison and there was a great rush to see the man as he alighted from the conveyance. The negro was badly frightened and breathed more freely when safely in a cell in the jail. While some talk of lynching was heard it is not thought the people would have taken the law into their hands, especially when not assured that the right man had been arrested.

---

[142] *The Baltimore Sun*, "Assault of Mrs. Maggie Foundes by a Negro Man in Cecil County; A Daring Desperado's Work; Left Bleeding and Unconscious in a Clump of Bushes Near the Road; Alarm Given in Elkton and Searching Parties Sent Out," Sep. 25, 1896

Chapter 11. Eastern Shore Cases

Rowlette was closely questioned by Sheriff Mackey and State's Attorney W.S. Evans, and told a straight story of his whereabouts for yesterday. He said he arrived in Elkton from Perryville on the 4:16 train and remembered asking the watchman at North street crossing the way to Chesapeake City. He described the conductor and brakeman of the train, and said that between the two stations a man had been put off the train. The conductor and brakeman testify to the truth of the man's story.

The other suspect, Richard Everitt, was also closely questioned, but he likewise is able to prove an alibi.

State's Attorney William S. Evans and Sheriff Mackey have been working on the case today, but up to late tonight no clue was forthcoming. [143]

---

[143] *The Baltimore Sun*, "The Cecil Outrage; Two Colored Men Prove an Alibi – Condition of the Victim," Sep. 26, 1896

William Andrews
Lynched June 1897 in Princess Anne, Maryland

Andrews was lynched in Princess Anne following his conviction and sentencing, after which a mob grabbed him while being transported from the court. He was punched, kicked, beaten with bats and clubs, cut with razors, dragged to a walnut tree, and hung. He was buried at the almshouse burial grounds. Andrews was convicted for "ravishing" Mrs. Benjamin T. Kelley in Marion.

As reported by *The Baltimore Sun* in its June 10, 1987 issue, on the morning of the trial, Andrews was transported to Princess Anne, arriving by train at 8:29 A.M., and placed in the jail. Officers escorted Andrews from the jail to the courthouse, entering the private entrance used by judges.

> His appearance in the court was the signal for a rush by the crowd to the rail which separated the bar from the courtroom proper. In this struggle to get a sight of the prisoner benches were overturned, hats were destroyed and clothing was disarranged. Judge Page attempted to check the rush by threatening to have the aisles cleared of all those who were not seated. Several persons in the crowd answered by saying: "We could not get back if we wanted to do so." [144]

At the end of the trial, Andrews was found guilty and Judge Henry Page sentenced Andrews to be hanged. The prisoner was to be escorted from the court to the jail located about a block away from the courthouse. *The Baltimore Sun* June 10th issue describes the lynching.

> *"At this moment one of the mob, wild with fury, inflicted a wound upon Andrews' thigh with a razor. The blood from the wound left its trail to the place where the lynching took place."*
>
> June 10, 1897
> The Baltimore Sun

The judge was notified that a mob had surrounded the courthouse and that fears were entertained that violence would be resorted to when the sheriff should attempt to remove the prisoner to the jail. Leaving the bench he addressed the mob, urging all law-abiding citizens to remain quiet, as the law thus far had been permitted to take its course. He said justice would surely be meted out to Mrs. Kelley's assailant. The judge was asked if the prisoner would again be removed to the Baltimore jail, and having been assured that this would not be done the mob promised to disperse.

---

[144] *The Baltimore Sun*, "His Doom Swift, Mob's Fury would not Brook the Law's Delay, Although William Andrews had been Sentenced to Death," Jun. 10, 1897

Chapter 11. Eastern Shore Cases

> This promise proved to be but a subterfuge, for as soon as the sheriff and his deputies appeared with the prisoner at the door of the private entrance to the court Andrews, trembling and cowering, was seized by the infuriated people. Amid curses and cries of "Kill him" he was soon reduced to a state of unconsciousness.
>
> The suddenness of the attack came as a surprise to the guards who had charge of the prisoner. They attempted to protect him, but were powerless to cope with the maddened throng.
>
> Deputy Samuel W. Kennerley, who had hold of Andrews, seized him around the neck and attempted to shield his head from the blows which were being aimed at it. In this position the deputy attempted to drag the prisoner across a small ravine which separated the courthouse yard from Church street, and for an instant it seemed that he would reach the street.
>
> At this moment one of the mob, wild with fury, inflicted a wound upon Andrews' thigh with a razor. The blood from the wound left its trail to the place where the lynching took place. Andrews had become unconscious in the meantime from blows and kicks which he received from the crowd.
>
> A rope was gotten, and the noose having been quickly adjusted around the doomed man's neck, he was hanged to the limb of a walnut tree and soon was dead.

The body was left hanging from the tree until 3 o'clock in the afternoon. It was eventually taken by undertaker William H. Smith and buried at the almshouse property.

Also included in the issue is the following,

> There is little indignation expressed on the part of the colored population at Andrews' fate. They say their only regret is that the law was not permitted to take its course. One colored man gave expression to disapproval of the lynching and somebody overheard this remark. The next seen of him he was making for the nearest woods. He had not returned to town up to a late hour at night.[145]

---

[145] *The Baltimore Sun*, "Deplored by Judge Page; 'There Was No Reason for Violence'—Expressions of Opinion Made by All Classes of People," Jun. 10, 1897

Mob Law on Delmarva

Figure 23 Old courthouse, Princess Anne, Maryland

Old Somerset County courthouse, built 1833, located at the site of the current Courthouse, built 1905. Courtesy Keith Vincent.

The above photograph is of the old courthouse, the one that was the site of Andrew's trial. The courthouse is on the left, the Clerk office building is on the right. The "private entrance to the court" may be on the left front side of the building or near the rear (Vincent 2010).

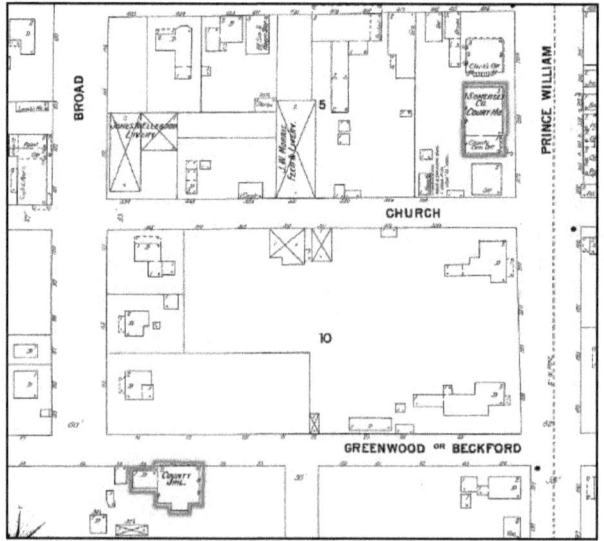

Figure 24 Map of Princess Anne structures at time of Andrew lynching

The 1899 Sanborn Fire Insurance Map of Princess Anne, Maryland with the jail and courthouse highlighted.

Chapter 11. Eastern Shore Cases

Garfield King

Lynched May 1898 in Salisbury, Maryland

Garfield King was taken from the Salisbury jail and hung from a tree in front of the jail yard. King had been arrested for shooting and killing Herman Kenney.

The May 23, 1898 issue of *The Baltimore Sun* reports,

> Salisbury, Md., May 22 – Garfield King, a colored youth of eighteen, shot and fatally wounded Herman Kenney, a white boy, at Twigg's store, near Allen, in Wicomico county, Saturday night. The wounded youth will die. The trouble was caused by a gang of ten negroes attacking several white boys in the store. Ongoing out of doors the trouble was continued, when, it is alleged, King pulled out his pistol and shot Kenney in the abdomen. Sheriff Dashiell arrested King this morning and placed him in jail here. He admits the shooting, but says he did it in self defense.[146]

The Baltimore Sun of May 26, 1898 reports,

> *"The men came to Salisbury to lynch the murderer, and as one of them said to* The Sun *correspondent, 'we would have accomplished it had we waded through blood to our necks.'"*
>
> May 26, 1898
> The Baltimore Sun

About 11 o'clock several men rode into town from Trappe district and halted in front of the jail. Every few minutes men dressed in gum trousers, tarpaulin hats and gum boots could be seen going around the courthouse in the direction of the jail. At midnight, when the electric lights were shut off, a cheer went up, and shortly afterward signals could be heard.

By this time the crowd had swelled to over 100 quiet, determined men, talking in whispers and awaiting their leader. At 12:30 A.M. the leader arrived with a shotgun, accompanied by three other men with large clubs.

At 12:35 ten men came up with a telegraph pole and the leader rapped on the door, calling to Sheriff Dashiell to open. The request being refused, the telegraph pole was brought into action as a ram. The first blow was given amid cheers and curses. After ten minutes of hard work the door was battered down and the crowd mounted the steps and called for a light. Sheriff Dashiell having extinguished all the lights in the jail as soon as the attack was made.

---

[146] *The Baltimore Sun*, "Shooting in Wicomico; A White Youth Fatally Wounded By a Young Negro With a Handy Pistol," May 23, 1898

A lantern was procured and search began for the negro. The crowd was so anxious to get hold of the right man that repeated cries of "Get the right man" were heard on all sides.

Sheriff Dashiell refused to give up the keys to the cell, and the leader, producing a sledge, broke the lock. While the men were breaking open the door the negro was on his knees begging for mercy.

The crowd dragged him from the cell, and someone said, "Shoot him," but the crowd down stairs, not wishing to be cheated out of their revenge, shouted, "No, bring him down."

A call was made and some delay was occasioned, but finally a small rope was procured and placed around the prisoner's neck. He was then dragged downstairs fighting for his life. At this time some one blew out the light. Fearing the murderer would escape one of the crowd struck him with a club.

Another light was procured. The prisoner all the while was fighting his captors and crying out for mercy. Before he could be strung up several of the gang kicked and stamped upon him.

The prisoner was then dragged to a tree and the line thrown over a limb, but as soon as the man was hauled up the rope broke and he fell to the ground. Some one then shot a bullet through the poor wretch who was still alive. He was pulled up again, a man climbing the tree and catching the rope.

After making the knot secure the second time, the leader called for the crowd to "stand on this side" and "line up, boys," after which more than one hundred bullets and gunshots were fired into the dangling body.

Some one called for three cheers, which were given.

The leader of the crowd called his followers to "fall in" and they marched away.

An examination of the body after the crowd had left revealed over fifty bullet holes. The face was battered and torn.

When taken from the cell the negro was dressed in a thin shirt and trousers, which were almost torn from his body.

Neither the leader of the lynchers nor any of the party wore masks. They called each other by name and no attempt at secrecy was made.

The men came to Salisbury to lynch the murderer, and as one of them said to The Sun correspondent, "we would have accomplished it had we waded through blood to our necks."

Most of the men were fishermen from along the Wicomico river and many of them leading citizens of their districts.

The lynched man was an educated negro, who graduated at the Colored Academy at Princess Anne, and has always been well thought of by his neighbors.

Chapter 11. Eastern Shore Cases

> An effort was made late tonight among the colored people to organize a fund [word unclear] to help defend the negro, and at one time during the lynching some one called out "Here come the negroes." In an instant a hundred pistols shown in the dim light. Fortunately the alarm was a false one, or there would probably be a still more awful story to tell.
>
> Considerable damage was done to the front of the jail.
>
> The lynching was witnessed by a number of citizens of Salisbury who were powerless to stop the mob. The body was left hanging to the tree.[147]

The lynching occurred the day before scheduled plans to remove King to Baltimore for safe keeping. "As the crowd left the leader called out, 'Let this be a warning to colored murderers.'"[147]

The *Salisbury Advertiser* of May 28, 1898, reports,

> Judge Holland was disturbed from his slumbers by the shooting and hurriedly dressing, he appeared upon the scene just as the mob was taking its orderly leave of the scene of bloody action. He ordered the remains of the lynched boy cut down from the tree and placed in the old engine house for protection till burial. Thursday morning hundreds of citizens visited the place. They saw the bloody, disfigured remains of a slightly built, intelligent faced mulatto youth about 18 years old. His body was clothed in a coarse shirt and pair of trousers, and on his feet were a pair of black cotton stockings. The shots of the mob had cut holes in his chest and face and blown away that part of his shirt that covered the upper part of his body.
>
> Thursday afternoon Undertaker Hill wrapped the body in a winding sheet, placed it in a neat coffin and interred it in the burial ground beyond the N.Y.P.&N. railroad.[148]

The burial ground described would be the public community cemetery sometimes referred to as the Potter's Field, a segregated cemetery, with the black section located at the east end. No marker exists and likely none was placed at the time of his burial.

---

[147] *The Baltimore Sun*, "Hanged at Salisbury; Garfield King, Colored, Taken from Jail and Lynched; Strung to a Tree and Shot; Summary Vengeance of a Mob in Wicomico County; The Victim was a Colored Youth of Eighteen Years Who Shot Herman Kenney, A White Boy, at Twigg's Store on Saturday Last," May 26, 1898

[148] *Salisbury Advertiser*, "A Murder and Lynching; Garfield King, Colored, Shot Herman Kenny, White, and a Mob Lynched the Negro; Details of the Lynching Which Took Place at the County Jail," May 28, 1898

Mob Law on Delmarva

Samuel Jones

Arrested October 1898 in Kent County, Delaware

The October 24, 1898 edition of The *Baltimore Sun*, gives accounts of local Delaware elections. Of particular note is a short description of the arrest in Felton, Delaware of Samuel Jones for shooting a white man. The article includes the following.

> *"Jones was locked up at Felton and lynching was threatened."*
>
> October 24, 1898
> The Baltimore Sun

The registration in Kent county yesterday at some points was exciting. At Master's Corner Democratic Challenger James M. Kemp was shot and seriously wounded by Samuel Jones, a negro. Jones declared that he would register or die. Kemp, it is alleged, threw a two-pound weight at the colored man, who fired into a crowd, wounding Kemp. Jones was locked up at Felton and lynching was threatened.[149]

Adam Stewart

Sentenced to imprisonment May 1903, Caroline County, Maryland

Adam Stewart, a farm seventeen-year-old farm hand employed by John Imler, was arrested and charged with shooting Imler at his farm about two miles from Ridgely in Caroline County. Stewart was transported to Baltimore to avoid a lynching, and Imler was hospitalized.

> Ridgely, Md., March 28 – John Imler, a highly respected farmer residing about two miles from Ridgely, Caroline county, was shot about 6 o'clock this morning by Adam Stewart, colored, a farmhand in his employ. Mr. Imler called to the negro to get up at the usual time, and after waiting some minutes called the second time. The negro failed to answer this summons, and Mr. Imler went the third time, when the negro opened the door and deliberately shot him in the abdomen.
>
> After the negro came down from his room he was met by the mother of Mr. Imler, who said to him: "Adam, you have shot John," whereupon the negro pointed the revolver in her face and said: "You had better not come this way." The negro made his escape, but the officers and a

---

[149] *The Baltimore Sun*, "Throughout Delaware; Democratic Leaders Predict a Victory for their Forces and Senator Gray's Re-election," Oct. 24, 1897

Chapter 11. Eastern Shore Cases

large posse went in hot pursuit of him, and he was captured at 4 o'clock P.M. by Deputy Sheriff Samuel Griffin and the posse.

> "Many rumors of lynching are current. The community is highly incensed at such a dastardly crime, which was committed without the least provocation.
>
> There was much excitement here tonight when it was learned that a crowd from the vicinity of the shooting was on the way to Denton. Sheriff Dukes and Deputy Griffin took Stewart from jail quickly and drove to Harrington, Del., where they took the train for Baltimore, where Stewart will be placed in jail for safekeeping."
>
> March 29, 1903
> The Baltimore Sun

Many rumors of lynching are current. The community is highly incensed at such a dastardly crime, which was committed without the least provocation.

There was much excitement here tonight when it was learned that a crowd from the vicinity of the shooting was on the way to Denton. Sheriff Dukes and Deputy Griffin took Stewart from jail quickly and drove to Harrington, Del., where they took the train for Baltimore, where Stewart will be placed in jail for safekeeping. [150]

On April 3rd, Imler died from his wounds after being transported to the Baltimore City Hospital. The funeral was held at Boonsboro, Caroline County, in the German Baptist Church. On April 16th, the trial was moved from Caroline County to Queen Anne's County in Centreville.[151]

Centreville, Md., May 12 – Judge Martin pronounced the sentence of the Circuit Court on Adam Stewart, who has been on trial for the last two days for the murder of John F. Imler on March 28 last. He found Stewart guilty of murder in the second degree and sentenced him to 15 years in the penitentiary. Stewart is but 17 years of age.

Last night the court was in session until nearly midnight. The last and only witness called by the prosecution was Z.C. Henry, a practicing physician of Berlin, Md. Dr. Henry was a physician at the Baltimore City Hospital at the time Imler was brought there in a dying condition, and the latter made his dying declaration, which was admitted by the court. In this declaration Imler said that he had not threatened Stewart in any way and declared that the assault was unprovoked. Both attorneys for

---

[150] *The Baltimore Sun*, "Mr. John Imler Shot Down By A Negro in Caroline County," Mar. 29, 1903; "Mr. Imler in Critical State. Adam Stewart, The Negro Who Shot Him, Brought To Jail Here," Mar. 30: "Mr. Imler May Recover," Mar. 31, 1903
[151] *The Baltimore Sun*, "Mr. John Imler Dead, Shot on March 28 By Adam Stewart, Negro Farm Hand," Apr. 4, 1903; "Funeral of Mr. Imler," Apr. 6, 1903; "Change of Venue, Imler Murder Case Removed to Queen Anne's Court," Apr. 17, 1903

the defense, William H. Deweese and Edward H. Brown, laid emphasis on the fact that Imler had seized a chair with which to strike Stewart, when the latter shot him.[152]

---

[152] *The Baltimore Sun*, "Adam Stewart Sentenced, Goes to the Penitentiary for 15 Years for Killing J.F. Imler," May 13, 1903

Chapter 11. Eastern Shore Cases

George White

Burned at Stake June 1903 near Wilmington, Delaware

George White was burned at the stake for the alleged assault and murder of a seventeen-year-old white woman. The case was widely reported in newspapers. The case has been widely researched and documented by historians including Dennis Downey and Yohuru Williams, and others. The following are just a few of the citations: (Downey, The "Delaware Horror," Two Ministers, a Lynching, and the Crisis of Democracy 2013), (Downey, Racial Lynching, History, and the Filmmaker's Craft; A Roundtable Discussion of Stephen Labovsky's In the Dead Fire's Ashes - The Lynching a Town Forgot 2005), (Williams, A Tragedy with a Happy Ending? The Lynching of George White in History and Memory 2005), and (In the Dead Fire's Ashes, The Lynching A Town Forgot 2004).

> *"The crowd which lynched White was composed of persons from Wilmington, Marshallton, Green Bank, Brandywine Springs, Newport, Stanton and the surrounding country, and some, it is said, came from Pennsylvania, Maryland and other States."*
>
> *June 24, 1903*
> *The Baltimore Sun*

The Baltimore Sun of June 23, 1903 reports,

A Delaware mob, led by a Virginian, burned a negro at the stake tonight within a few miles of Mason and Dixon's line.

The victim was George White, a negro, who feloniously assaulted and then stabbed to death Miss Helen S. Bishop, the 17-year-old daughter of Rev. Dr. E.A. Bishop. The crime was committed Monday afternoon, June 15, and ever since that time there had been threats of lynching.[153]

Arthur Corwell was arrested for participating in the lynching. Corwell was quickly prosecuted, but on June 26th at a hearing of crowd sympathizers, the charge was dropped.

White was held in the workhouse pending trial when the mob entered. On June 22, sometime after 10:00 P.M., a mob stormed the workhouse. During the melee, gunfire discharged by mob members, accidentally killed seventeen-year-old Peter Smith.

Once White was removed from the workhouse jail, he was taken to a spot on Price Road where he was to be burned to death as planned. White

---

[153] *The Baltimore Sun*, "Delaware Lynchers Burn Negro To Death," Jun. 23, 1903

reportedly confessed his guilt and begged for mercy. Mob members created a circle and split rails for the pyre. Reports *The Baltimore Sun* of June 24, 1903,

> The crowd which lynched White was composed of persons from Wilmington, Marshallton, Green Bank, Brandywine Springs, Newport, Stanton and the surrounding country, and some, it is said, came from Pennsylvania, Maryland and other States. ....
>
> While White was praying and confessing in the background and the crowd was struggling to form a circle, three or four stern-faced men began splitting rails with which to burn the wretch. It took so long to get the fuel ready that the crowd cried to the leaders to proceed with the burning. The crowd numbered about 6,000 persons by this time, and surged back and forth, pushing to gain or retain a good position from which to see the burning. ....
>
> When the negro had ceased to show any signs of life his body was placed on its back and fuel was piled upon it until a roaring fire was soon consuming it. .....
>
> After the mob had completed its awful work of vengeance the body was left chained to the stake with the fire burning all around it and the members of the lynching party went to their homes. A rain which began falling later extinguished the fire, but it was seemingly rekindled later....[154]

> *"While there is excitement, it is of that calm, satisfied order that a tigress might manifest as she licked her bloody jaws after a conquest that furnished her with a meal."*
>
> June 24, 1903
> The Philadelphia Inquirer

Some mob members collected souvenirs such as pieces of wood and rope, as well as pieces of the body.

An account from a correspondent from *The Philadelphia Inquirer* describes the day following the lynching.

> Everywhere throughout the city the one topic of conversation today was the lynching. Men were found who did not hesitate to say that they took a hand in the affair. Others look up to them as heroes. Minor officials of the Commonwealth of Delaware express satisfaction over the result.

---

[154] *The Baltimore Sun*, "Led Mob Like An Army; Remarkable Thoroughness of the Lynchers' Plans; Confession the Negro Made; Once he Broke From the Fire, But was Struck With A Fencerail and Hurled Back on the Pyre," Jun. 24, 1903

Chapter 11. Eastern Shore Cases

While there is excitement, it is of that calm, satisfied order that a tigress might manifest as she licked her bloody jaws after a conquest that furnished her with a meal.[155]

(See page 22 for the section on "The Spectacle of Lynching" for more discussion about the George White lynching.)

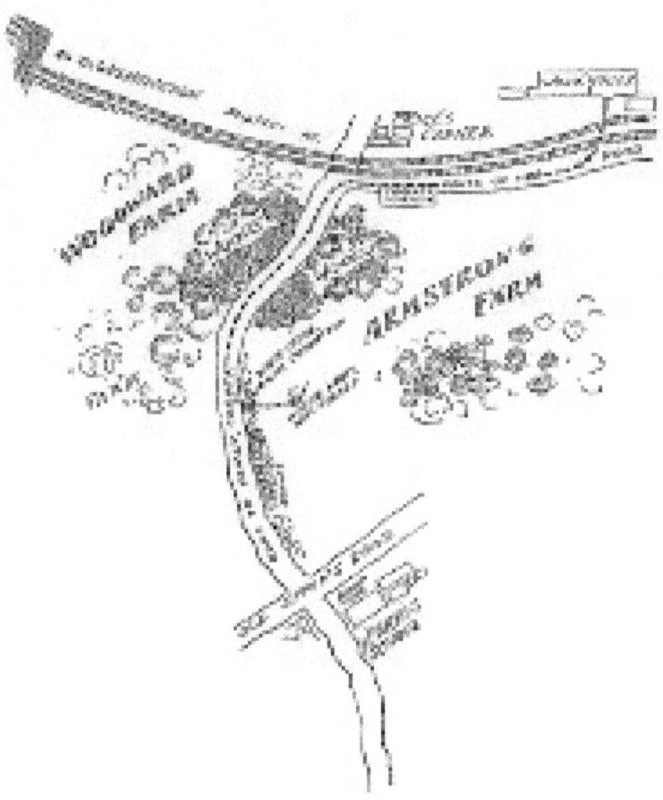

Figure 25 Map of vicinity of George White lynching
The Philadelphia Inquirer, June 24, 1903

---

[155] *The Philadelphia Inquirer,* "Delaware Calmly Views Death at Stake; One man in Custody on Murder Charge," Jun. 24, 1903

Figure 26 Image of souvenir hunters at site of George White lynching

The image is from the June 24, 1903 edition of *The Philadelphia Inquirer* depicting the crowd at the site of the lynching.

Chapter 11. Eastern Shore Cases

Eugene Harris
Arrested June 1903 in Kent County, Delaware
The Baltimore Sun of June 21, 1903 reports,

> *"Harris and the other prisoners confined in the county prison were so alarmed at the report last night that a mob would come here and lynch Harris that the Sheriff was appealed to for protection."*
>
> June 25, 1903
> The Baltimore Sun

Dover, Del., June 20 – Ferris J. Davis, a prominent farmer of Pearson's Corner, who recently purchased and moved upon the Voshell farm there, appeared before Magistrate Wood and caused the arrest later of Eugene Harris, colored, charged with attempting to feloniously assault Mrs. Davis.

Sheriff Melvin and Constable Williams found Harris and brought him to prison. He protested that he was innocent and could prove an alibi. Harris asked the Sheriff how much money it would cost to settle the case, as he had a family at home and wanted to get back.

Mrs. Nora Davis, wife of the farmer, was at home Thursday evening alone. The farmhands had not returned when a negro approached the house and asked to be shown a cornsheller which he desired to purchase. She accompanied him to the granary, where she pointed out the machine. The negro, she said, then attacked her, and a fierce encounter ensued, the woman fighting herself free and making her escape.[156]

The June 25, 1903 edition of *The Baltimore Sun* reports,

> Dover, DE -- Eugene Harris, a negro, who was committed to jail here last Saturday in default of $1,000 bail on a charge of attempting to assault Mrs. Ferris J. Davis, wife of a farmer near Corson's Corner, secured bail today and was released by Sheriff Melvin. His bondsmen are farmers in the vicinity where the assault took place and who believe him to be innocent.
>
> Harris and the other prisoners confined in the county prison were so alarmed at the report last night that a mob would come here and lynch Harris that the Sheriff was appealed to for protection. The Sheriff assured the prisoners that every precaution would be taken to protect them.
>
> Mrs. Davis and her husband are making arrangements to leave Delaware as soon as they can dispose of their farm.[157]

---

[156] *The Baltimore Sun*, "Woman Accuses Negro, Mrs. Nora Davis Charges Eugene Harris With Attempted Assault," Jun. 21, 1903
[157] *The Baltimore Sun*, "A Scare at the Dover Jail," June 25, 1903

Leander Moore and Joseph Shockley
Arrested June 1903 in rioting following Wilmington lynching

The June 26, 1903 edition of *The Daily Star* of Fredericksburg, Virginia reports,

> Wilmington, Del., June 26 – A riot broke out on the streets here last night between whites and negroes which for a time assumed serious proportions. The arrival of a squad of police, however, quickly dispersed the participants. Two arrests were made. A large gang of negroes, numbering probably 200, who had been marching up and down Ninth street, were challenged by about 25 white men, and in the battle that followed over 100 shots were exchanged.
>
> A squad of policemen, under Captain Evans and Sergeant McDermott, rushed to the scene and charged upon the mob. The negroes and whites scattered and fled in all directions, but the police succeeded in capturing two negroes, Leander Moore and Joseph Shockley. The policemen used their clubs freely, and in the melee attendant upon the arrests McDormott and Patrolman Green received slight wounds. One negro, James Mercer, was shot in the head during the riot, but his wound is not believed to be serious.
>
> In a brawl in another part of the city William Cramer, a negro, was shot in the stomach by a white man. He was taken to a hospital in a serious condition.
>
> The leaders of the party of negroes who were marching on Ninth street declared that they intended to resent the attacks made upon members of their race. They say they have been badly abused and that they do not intend to quietly submit to such abuse.[158]

---

[158] *The Daily News*, Fredericksburg, VA, "Riots in Wilmington, Negroes Resent Attacks on Them Since Lynching of White," Jun 26, 1903

Chapter 11. Eastern Shore Cases

Fletcher Hollis
Manhunt August 1903 in Smyrna and Wilmington, Delaware
The August 4, 1903 edition of *The Baltimore Sun* reports,

> *"Delaware is on the eve of another lynching if 300 men armed with shotguns and pistols who are in three separate posses succeed in catching Fletcher Hollis."*
>
> August 3, 1903
> The Baltimore Sun

Smyrna, Del., Aug. 3 – Delaware is on the eve of another lynching if 300 men armed with shotguns and pistols who are in three separate posses succeed in catching Fletcher Hollis, a desperate negro, of Smyrna, aged 22 years, who tonight shot and fatally wounded Constable James D. Wright at Clayton, one mile from this town, while resisting arrest. ....

The posses, who are under the leadership of Chief of Police Benjamin Turner, Policeman Joseph Cummins and Constable Charles H. Jones, of Smyrna, and W. D. Venn and William King, of Clayton, are surrounding every outlet for a radius of half a dozen miles, and they will spend the night on guard. If they catch the negro it is believed that he will be shot.

Constable Jones and Constable Wright, of Clayton, were co-operating in an effort to arrest Hollis on the double charge of shooting at a man in Dover last Saturday night and creating a disturbance at the Friendship colored camp-meeting, four miles from Smyrna, last evening. Neither constable was armed.[159]

The article further describes the Constables' attempt to arrest Hollis in front of the Hotel Steckle in Clayton that evening. Hollis was pursued. The August 6th edition of *The Baltimore Sun* reports that he might be with relatives in Chester, Pennsylvania, but that it was believed Hollis was in the Duck Creek area about a mile from Wilmington. The August 7th issue reports that a posse was still hunting Hollis, that he was suspected of hiding in or near Smyrna, and "A posse from Clayton, all armed with shotguns, searching for the negro for several hours last night, but secured no clue."

---

[159] *The Baltimore Sun*, "Posses Chasing Negro, Another Lynching Is Expected In Delaware, Constable was Shot Down, Fletcher Hollis, Colored, Who Resisted Arrest, Aroused A Storm of Popular Wrath," Aug. 4, 1903

Oliver Cephus

Arrested July 1906 in Seaford, Delaware

Oliver Cephus was arrested and charged with the murder of Robert Passwaters and jailed on threat of lynching. A second man was also mentioned as committing the murder, but no information yet determined.

The Baltimore Sun of July 25, 1906 reports,

> While returning to his home near Horsey's road last Saturday night Robert Passwaters was the victim of a brutal assault by two negroes, which resulted in a murder.
>
> Passwater, who was in company with his father, met the negroes and demanded that they drive out of the road and let him pass. This they refused to do, and Oliver Cephus, one of the negroes, seized a stick of wood and felled young Passwater, splitting his head open. His father took him to a nearby house, where he remained unconscious until his death late last evening.[160]

The Baltimore Sun of July 27, 1906 reports,

> *"The detective eluded the mob which, it is believed, would have lynched the negro, and he was taken to the county jail."*
> July 27, 1906
> The Baltimore Sun

Seaford, Del., July 26 – State Detective James L. Hawkins late this evening captured Oliver Cephus, charged with murdering Robert Passwaters late Saturday evening by splitting his head open with a stick of wood because he would not give him the right of way.

The detective eluded the mob which, it is believed, would have lynched the negro, and he was taken to the county jail.[161]

---

[160] *The Baltimore Sun*, "Two Negro Outrages. Murder And Hold-Up Near Seaford, Del.—Lynching Expected," Jul. 25, 1906
[161] *The Baltimore Sun*, "Eluded Mob With Negro," Jul. 27, 1906

Chapter 11. Eastern Shore Cases

William Lee

Executed July 1906 in Somerset County, Maryland

William Lee was arrested June 11, 1906, in Eastern Shore Virginia for the crime of assault and rape on Mrs. Robert Barnes and assault on Miss Frances Powell near Kingston in Somerset County, Maryland. He would be convicted and sentenced. His execution was held at Solomons Lump on Smith Island in Somerset County.

> *"It would take a regiment of soldiers to save the brute from being literally torn to pieces if he should fall into the hands of the people,' a Crisfield man warned."*
>
> Gallows on the Marsh
> by Brooks Miles Barnes
> 2006

Details of the case are described in the 2006 book, *The Gallows on the Marsh: Crime and Punishment on the Chesapeake, 1906,* by Brooks Miles Barnes.

Lee's execution was most unusual. Because at that time executions were held in the counties where the crimes were committed, Lee was required to be executed in Somerset County. At Governor Warfield's direction, the entourage for Lee's execution boarded the *Gov. Robert M. McLane*, the flagship of the Maryland Oyster Navy, in Baltimore, and departed for the Eastern Shore. As the ship traveled down the Chesapeake Bay towards Somerset County, Somerset County Sheriff George W. Brown and Commander Thomas C. B. Howard of the Maryland Oyster Police, charged with commanding the *McLane*, met to discuss plans for Lee's execution. As described in Barnes' book,

> Before leaving the shipyard, they had heard rumors that the mob had gathered at the Somerset County almshouse and had torn down the scaffold. Also, Brown had been assured by one of his deputies, an erstwhile mob leader whom, along with Robert Barnes, the sheriff had shrewdly co-opted, that the lynching spirit remained strong in Somerset. Howard and Brown agreed that an attempt to execute Lee on the mainland would be foolhardy.

Mob Law on Delmarva

So the two looked for an isolated area of the county to conduct the execution, and the ship had been equipped with a scaffold to be erected for that purpose if needed. A remote, sandy, and deserted area of Smith Island known as Solomon's Lump was selected. The gallows, Lee, and witnesses were delivered to the beach where the scaffold was erected and Lee was executed, to the amazement of a few curious onlookers, mostly Smith Island watermen.

Figure 27 William Lee
Courtesy Brooks Miles Barnes

Lee had been arrested in Cape Charles on the Virginia Eastern Shore as Lee left the train. He had hopped on in Pocomoke, Maryland, and exited at its southernmost terminus. Lee was delivered to the jail in Eastville. In the meantime, Somerset County mobs searched Pocomoke, the Princess Anne jail, and trains in search of Lee. Brooks Miles Barnes writes, "'It would take a regiment of soldiers to save the brute from being literally torn to pieces if he should fall into the hands of the people,' a Crisfield man warned" (1906, 11).

It indeed did take a regiment of soldiers and fortuitous circumstances to save Lee from being lynched in Eastville. Somerset County residents and authorities confronted those of Eastville, militia from Norfolk intervened, and Lee was transported first to Norfolk and then eventually to Baltimore where he was held for trial. The threats of lynching in Eastville came to a head before the arrival of militia, with Somerset County mob, verbally threatening and brandishing weapons, prevented from obtaining Lee due to Sheriff Jarvis and the local posse formed to protect the prisoner against a lynching. "The Somerset men promised Sheriff Jarvis that should Lee be given up without a struggle they would forbear lynching him on Virginia soil." But the Virginians succeeded in protecting Lee (1906, 19).

Chapter 11. Eastern Shore Cases

Following the execution on Solomon's Lump, Lee's body was transported to the wharf at Mt. Vernon. From there his body was interred at the county almshouse a few miles outside of Princess Anne.

Figure 28 Images from William Lee Execution

Images courtesy Brooks Miles Barnes. Several photographs were taken of the execution on Solomon's Lump on Smith Island. The second photograph was taken of Lee's body delivered to the wharf at Mt. Vernon before being buried at the Somerset County almshouse.

Mob Law on Delmarva

John Henry

Executed July 1906 in Worcester County, Maryland

John Henry was arrested for assault on Mrs. Frederick Selby of Berlin. Later the charge was changed to rape. Henry would avoid lynching, be tried, convicted, and executed by hanging on July 27, 1906, the day after the execution of William Lee.

> *"Had the whole truth been known when he was arrested, he would have been lynched. This is admitted freely in Berlin."*
>
> February 19, 1906 excerpt from the Messenger, printed in The Baltimore Sun

On November 22, 1905, a warrant was issued for the arrest of Henry for attempted assault on Mrs. Selby. Henry was arrested by Constable Scott about an hour after the assault in Berlin.

….He denied any knowledge of the crime, but was positively identified by Mrs. Selby. He was found standing on a street corner, as if nothing had happened. It was thought he would be lynched by a mob which quickly assembled, and the officers had hard work to keep them back. It was necessary to keep an armed guard with him all night to prevent lynching. A hearing was had before Magistrate Massey today and he was committed to Snow Hill Jail to await the action of the grand jury. Henry has served a term in the House of Correction.[162]

The following excerpt from the Snow Hill *Messenger* was printed in *The Baltimore Sun* on February 19, 1906.

> "John Henry, a negro, who is in jail charged with assaulting Mrs. Fred Selby, while on her way home from Berlin one night in December last, can thank his victim that he is still alive and will be permitted to face a jury. He is now charged with a crime that may cause him to swing from the hangman's scaffold.
>
> "When Henry was committed to jail it was for a crime in connection with his assault upon Mrs. Selby entirely different from the one now laid against him by his victim, who alleges that the villain accomplished his purpose, and that she did not have the courage to admit all when she made the first charge against him.

---

[162] *The Baltimore Sun*, "White Woman Assailed; Daring Attempt By A Negro On A Public Highway; People Excited in Berlin; Mob Restrained With Difficulty From Lynching Prisoner, Who Is Now In Snow Hill Jail," Nov. 23, 1905

Chapter 11. Eastern Shore Cases

> "Had the whole truth been known when he was arrested, he would have been lynched. This is admitted freely in Berlin."[163]

Henry reportedly confessed following his conviction and sentencing but secured secrecy for the hopes of avoiding a lynching.

> At 8:30 Sheriff Anderson, with Deputies Lewis, McNeal, Campbell, Shockley, Johnson and Archer, led him to the hack standing at the jail entrance. A few yards from the jail the hack was stopped to wait for the other guards to get in carriages. Henry knelt on the floor of the hack, and with Rev. E.J. Henry by his side, sang alone two verses of "God Be With You Till We Meet Again." His voice was firm and showed no sign of nervousness.
>
> The scaffold was erected on the almshouse farm, about three miles from Snow Hill, on the same spot where stood the scaffolds on which Asbury Dixon and Summerfield Dennis were hanged a few years ago. It was built by George W. Truitt, of Snow Hill, who also built the other two. During the three-mile drive Henry said little and showed almost no sign of nervousness. At the scaffold, in reply to Sheriff Anderson's inquiry as to whether he had anything to say, Henry, in a very low town, asked the Sheriff to say for him that he had nothing against anybody. The straps about Henry's wrists and legs were adjusted by Deputy Sheriff J.G. McNeal, of Berlin. The rope which held the drop was cut by Sheriff Anderson in person.
>
> Long before day the crowd began to gather, and by 8 o'clock probably 1,000 persons were congregated about the place of execution. The bars were closed to aid in preserving order.
>
> The crowd was very orderly and there was no disturbance of any kind. None of Henry's family was present. His brother, Charles Henry, visited him in jail last night. It is considered fortunate that his confession was not made public until after the execution.[164]

---

[163] *The Baltimore Sun*, "Saved From, Lynching; Case of the Negro John Henry In Worcester County," Feb. 19, 1906, reprinted from the Snow Hill *Messenger*

[164] *The Baltimore Sun*, "John Henry is Hanged; Another Negro Ravisher Gives Up Life for His Crime; He Assaulted Mrs. Selby; Confessed Several Times That He Was Guilty – Crowd Of About 1,000 Assembles To See Him Die," Jul. 28, 1906

Charles Conley
Sentenced 1906 to imprisonment in Wilmington, Delaware

> "The community is thoroughly aroused, the crime having been committed near where the negro George White was burned at the stake in June, 1903, for assaulting and murdering 17-year-old Helen Bishop."
>
> September 13, 1906
> The Baltimore Sun

The Baltimore Sun reported from Wilmington, Delaware that on September 10, 1906,

Walter Russell, colored was arrested today on suspicion that he is the negro who committed the assault on Mrs. Beatrice Frankish and her daughter, Miss Gussie Leech, near Price's Corner last night. Russell was found near Centreville, and was at once brought to the police station in Wilmington to avoid an attempt at lynching.

Russell denied his guilt. He had trouble with Mrs. Frankish recently, and she had a warrant issued for his arrest on the charge of attempting to entice a colored girl from her employ.

Mrs. Frankish and her daughter are better today, and an examination of their wounds shows that they did not, as was feared, sustain fractured skulls as a result of the terrible beating they received at the hands of their assailant.[165]

The Baltimore Sun of September 13, 1906 reports,

> Wilmington, Del., Sept. 12 -- State Detectives Hawkins and Gray and the Wilmington police are making strenuous efforts to run down the negro who murderously assaulted Mrs. Beatrice Frankish and her daughter, Miss Gussie Leitch, on a country road near here Sunday night. The mother successfully resisted felonious assault. Both victims were seriously injured, but will recover.
>
> Several arrests have been made, the authorities scouring the country in automobiles. Today the arrest of Harold Reed, a negro 21 years old, was announced. He was captured near the scene of the crime and has failed to account for his whereabouts Sunday night. Robert Lee, another negro suspect, will be released. Mrs. Frankish declared she thought Walter Russell, colored, but established an alibi. He will be tried for disorderly conduct on the Frankish farm over a week ago.
>
> Other arrests are expected. The community is thoroughly aroused, the crime having been committed near where the negro George White was

---

[165] *The Baltimore Sun*, "Negro Held on Suspicion. Thought To Have Attacked Mrs. Frankish And Daughter," Sep. 11, 1906

Chapter 11. Eastern Shore Cases

burned at the stake in June, 1903, for assaulting and murdering 17-year-old Helen Bishop.[166]

The Baltimore Sun of September 19, 1906 reports,

> Wilmington, Del., Sept. 18 – Charles Conley, a desperate negro, who was arrested by State Detectives Hawkins and Gray on the charge of murderously assaulting Mrs. Albert Frankish and her daughter, Miss Gussie Leitch, on a country road near Brandywine springs on Sunday night, September , today made a full confession.
>
> The negro told the story between moans in his cell at the New Castle County Workhouse. He declared in the presence of Deputy Attorney-General Hastings that he was drunk at the time.
>
> The negro will be tried at the present term of the County Court and will be "railroaded." The penalty is 20 years' imprisonment. The victims, who were badly injured, are recovering.
>
> Conley begged the officials to protect him from lynching.[167]

> *"The negro told the story between moans in his cell at the New Castle County Workhouse."*
>
> September 19, 1906
> The Baltimore Sun

> *"Conley begged the officials to protect him from lynching."*
>
> September 19, 1906
> The Baltimore Sun

Charles Conley was "sentenced to serve 50 years in prison and to receive 30 lashes at the whipping post," for the crimes of assaults on Frankish and Leech. "His term of imprisonment begins today and he will be whipped Saturday."

A lynching during the night had been feared, and though some people were in the vicinity of the workhouse, chiefly to see if anything of the kind would be done, there was no attack on the institution.[168]

---

[166] *The Baltimore Sun*, "Seek Negro Assailant. Delaware Police After Black Who Attacked Two White Women," Sep. 13, 1906
[167] *The Baltimore Sun*, "Admits Attacking Women," Sep. 19, 1906
[168] *The Baltimore Sun*, "Swift Justice for Negro. Conley, Who Confessed, Gets 50 Years And 30 Lashes," Sep. 20, 1906

> "Before the eager gaze of nearly 500 persons, Charles Conley ... was publicly whipped today in the yard of the New Castle County Workhouse. More than 2,000 persons clamored for admission to the workhouse yard, which was too small to accommodate all of them.
>
> September 23, 1906
> The Baltimore Sun

The Baltimore Sun of September 23rd reports,

Wilmington, Del., Sept. 22 – Before the eager gaze of nearly 500 persons, Charles Conley ... was publicly whipped today in the yard of the New Castle County Workhouse. More than 2,000 persons clamored for admission to the workhouse yard, which was too small to accommodate all of them.[169]

The article described the administering of the 30 lashes and his walk without assistance to his cell to begin his fifty-year sentence.

The fate of Reed or Lee is not reported.

---

[169] *The Baltimore Sun*, "Negro Gets 30 Lashes. Is Then Taken To Prison For 50-Year Sentence," Sep. 23, 1906

Chapter 11. Eastern Shore Cases

Edward Watson

Sentenced October 1906 to imprisonment for crime in Somerset County, Maryland

Edward Watson was arrested for the assault on June 12, 1906, of Somerset County farmer Samuel S. Barnes, narrowly escaping lynching following his arrest. Tried in October, Watson was found guilty and sentenced to ten years in the penitentiary.[170]

> "Bailiff Stroud demanded that he be given up to their care and a determined effort was made by the authorities to get the negro off to Princess Anne on the 8:30 train, but the violence of the mob which was pressing closely on all sides prevented the attempt. The negro was then quickly rushed up Clarke avenue and placed in the lockup, which was surrounded by a mob numbering nearly 500 persons.
>
> "While on his way from the station the negro was beaten severely on the head by clubs and bricks thrown at him by the mob and received also a bullet wound. He is not dead, however, as had at first been reported."
>
> June 13, 1906
> The Baltimore Sun

The Baltimore Sun of June 13, 1906 reports,

Pocomoke City, Md., June 12 – Edward Watson, a negro farm hand, was severely beaten ad wounded here tonight by an infuriated crowd of Somerset county people for a murderous assault he made upon his employer, Samuel S. Barnes, in the afternoon. The negro narrowly escaped lynching.

The assault took place on the Barnes farm, about a mile from King's Creek, Somerset county. Mr. Barnes, who is one of the most prominent farmers of Somerset county, had a dispute with the negro over some farm work, when the negro struck him with a piece of scantling, dealing several blows over the head, after which he stamped upon him and kicked him in the face several times. Watson then hurriedly left the place, going toward Virginia. News of the assault soon spread over the neighborhood and a posse of white men, armed, started in pursuit of the negro, while Drs. Fisher and Lankford hurried to Salisbury with Mr. Barnes, who was operated on by Drs. Dick and Tull for fracture of the skull.

The negro was caught at Pocomoke City, near the railroad station, at 8 o'clock tonight and almost in an instant a large mob gathered around.

Bailiff Stroud demanded that he be given up to their care and a determined effort was made by the authorities to get the negro off to

---

[170] *The Baltimore Afro-American*, "Maryland State News," Oct. 20, 1906

> Princess Anne on the 8:30 train, but the violence of the mob which was pressing closely on all sides prevented the attempt. The negro was then quickly rushed up Clarke avenue and placed in the lockup, which was surrounded by a mob numbering nearly 500 persons.
>
> While on his way from the station the negro was beaten severely on the head by clubs and bricks thrown at him by the mob and received also a bullet wound. He is not dead, however, as had at first been reported.[171]

Local tensions were particularly heightened due to the William Lee case, which influenced the Watson case.

> Salisbury, Md., June 19 – Two deputy sheriffs of Somerset county brought the negro, Edward Watson, who assaulted Mr. Samuel S. Barnes in Somerset county last week, to Salisbury tonight and put him in the county jail here. This precaution was taken on account of the fear that the large number of persons assembling in Princess Anne for the hearing of the negro [William] Lee, accused of assault, might do harm to Watson.[172]

The October 20, 1906 issue of the *Baltimore Afro-American* reports that Watson was tried in Circuit Court of Baltimore with Gordon Tull representing him. Judge Lloyd sentenced Watson to ten years in the penintentiary.[170]

> Edward Watson, colored, charged with murderous assault upon Samuel G. Barnes, of near Kings Creek, Princess Anne County, was tried in the Circuit Court. Gordon Tull represented Watson. The jury returned a verdict of guilty and Judge Lloyd sentenced Watson to 10 years in the penitentiary.[170]

---

[171] *The Baltimore Sun*, "Negro Had Close Call; Crowd Shoots Him at Pocomoke City for Attempted Murder, Jun. 13, 1906
[172] *The Baltimore Sun*, "Watson Taken to Salisbury; Negro Who Nearly Killed Mr. S. S. Barnes Removed To Safety," Jun. 20, 1906

Chapter 11. Eastern Shore Cases

James Reed, Lemuel Showers, Hildred
Lynched July 1907 in Crisfield, Maryland
James Reed, apprehended for the alleged murder of Chief of Police John Daugherty, was lynched in Crisfield; outcomes of others not known.

Figure 29 Postcard of 1907 lynching of James Reed
Image courtesy Frank Rhodes.

Reed was lynched in Crisfield where he was attacked by a mob when a search party was returning him to Crisfield. Reed was killed by blows to his skull. His body was hung from a telegraph pole and later buried in the marsh. His body was then dug up, further abused and shot with bullets, and thrown onto a bonfire. The rioters continued to run through the black community of town, pulling people from their homes, beating them, and threatening them to leave town.

According to the July 29, 1907 edition of the *Evening Star*, Reed "came to Crisfield as a waiter on the geodetic survey steamer *Endeavor*. He hailed originally from Oklahoma and was half Indian and half negro. He was twenty-two years old, quite tall, straight, with straight hair."[173]

---

[173] *Evening Star*, Washington, D.C., "Life Pounded Out of Him," Jul. 29, 1907, page 10

Mob Law on Delmarva

Reed was apprehended for murdering Chief of Police John H. Daugherty. Lemuel Showers, owner of the revolver that Reed allegedly used to kill Chief Daugherty was arrested after leaving town. He was jailed at Princess Anne jail to await his trial. Another person implicated, prisoner Hildred, is believed to have escaped.

> "The excitement over the murder of Policeman Daugherty Saturday night and the lynching of the murderer, James Reed, a North Carolina negro, yesterday is still intense.
>
> At a late hour last night the body of the lynched negro was dug up from his grave on the marsh and a large bonfire made. The mangled body was riddled with bullets and then thrown into the fire.
>
> "The whole town seemed to be in a frenzy. Half of the people did not sleep during the entire night. The morning brought a condition a little less serious, but feeling was still intense and there was fear of more trouble between the blacks and the white population of the town."
>
> July 30, 1907
> The Baltimore Sun

The July 28th edition of *The Baltimore Sun* reports on the killing of Daugherty.

Crisfield, Md., July 27 – Patrolman John H. Dougherty [sic] was shot and instantly killed late tonight by James Reed, a negro, who escaped.

The officer was trying to arrest one of a group of negroes who were disorderly on Lower Maryland avenue. It was alleged some were peddling whisky, and when Dougherty went to make an arrest he was fired upon.

The negroes escaped and are said to have taken a boat and gone to Tangier Sound. Patrolman Evans, who had tried to make an arrest first, was not hurt.

The negro Reed is alleged to have deliberately fired at Mr. Dougherty, the shot piercing his head. It is also said there were two armed negroes who escaped. One went toward the railroad and the other to the river.

The police in the upper part of the county have been notified, and large searching parties have gone down the railroad. A lynching is regarded as likely if Reed is caught.[174]

After firing the shot, he [Reed] ran down the back street toward the wharf and through an alley to Main Street where he followed the railroad up far as Ward's crossing. At this point he stole a wheel the property of

---

[174] *The Baltimore Sun*, "Officer Killed By Negro," Jul. 28, 1907

Chapter 11. Eastern Shore Cases

a young man, by the name of Ward, and rode on up the track in the direction of Marion. Here he was met by a posse who fired at him, but the negro dropped his wheel and took to the woods.

He succeeded in making his way to Coulbourne's Creek where he stole a boat intending to make his escape to the Western Shore. Instead of going down the creek, he went up it and ran his boat ashore where he was compelled to leave her. This was the cause of his undoing. After having abandoned this vessel, he sought around for another and having found one he set sail for Tangier Sound.

At an early hour on Sunday morning a telephone message was received from Coulbourne's Creek stating that a boat was missing at that point and that it was believed that the negro had stolen her.

The Crisfield town authorities acting upon this [clue] immediately took steps to apprehend the fugitive. The mail boat *Erecliffe*, the *Helen Avetta*, and several other gasoline Steamers were dispatched to search Tangier Sound. After a short run, the Erecliffe sighted the boat, and when within hailing distance the crew, who were heavily armed ordered its occupant to throw up his hands and surrender. He instead jumped to drown himself.

With the aid of boat hooks the negro was hauled before the Erecliffe. .... He first declared that he was the wrong man, but as his identity was established beyond a doubt by persons aboard, he confessed his guilt, saying he did not intend to commit a murder, his purpose being only to frighten the officers that his companion might escape.

By the time the Erecliffe had steamed into the river a large crowd of persons from all over Somerset County had denigrated but as they were orderly, no danger was feared from them. When the steamer was within hailing distance, and it was known that the murderer had been caught a revulsion of sentiment became evident, and cries of "Lynch him!" "Lynch him!" were heard on every side.

To land the prisoner at that time was out of the question and the Erecliffe, taking on board Police Justice P. M. Tilghman, steamed up and down the river for more than half an hour. ... [*portion of article torn and missing*]

When the Steamer had made landing and [the] plank run out, down which the prisoner walked ... the frenzy of the mob as the negro's life became apparent. He was hit with clubs, stones and missiles of every description before he had proceeded ten feet, and when about 50 yards had been covered a member of the mob struck him on the face and head with a huge club, crushing his skull and knocking him to the ground. The officers were then swept away from him by the irresistible force of the mob and a rope produced which was quickly put about the negro's neck. Bleeding and dying he was dragged through the streets to the place where the night before he had committed his cold-blooded crime and strung up a telephone pole, where missiles were again showered on him until every possible spark of life was extinct.

Mob Law on Delmarva

> The body hung from the pole all day and was viewed by thousands, sightseers coming from points 30 to 40 miles away. At 3:30 o'clock Justice Tilghman held a coroner's inquest, with Lloyd Riggin as foreman of the jury and Dr. C. E Collins as medical examiner, and as the body of the dead officer was being carried to his grave the jury rendered a verdict of death by mob violence at the hands of unknown men.[175]

The July 30, 1907 edition of *The Baltimore Sun* reports,

> Crisfield, Md., July 29 – The excitement over the murder of Policeman Daugherty Saturday night and the lynching of the murderer, James Reed, a North Carolina negro, yesterday is still intense.
>
> At a late hour last night the body of the lynched negro was dug up from his grave on the marsh and a large bonfire made. The mangled body was riddled with bullets and then thrown into the fire.
>
> The whole town seemed to be in a frenzy. Half of the people did not sleep during the entire night. The morning brought a condition a of little less serious, but feeling was still intense and there was fear of more trouble between the blacks and the white population of the town. ....
>
> Photographs of the lynching have been made into souvenir postal cards and the dealers are rushed to supply the demand of those who wish to send them to their friends, relatives and acquaintances in all parts of the country. The rope with which the negro was hanged was cut up into small pieces as souvenirs. Large crowds of white people congregated on the streets all day, but very few negro inhabitants of the town were to be seen on the streets.
>
> Lemuel Showers, proprietor of the negro billiard room, who lent the negro Reed the pistol with which Daugherty was murdered, managed to escape from the town yesterday, but was captured up the county today and lodged in jail at Princess Anne to await trial. A large number of persons have met each train today with the hope that he would be brought back to Crisfield. They intended to lynch him as soon as he arrived, but the officers knowing the fate which awaited him if he was brought here took him to Princess Anne.
>
> The negro Hildred, who was under arrest when the tragedy occurred and who was a partner of the negro Reed, is still at large, but the authorities are continuing the search for him. It will probably go hard with him if he is captured.[176]

The July 29th issue of the *Evening Star* reported of the lynching that the boat carrying Reed landed at the Tangier Packing Company's wharf. The issue describes the following:

> As soon as the negro was taken inshore some one in the crowd shouted: "I am from Virginia, and down there we would kill him."

---

[175] *The Crisfield Times*, "Mob Lynches," Aug 3, 1907
[176] *The Baltimore Sun* "Crisfield In a Frenzy, Body of Lynched Negro Reed Dug Up and Burned," Jul. 30, 1907

Chapter 11. Eastern Shore Cases

The man then struck the negro, knocking him senseless. He was kicked in the face and stomach. The life was literally pounded out of him. His skull was crushed.[173]

Moses Driver, James Pitt, Arthur (Artemus) Miles

Arrested August 1907 for crime in Seaford, Delaware

The Baltimore Sun August 29, 1907 reports,

> Marshal Farnan is searching the city for three negroes who are wanted in Seaford, Del., to answer the charge of assaulting and shooting Constable Steen.
>
> The negroes are James H. Pitt, Arthur Miles and Moses Driver. All have followed the water, and the police believe they may have come to this city for employment.[177]

The Baltimore Sun September 12, 1907 reports,

> *"After a severe 'sweating' process, conducted by Captain McGee, the negro is said to have admitted that he was the man wanted, but added that he was with another negro named Pettitt, who, he affirms, did the shooting."*
>
> September 12, 1907
> The Baltimore Sun

Locked up at the Southern Police Station is Moses Driver, colored, 25 years old, who is wanted in Seaford, Del., on the charge of assaulting and shooting Constable Richards [sic, should be Steen], of the county force.

Patrolman Harry Knight arrested the negro on description. Shortly after 6 P.M. Patrolman Knight spied the man at Light street wharf.

"Hello, Moses! How long have you been in town?" asked the patrolman.

The negro wheeled, and when he saw the brass buttons he was about to take to his heels, but Patrolman Knight was quicker.

---

[177] *The Baltimore Sun*, "Negroes Wanted For Shooting," Aug. 29, 1907

> "Four negroes recently arrested for the crime narrowly escaped lynching at Seaford."
>
> September 13, 1907
> The Baltimore Sun

After a severe "sweating" process, conducted by Captain McGee, the negro is said to have admitted that he was the man wanted, but added that he was with another negro named Pettitt, who, he affirms, did the shooting.[178]

The Baltimore Sun September 13, 1907 reports,

Wilmington, Del., Sept. 12 – State Detective Hawkins returned here tonight from Baltimore with Moses Driver, a negro, who was arrested in that city for complicity in the recent shooting of Constable Steen in a grove at Seaford, Del. This is the fifth arrest in the case.

Four negroes recently arrested for the crime narrowly escaped lynching at Seaford.[179]

The Crisfield Times of March 28, 1908 reports on Artemus Miles, possibly Arthur Miles,

Artemus Miles, colored, who was arrested in Elizabeth City, N.C., was brought to Seaford, Del., Thursday morning of last week, by State Detective Hawkins and John E. Martin, who went to that city to identify Miles as the man who shot Constable Curtis Steen last August. Miles claims he was never in Delaware before Thursday, and no one could positively identify him, although Martin thinks he is the man he shot at. The name which he answers to is the same and he also bears a bullet wound in the arm which fits the description. Detective Hawkins asked that he be held for court until he could produce other evidence. Magistrate Parks committed him to jail without bail.[180]

---

[178] *The Baltimore Sun*, "Negro Accused of Shooting," Sep. 12, 1907
[179] *The Baltimore Sun*, "Fifth Arrest in Steen Case; Negro Found in Baltimore Taken To Wilmington, Del.," Sep. 13, 1907
[180] *The Crisfield Times*, "Held in Jail," Mar. 28, 1908

Chapter 11. Eastern Shore Cases

Henry Taylor

Sentenced June 1908 to imprisonment for crime in Pocomoke, Maryland

The Baltimore Sun of January 12, 1908 reports,

> *"Since the death of Mr. Lankford excitement among the whites has been intense and it would not be surprising if an attempt were made to get the negro out of the jail and string him up on the nearest tree."*
>
> January 12, 1908
> The Baltimore Sun

Pocomoke City, Md., Jan. 11 – Mr. William S. Lankford, who was assaulted Thursday by Henry Taylor, alias Henry Tink, colored, died today of his wounds, never having regained consciousness.

The assault occurred at the factory of the Marvil Package Company, of which Mr. Lankford was an employee, and seems to have been entirely uncalled for. Taylor struck Mr. Lankford with a stick 4 feet long and 3 inches wide.

The victim was a quiet man and that he should have been assaulted by such a worthless outlaw as Taylor is has aroused race sentiment to a high pitch. Taylor had a hearing before Justice William W. Quinn Thursday afternoon and was promptly committed to jail to await action by the grand jury. Indignation of the whites was at such a high pitch that Sheriff Townsend immediately removed the prisoner to Snow Hill, where he was placed in the county jail.

Since the death of Mr. Lankford excitement among the whites has been intense and it would not be surprising if an attempt were made to get the negro out of the jail and string him up on the nearest tree.[181]

The January 15, 1908 issue of *The Baltimore Sun* reported,

The excitement caused by the killing of William S. Lankford in Pocomoke City last week by a negro now in jail, has subsided so far as any danger from mob violence is concerned. Indignation at the crime has been and still is high throughout the county, but there seems to be no disposition to prevent the law taking its course.

There was some talk at Pocomoke City of a possible lynching Saturday night, but it was more talked of as a possibility than of any actual plan to carry it out.[182]

Taylor was employed by Lankford at a sawmill. *The Crisfield Times* of June 6, 1908 reported on Taylor's trial and sentencing and included the following description of the testimony.

---

[181] *The Baltimore Sun*, "Lynching May Follow. W.S. Lankford Dead and Henry Taylor, Colored, Arrested. Prisoner in Snow Hill Jail," Jan. 12, 1908
[182] *The Baltimore Sun*, "No Danger of Lynching," Jan. 15, 1908

While at his work, Lankford accidentally displaced an empty nail keg, which rolled down an embankment and struck Taylor on the leg. Taylor threw it back and struck Lankford a stinging blow. Lankford returned the blow, and went about his work. Everybody thought the episode was closed, as neither man seemed very angry. A short while afterward Lankford was missed, and upon search being made was found lying unconscious on the floor of the supply-room, where he had gone for some machine oil.

Suspicion at once pointed to Taylor. He had left his work and disappeared, but, after a short search, he was found hiding under a bed at his lodging-house. At the time of his arrest he admitted striking Lankford but said he did not mean to kill him

He was found guilty and sentenced to 18 years in the Maryland Penitentiary.[183]

Charles Anderson (Granger)
Arrested November 1909 in Centreville, Maryland

Note, Anderson was reported with different names both as Grantner and Granger in different articles. *The Baltimore Sun* of November 14, 1909 reports,

> "It is believed that should the man – Charles Anderson, alias Grantner – prove to be the person for whom the authorities have been looking, summary justice will be dealt out at a rope's end."
>
> November 14, 1909
> The Baltimore Sun

Centreville, Md., Nov. 13 – Centreville is in the throes of intense excitement as the result of the arrest of a negro suspect in the case of Mrs. Henrietta Meredith, who was assaulted in her bedroom in the suburbs of Centreville last Wednesday night and left bound and helpless. The affair is the sole topic of conversation, and feeling is running high against the suspect, the officers having declared that they have considerable evidence against him. How far their investigations have gone they will not disclose. It is believed that should the man – Charles Anderson, alias Grantner – prove to be the person for whom the authorities have been looking, summary justice will be dealt out at a rope's end.

The case is aggravated by the fact that there are several hundred women in Centreville who live in isolated sections of the city, where

---

[183] *The Crisfield Times*, "Murderer Sentenced," June 6, 1908

Chapter 11. Eastern Shore Cases

> crimes of this sort might easily be perpetrated at any time. As a result the people of the city are incensed to the degree of expressing their sentiments in a manner similar to that in the case of Asbury Green, colored who was lynched here in 1891 by a mob after he had been found guilty of assaulting a young woman of Kent Island. ... Owing to the intense feeling aroused the hearing will be held in a cell in the county jail.[184]

The Baltimore Sun of November 18, 1909 reports,

> Centreville, Md., Nov. 17 – Following a hearing this afternoon behind closed doors, Charles Granger, colored, was committed to jail for court on the charge of assaulting Mrs. Henrietta Meredith at her home a week ago today. The negro denied all knowledge of the crime, but, it is said, the evidence against him is strong. ...
>
> Mrs. Meredith testified that so great was her terror and so brutal her treatment at the hands of her assailant that she was unable to identify him positively. His voice, she said, was like that of Granger. Her description, of the man's clothing, too, tallied with that worn by the negro when arrested.
>
> The strongest evidence against the prisoner was given by Eugene Wooden, a white prisoner, under sentence for bigamy. Wooden swore that Granger told him after his arrest that he had assaulted Mrs. Meredith and that he was sorry for it.
>
> Other witnesses testified to seeing Granger in the neighborhood of the Meredith home about the time of the crime.
>
> Granger, on the stand, admitted telling Wooden he was guilty, but protested his innocence. When asked why he had told Wooden he had committed the crime, Granger said: "I don't know." It is said he has told half a dozen conflicting stories of his whereabouts the night of the assault.
>
> The authorities anticipate no trouble, it is said, the people being content to allow the law to take its course and feeling confident that justice will be done.[185]

---

[184] *The Baltimore Sun*, "Centreville in Uproar. Arrest of Negro Suspect In Assault Case Stirs Residents. Will Hold Hearing In Cell," Nov. 14, 1909

[185] *The Baltimore Sun*, "Negro Held for Court, Alleged Assailant of Mrs. Meredith Says He Is Innocent, The Hearing Held in Secret," Nov. 18, 1909

Wesley Miles
Executed December 1912 in Princess Anne, Maryland

> "A frenzied mob from Somerset county has drawn a cordon around Salisbury and is searching all the country around the town for Sheriff Tull, of Somerset, and a negro prisoner, Wesley Miles, who committed an assault on the 14-year-old daughter of ex-Sheriff William Phillips, of Somerset. The negro will be lynched if he is captured."
>
> *June 4, 1912*
> *The Baltimore Sun*

Wesley Miles was executed on December 6, 1912 after being convicted for the crime of assaulting Margaret E. Phillips, 15-year-old daughter of former Sheriff Phillips, Miles' employer. The December 7th edition of *The Baltimore Sun* recorded that Miles was survived by a wife and a 21-year-old son.[186]

The Baltimore Sun of June 4, 1912 describes a mob in pursuit of Miles, a dispatch from Salisbury.

Salisbury, Md., June 3 – A frenzied mob from Somerset county has drawn a cordon around Salisbury and is searching all the country around the town for Sheriff Tull, of Somerset, and a negro prisoner, Wesley Miles, who committed an assault on the 14-year-old daughter of ex-Sheriff William Phillips, of Somerset. The negro will be lynched if he is captured.

The assault has thrown Princess Anne into a frightful rage and this feeling has been communicated to Salisbury. It seems that the negro, who is 40 years old, married and with a family, had been employed by Mr. Phillips for about three years. Mr. Phillips has a store and bakery in Princess Anne and Miles worked around the place and attended to the stables and the teams. .....[187]

The Crisfield Times provides additional detail.

The issuing of the warrant was kept very quiet. The negro went to work as usual Monday morning and was not arrested until night. He was taken before Lyons and was held without bond for the action of the grand jury.

Sheriff Harding P. Tull, realizing that as soon as the news of the assault could get about the town his prisoner would be taken out and lynched, got an automobile and, Washington Revell and State's Attorney Gordon Tull, put the negro in the bottom of the machine and started out of town.

---

[186] *The Baltimore Sun*, "Wesley Miles Hanged. Negro Goes Coolly To Gallows At Princess Anne. Made Confession of Crime," Dec. 7, 1912
[187] *The Baltimore Sun*, "Mob After Negro, Pursues Sheriff With Prisoner, Picketing All the County Roads," Jun. 4, 1912

Chapter 11. Eastern Shore Cases

Some distance away from town they left their automobile and got into a more powerful one belonging to Washington Revell and started for Salisbury.

> *"Convinced that their man was not there, the pursuers then threw their cordon around town so that no one could get in without their knowing it. Men in fast automobiles were rushed to Delmar, Laurel, Pocomoke City, and even to Cambridge in the hope of heading off the negro and stringing him up."*
>
> *June 8, 1912*
> *The Crisfield Times*

They had hardly gotten out of the town before the news of what had happened spread. There was a scurry for motorcars, and almost every one in the place was pressed into service, loaded with as many men as they could carry, and started off in pursuit of the Sheriff and his prisoner. In addition about 100 men took the train for Salisbury, expecting to arrive there in time to head off Sheriff Tull and his charge.

The men who started out in automobiles arrived at Salisbury soon after those who came by train and at once surrounded the jail, supposing that the Sheriff and the negro had arrived and that the negro had been locked up. About 10 o'clock Sheriff Smith, of Wicomico, went to the jail door and assured the crowd that the man they wanted was not there. He threw open the jail doors and invited them to take a look. They took him at his word and surged into the prison and ransacked it from top to bottom. They looked into all the cells, into every room and closet, under the beds, in the coal bins and even in the furnace. There was not a nook or a cranny that was left unsearched.

Convinced that their man was not there, the pursuers then threw their cordon around town so that no one could get in without their knowing it. Men in fast automobiles were rushed to Delmar, Laurel, Pocomoke City, and even to Cambridge in the hope of heading off the negro and stringing him up.

Then the pursuers picked up the chase again and darted away toward Delmar, six miles distant. The tracks of the escaping car were followed down the Shell road, through Laurel, into Seaford, where the officers and their prisoner finally eluded the would-be lynchers.

At Seaford Sheriff Tull and his deputy, E.O. Townsend, left the machine and took to the woods, which are dense at that point. There in darkness with their frightened prisoner they lay until dawn, fearful to move lest the pursuers should learn their whereabouts.

Leaving their shelter early Tuesday morning, the two officers hired a team and with the negro between them, drove to Greenwood, Del., where they boarded a train for Love Point, Md., keeping the identity of the negro a secret. From Love Point the trio rode by boat to Baltimore and Miles was hurried across the city from the wharf and placed in jail before the route of the escaping party became known. Miles will be held in Baltimore until the authorities think it safe to return him to Princess Anne for trial.[188]

Wesley Miles was tried in Baltimore on October 10th and convicted on October 11th. Miles was described as aged about fifty and having a wife and eight children.[189] On October 12th, he was sentenced to hang.[190]

The Marylander and Herald of Princess Anne reports the execution of December 6th.

> Wesley Miles, a Princess Anne negro, paid the penalty for his crime on the gallows on the Poor House Farm at 7:00 o'clock Friday morning. Sheriff Harding P. Tull wielded the hatchet that cut the rope, releasing the trap an sending the condemned man to his doom.
>
> Rev. John Nutter, colored, stood at one side of the platform and began a prayer. Every hat in the group of about 100 men was raised. He implored the protection of the Father in Heaven on the officers to carry out the law in the execution of a man charged with a heinous crime and also asked that the soul of the man condemned, because of his weakness, be cleansed. Then he sang "Jesus Lover of My Soul" and the voice of the condemned man could be heard plainly above the others as the singing proceeded.
>
> Just as the first rays of the sun broke through the clouds the black cap was pulled over Miles' eyes by former Sheriff George W. Brown, who aided the officials in properly adjusting it. Sixteen minutes after the trap had been sprung the negro was declared dead by Drs. Henry M. Lankford, of Princess Anne, and R. R. Norris, of Crisfield.[191]

After Miles was readied for the hanging he made a statement, saying that following the devil had brought him to do this. Despite the early hour, "at least three scores of vehicles" were gathered at the site. The article reported, "The fence which had been placed about the scaffold had been torn down and the boards were strewn about the place. The scaffold had been placed in a sort of low ravine in the midst of a half dozen gigantic foxtail pines."

> Almost immediately after the body was cut down it was lowered into the grave on the Poor House farm which had been dug not very far from

---

[188] *The Crisfield Times*, "Negro Assaults a White Girl; Daughter of Ex-Sheriff Phillips the Victim; Girl's Assailant Hidden in the Woods by Sheriff and Deputy of Somerset County," June 8, 1912
[189] *The Baltimore Sun*, "Somerset Negro Guilty; Wesley Miles Convicted of Assaulting Ex-Sheriff's Daughter; To Penitentiary or Death," Oct. 11. 1912
[190] *The Baltimore Sun*, "Negro Sentenced to Hang; Somerset County Assailant of White Girl Hears It Stoically," Oct. 12, 1912
[191] *The Marylander and Herald*, Princess Anne, MD, "Miles Dies on Gallows, Joins in Singing Hymn and Meets His Doom With Calmness," Dec. 10, 1912

Chapter 11. Eastern Shore Cases

where William Lee, the negro whom Governor Warfield was forced to resort to all kinds of means to prevent being lynched, is buried.

Norman Mabel and James Paraway
Sentenced in March 1914 to prison for crime in Kent County, Maryland

Norman Mabel and James Paraway were indicted in Chestertown on December 30, 1913 for robbing and killing James R. Coleman a week prior. Two days before the indictment, a mob entered the jail with an unsuccessful attempt to lynch Mabel.

The Baltimore Sun of December 28, 1913 describes the attempted lynching.

> *"In silence the mob withdrew a short distance, but only to open fire upon the windows on the second story, where Mabel and the other negroes under arrest in connection with the crime are confined. Volley after volley from half a hundred pistols and shotguns was directed at the second story and scarcely a pane of glass in the windows was left."*
>
> *December 28, 1913*
> *The Baltimore Sun*

Chestertown, Md., Dec. 28 – Just at midnight the mob which had been gathered around the jail all day determined upon lynching Norman Mabel, the negro who confessed having murdered James R. Coleman, forced two of the jail doors.

It was met by State's Attorney Vickers, Sheriff Brown and his corps of 15 special deputies with drawn revolvers. Mr. Vickers pleaded with the band to leave the jail, and when this proved ineffectual the Sheriff ordered the deputies to fire over the heads of the mob. Two volleys brought the infuriated invaders to a stop. A suppressed growl ran through the attacking party. Cries of vengeance not alone against the negro but against his protectors were heard.

Here and there from the crowd came scattered shots, but none of the bullets entered the corridor.

The determined front presented by the officers held the crowd at bay, but apparently did not lessen its determination to wreak vengeance upon the negro. It refused to disperse and pressed close to the broken doors, simply waiting for some one to make the first rush upon the little band of officers.

Finally five men bolted the into the corridor, the leader bearing a sledge hammer with which the cell door was to be broken. The officers pressed around the door waiting to rush, to the assistance of the leader.

For a moment it looked as if the little band of guards would be overpowered. Former Sheriff William H. McKee, who is acting as deputy, faced the would-be lynchers single-handedly, wrenching the hammer from the leader's hand and forced them from the corridor.

In silence the mob withdrew a short distance, but only to open fire upon the windows on the second story, where Mabel and the other negroes under arrest in connection with the crime are confined. Volley after volley from half a hundred pistols and shotguns was directed at the second story and scarcely a pane of glass in the windows was left.

Sheriff Brown ordered the negroes to lie down close under the windows so as to escape the flying shots.

Crowding around the jail, the mob flourished revolvers, knives and pistols in the air and demanded that the murderer be given up. Only a leader was needed to take the first step in charging the door.

Former Judge James Alfred Pearee, who had spent several hours in the jail, went to the door and begged the mob to disperse. The men heard him in silence, but did not relax from their hostile attitude. State's Attorney H.W. Vickers then attempted to address them, but his appearance was a signal for an outbreak.

"We will lynch the negro before morning," was cried by hundreds of voices. "You had better give him up now and save trouble."

Another attempt to reach the negroes was made a half hour later. About 20 men dashed over the broken door and rushed up the stairs. They were met by Sheriff Brown and Deputy McKee and ordered to disperse.

They refused and McKee fired one shot over the heads of the invaders and a second into the floor at their feet. Sheriff Brown warned them that the third shot would be into their midst. He gave them one minute to leave the jail.

The mob slowly filed out. State's Attorney Vickers and Sheriff Brown followed the men and, selecting half a dozen who appeared to be the leaders, deputized them and ordered them to come into the jail and aid in the defense. The men selected obeyed.

The crowd then began to disperse and by 3 o'clock the yard was practically deserted.[192]

The next day, the prisoners were transported from the jail, but not without threats from violent crowds. The article of *The Baltimore Sun* referred to the 1892 murder of Dr. Hill also in Kent County.[192]

During the trial, James Paraway took the stand and testified to killing James R. Coleman, reportedly admitting guilt in order to save Norman Mabel from the gallows. David Mabel, father of Norman, took the stand in defense of his son. Also during the trial, defense attorney T. Alan

---

[192] *The Baltimore Sun*, "Mob Enters Jail; Would-Be Lynchers at Chestertown Held at Bay in Prison Corridor; Deputies Fire Over Heads; Determined Rush Checked By Ex-Sheriff William McKee; Cell Windows Broken," Dec. 28, 1913

Chapter 11. Eastern Shore Cases

Goldsborough challenged the confessions and the testimony of the witnesses for the prosecution.[193]

In Elkton on March 7, 1914, both Mabel and Paraway were found guilty of murder in the first degree and sentenced. James Paraway, aged 15, was sentenced to prison for life. The day before, Norman Mabel was found guilty of murder in the second degree and sentenced to 18 years, reportedly the maximum penalty. *The Baltimore Sun* includes,

> The masterly defense put up by T. Alan Goldsborough, Herbert E. Perkins and Omar D. Crothers undoubtedly saved the boys from the gallows. Fighting every step of the way, they took advantage of every opportunity to help their case. Mr. Goldsborough did the brunt of the fighting. His argument before the jury yesterday morning had great influence as the jurors showed by nodding their heads in agreement with him.[194]

James Dutton
Commuted Sentence March 1915 for crime near Cambridge, Maryland

In July of 1913, James Dutton was arrested for the crime of attacking a seventeen-year-old daughter of a farmer near Cambridge, Maryland. Dutton was tried on appeal in the Wicomico County court, following a conviction at a trial in Dorchester County. In October of 1914 he was convicted a second time and sentenced to hang. In March of 1915 the Governor commuted his sentence to life imprisonment.

The first account of the crime reported by *The Baltimore Sun* on July 29, 1913, includes the following,

> Cambridge, Md., July 28 – Miss Marguerite Gillis, the pretty 17-year-old daughter of Ernest Gillis, a farmer living near Dailsville, four miles from Cambridge, was attacked about 10 o'clock this morning by a negro, said to have been James Dutton, a young mulatto.
>
> Miss Gillis had driven to town and was returning home. As she was passing a wooded road the negro jumped into the buggy and seized Miss Gillis by the throat and choked her almost into unconsciousness.

---

[193] *The Baltimore Sun*, "Paraway Takes Blame; Testifies Mabel Did Not Plan To Murder Mr. Coleman; Robbery the Motive, He Says; Negro Youth Declares He Struck the Fatal Blow Without His Companion's Knowledge," Mar. 6, 1914

[194] *The Baltimore Sun*, "Life Term For Paraway, Judges Return First-Degree Murder Verdict Against Negro Youth. Judge Constable Dissents," Mar. 8, 1914

> The girl did not give up, however, but struck her assailant in the face with the butt end of her whip and scratched him. Frightened by her resistance, he leaped from the vehicle and returned to work on the farm of James Slocum, near by.
>
> Miss Gillis drove to the home of her uncle, Henry Gillis. A telephone message was sent to Sheriff Bradshaw and to Waldo Jackson, a neighbor. The former went to the Gillis farm in an automobile and got a description of her assailant from Miss Gillis. The negro was found on the Slocum farm.
>
> Dutton made no attempt to escape and pretended not to notice the officers. He was taken before Miss Gillis, who identified him as her assailant and he was hurried to the Cambridge Jail.
>
> Mr. Jackson and his son Ralph, accompanied by Henry Gillis, visited the scene of the attack and obtained a measure of the assailant's foot.[195]

Dutton was tried and convicted and sentenced to hang. The case was appealed.

The September 19, 1914 edition of the *Salisbury Advertiser* of Wicomico County reported the Dutton case as one of several cases removed from adjoining counties, noting "His council took an appeal to the Court of Appeals and a new trial was granted."[196]

The October 3, 1914 edition of the *Salisbury Advertiser* describes the following.

> The court held a night session for the trial of James Dutton, a colored man, for an assault upon a white girl with intent to rape. This case held the court into the early hours of Saturday morning. The jury was out but a short time in finding the accused negro guilty, and on Saturday morning he was for the second time sentenced to be hanged. This case had been tried in Dorchester county last spring and sentence was passed there to hang Dutton, but he obtained a new trial on an appeal to the Court of Appeals. It is not generally believed that the negro will ever hang, owing to the fact that he failed of the purpose of his assault, but it is not probable that he will ever again see freedom.[197]

In the March 5, 1915 edition of *The Baltimore Sun* reports that Dutton's sentence had been commuted by the Governor to life imprisonment.

> Spirited out of the jail at Cambridge, Dorchester county, Wednesday night while the residents of the community were asleep and driven six miles to Travers' Wharf, on the Choptank river, James Dutton, a negro,

---

[195] *The Baltimore Sun*, "Negro Attacks Girl; Miss Gillis, Near Cambridge, Choked by Mulatto, Who Jumps into her Buggy," Jul. 29, 1913
[196] *Salisbury Advertiser*, "A Week in Wicomico Court; Several Removal Cases," Sep. 19, 1914
[197] *Salisbury Advertiser*, "Court News to Date," Oct. 3, 1914

Chapter 11. Eastern Shore Cases

twice convicted of attempted criminal assault on Miss Marguerite Gillis in 1913 and twice sentenced to be hanged, will today begin a life sentence in the penitentiary, his former sentence of death having been commuted by Governor Goldsborough late yesterday afternoon.

It was not until after Dutton had been taken out of Cambridge and was practically on his way to the penitentiary that the Governor announced that he had commuted the death sentence. This delay was intended to prevent any hostile demonstration in the neighborhood.

> *"The reason the negro was spirited out of the Cambridge jail was due to the fact that Governor Goldsborough had heard that threats had been made against the prisoner."*
>
> March 6, 1915
> The Baltimore Sun

That Dutton was to be taken from the jail was known only to the Sheriff and others particularly interested in the case. It is thought the negro was taken aboard the steamer Talbot, of the Baltimore, Chesapeake and Atlantic Railway line, due in Baltimore early this morning.[198]

The March 6, 1915 edition of *The Baltimore Sun* reports more on the Governor's instructions to the Baltimore city jail warden.

> It was not officially stated until after 1 o'clock yesterday afternoon by the jail authorities that the negro had been brought there at 7 o'clock Thursday morning by the Sheriff of Dorchester county. The announcement came after Warden Lee had been in conference with Governor Goldsborough.
>
> After leaving Dutton Thursday morning in the custody of Warden Lee, the Sheriff of Dorchester county returned immediately to Cambridge to get the papers in the case to be presented to John F. Leonard, Warden of the penitentiary, when the negro is delivered to him. It is expected the Sheriff will arrive with the papers today.
>
> The reason the negro was spirited out of the Cambridge jail was due to the fact that Governor Goldsborough had heard that threats had been made against the prisoner.[199]

---

[198] *The Baltimore Sun*, "Negro on Way to 'Pen'; Governor Commutes Death Sentence in Dorchester Case," Mar. 5, 1915
[199] *The Baltimore Sun*, "Secret to Save Negro, Warden Lee Says Governor Advised Him in Case of Dorchester Prisoner," Mar. 6, 1915

Aloysius "Wish" Sheppard
Executed August 1915 in Denton, Maryland

Justice was quick for Aloysius "Wish" Sheppard. He was arrested in Caroline County, Maryland on July 16, 1915 for the assault of the fourteen-year-old daughter of a white farmer. Within a day he was quickly removed from the jail in Denton and transported to Baltimore. He was hanged on August 27, 2915 in Denton.

The Baltimore Sun of July 16, 1915 reports on a posse scouring parts of Caroline County for the then unknown assailant of Mildred Clark, teenaged daughter of a farmer, Enoch S. Clark. "Sheriff Temple and the posse have run down several clues, but none has resulted in an arrest. Tonight the whole country for miles around Federalsburg is being searched and indignation is so high that a lynching is expected if the negro is captured."[200]

> *"Thank God that I am away from that county. If they had caught me I know they would have beat me to death."*
>
> *July 17, 1915*
> The Baltimore Sun

Sheppard was arrested at his home, located near the Federalsburg railroad station. From the Denton jail, Sheriff James Temple and Deputy Sheriff A. E. Cooper transported Sheppard to Love Point where they and their prisoner boarded the *Westmoreland* for Baltimore. When placed in the Baltimore jail, Sheppard was heard to sigh and say, "Thank God that I am away from that county. If they had caught me I know they would have beat me to death."[201]

Ten days later, with Sheppard pleading to remain in Baltimore to avoid a lynching, Sheppard was delivered to Denton for trial. Sheriff Temple stationed his deputies around the jail and directed others to patrol the town for trouble. About fifteen special deputies were sworn in. The Baltimore Sun reported willingness expressed local residents to allow the state to execute Sheppard but vowed a lynching if Sheppard were let off with a penitentiary sentencing.[202]

---

[200] *The Baltimore Sun*, "Negro Assaults Girl," Jul. 16, 1915
[201] *The Baltimore Sun*, "Negro Smuggled to City, Aloysius Sheppard Accused Of Assault In Caroline County," Jul. 17, 1915
[202] *The Baltimore Sun*, "Sheppard's Trial On, Negro Faces Charge of Criminally Assaulting Girl, Hearing Draws Big Crowd, Sheriff Temple And 20 Deputies Guard Jail To Prevent Mob Violence," Jul. 27, 1915

Chapter 11. Eastern Shore Cases

Sheppard was tried and convicted. On July 27, 1915 he was hanged in Denton. *The Cambridge Record* of August 30, 1915 reports the execution.

> Sheriff Temple's plan to hang Aloysius ("Wish") Sheppard, the negro assailant of Miss Mildred Clark, of Federalsburg, in the barn attached to the Denton Jail, as affording the degree of privacy required by the Maryland law in the execution of the death penalty, had to be changed because of well-founded rumors that the barn would be burned down last night or torn down by the crowd which came to town to see the execution. Sheppard was hanged two minutes before 6 o'clock this morning, on the bank of the Choptank river, west of the jail, where the gallows had been removed from the barn. Ten minutes afterward the negro was pronounced dead by Drs. P.R. Fischer and Dawson O. Stevensville, physicians summoned to witness the execution.
>
> A large crowd was in Denton and many saw the hanging from points on the curving river bank, but there was no disorder. Guards kept the one narrow roadway from the street to the side of the jail clear of all persons except the official witnesses. From scows and boats on the river a number of spectators saw the gruesome sight, but boatmen who had expected to do a thriving business selling seats were disappointed, because of the early hour of the hanging.[203]

Aaron Johnson

Arrested August 1915 in Talbot County, Maryland

The Baltimore Sun of August 7, 1915 reports the following.

> Easton, Md., Aug. 6 – Following the criminal assault upon Mildred Clark, near Federalsburg, by "Wish" Sheppard, a negro, comes the news of an alleged criminal assault Monday upon Mrs. Lulu S. Willey, aged 30 years, wife of Charles Willey, a farmer of Pea Neck, between Royal Oak and St. Michaels. Aaron Johnson, a negro, who worked on Mr. Willey's farm, is accused.
>
> Mrs. Willey, who identified the negro, said at the hearing that while her husband was away Johnson came into the house between 11 o'clock and midnight, drover her small children out and fastened the doors. He then threw his arms around her, she declared. She attempted to get away from him, but he threw her to the floor.
>
> When Mr. Willey came home the next day she told him what had occurred. They went to St. Michaels to report to the authorities. In order not to frighten the negro away the affair was kept secret until Constable Mortimer had made the arrest and Sheriff Stevens had placed Johnson in jail.

---

[203] *The Cambridge Record*, Cambridge, Maryland, "Sheppard Hanged in View of Public," Aug. 30, 1915

> "The majority of the people seem disposed to await the action of the courts, though it is freely predicted by many of the rougher element that trouble may be expected unless a verdict similar to that imposed on 'Wish' Sheppard at Denton a few weeks ago be rendered."
>
> August 8, 1915
> The Baltimore Sun

Johnson admitted today that he worked for Mr. Willey off and on for four or five years, but he denied that he committed the assault. He said he wanted a speedy trial.[204]

The August 8, 1915 account of *The Baltimore Sun* reports,

Easton, Md., Aug. 7 – Though excitement is running high against Aaron Johnson, in jail here charged with an alleged criminal attack upon Mrs. L. S. Willey, of near Royal Oak, it is not thought that any attempt will be made to lynch him. The majority of the people seem disposed to await the action of the courts, though it is freely predicted by many of the rougher element that trouble may be expected unless a verdict similar to that imposed on "Wish" Sheppard at Denton a few weeks ago be rendered.[205]

The September 3, 1915 account of *The Baltimore Sun* includes,

Easton, Md., Sept. 2 – The Circuit Court for Talbot County was convened today in special session, with Chief Judge Albert Constable and Associate Judge P.B. Hopper on the bench, at the solicitation of State's Attorney Charles J. Butler, to take up the cases of James R. Smith and Aaron Johnson, both negroes, who are charged with criminal assault.

Johnson was indicted for criminally assaulting Mrs. Lulu Willey, wife of Charles Willey, a farmer living near St. Michaels, on August 2. The maximum punishment for both crimes, in case of conviction, is death.[206]

The September 11, 1915 account of *The Baltimore Sun* reports that Johnson's case had been removed and was scheduled to be tried in Elkton on September 24.[207]

---

[204] *The Baltimore Sun*, "Woman Accuses Negro; Mrs. Willey, of Talbot County, Says Farm Hand Assaulted Her; Children Driven from House; Black Forced Way Into Room At Night During Husband's Absence; Speedy Trial Demanded," Aug. 7, 1915
[205] *The Baltimore Sun*, "No Danger of Lynching," Aug. 8, 1915
[206] *The Baltimore Sun*, "Two Negroes Indicted; Talbot Grand Jury Charges Smith and Johnson with Criminal Assault," Sep. 3, 1915
[207] *The Baltimore Sun*, "Assault Case Removed," Sep. 11, 1915

Chapter 11. Eastern Shore Cases

Robert J. Smith (or James Smith)
Arrested August 1915 in Talbot County, Maryland

The Royal Oak area again became the focus of arrest. Robert Smith was arrested for assaulting Annabel Denny, daughter of Mr. and Mrs. Elbert Denny of Royal Oak. Articles of *The Baltimore Sun* were downloaded reporting a talk of lynching. Note, some accounts refer to him as Robert Smith, others as James Smith. Robert is likely his middle name. *The Baltimore Sun* of August 28th reports,

> "...the feeling against the accused here in the county is so strong that State's Attorney Charles J. Battler is trying to arrange for a speedy trial in order to prevent lynching."
>
> *August 28, 1915*
> *The Baltimore Sun*

Easton, Md., Aug. 27 – Robert Smith, a young negro, is in jail here on the charge of having assaulted Annabel Denny, 15-year-old of Mr. and Mrs. Elbert L. Denny, at her home near Royal Oak last Tuesday night, and the feeling against the accused here in the county is so strong that State's Attorney Charles J. [Butler] is trying to arrange for a speedy trial in order to prevent lynching. ...[208]

The August 29, 1915 account of *The Baltimore Sun* includes,

> Since the people in and around Royal Oak, where Annabel Denny, the 13-year-old daughter of Mr. and Mrs. Elbert Denny, upon whom a criminal assault was committed at her home a few days ago by Robert Smith, colored, had definite assurance today from State's Attorney Charles J. Butler that Judge Hopper, of this judicial circuit, would convene the grand jury for Talbot county next Wednesday or Thursday for the purpose of hearing the evidence in the case, all incipient talk of lynching was stopped. The neighbors of the Denny family have become more reconciled to the situation and tonight everything is quiet in the locality. For a time, though, fear of a lynching kept the county authorities on alert.
>
> Sheriff Sewell is keeping a diligent watch on his prisoner to see that he does not escape and to see that no crowds loiter around the jail.[209]

The September 3, 1915 account of *The Baltimore Sun* includes the following.

> Easton, Md., Sept. 2 – The Circuit Court for Talbot County was convened today in special session, with Chief Judge Albert Constable and Associate Judge P.B. Hopper on the bench, at the solicitation of

---

[208] *The Baltimore Sun*, "Girl, 15, Accuses Negro, Annabel Denny Tells Story Of Fighting Assailant, Lynching in Talbot Feared," Aug. 28, 1915
[209] *The Baltimore Sun*, "Lynching Talk Stops," Aug. 29, 1915

> State's Attorney Charles J. Butler, to take up the cases of James R. Smith and Aaron Johnson, both negroes, who are charged with criminal assault.
>
> Smith was charged with criminally assaulting Anna Lee Denny, the 13-year-old daughter of Mr. and Mrs. E.L. Denny, near Royal Oak, on August 22...[206]

The September 11, 1915 account of *The Baltimore Sun* reports on both two cases, of Aaron Johnson and James Smith.

> The case of Smith was taken up first. His counsel, George H. Pendleton, a negro lawyer of Baltimore, filed an affidavit made by Smith before a notary public setting forth that he did not believe he could get a fair and impartial trial in Talbot county and asked to have his case removed to another county.[207]

The article reported that the case would be removed to Cecil County and was scheduled for September 24.

The article was likely referring to George L Pendleton (1866-1943), an attorney practicing in Baltimore at that time, and best known for his work later defending John Snowden of Annapolis, whose case was unsuccessfully commuted; Snowden was executed at the Annapolis jail in 1919.

Chapter 11. Eastern Shore Cases

Bailey Jonabe

Arrested November 1915 in Somerset County, Maryland

The November 9, 1915 edition of the *Maryland and Herald* of Princess Anne reports the following.

> *"...the cry to 'put him up a pole' was heard on every side."*
>
> November 9, 1915
> Maryland and Herald

At an early hour Monday morning of last week Carroll Hurley, mate on the oyster boat *Emma Florence*, was struck on the head by Bailey Jonabe, a negro deck hand, with a spike and seriously injured. Jonabe seemed to have run amuck on the boat, hitting another negro, T. L. Brown, over the head with a piece of wood before assaulting Hurley.

Jonabe, a shipped man from Baltimore on the schooner *Minnie V.*, lying in the harbor at Smith's Island, acted queerly Sunday afternoon and a doctor was called to see him by Capt. Charles Middleton, owner of the boat. The doctor not finding anything the matter with him, Captain Middleton told the negro if he did not wish to work he would send him to Crisfield on the mail boat Monday morning.

When Hurley went to the boat Monday morning to put Jonable on board the mail boat for Crisfield, the negro attacked him. He was overpowered after a stiff fight and tied in a sailboat and taken to Crisfield by Capt. John Evans, where he was given a preliminary hearing before Justice Britton, who committed him to jail to await the outcome of Hurley's injuries.

During the hearing a large number of the island men arrived in Crisfield in gasoline boats, and, the news having spread over the town, a crowd gathered and the cry "put him up a pole" was heard on every side. While the crowd had about decided to rush to the local jail and get the negro, Sheriff Sterling, with his deputies, put the negro in his high-powered automobile and started at full speed for Princess Anne and lodged the prisoner in jail here.

Carroll Hurley was taken to the General and Marine Hospital at Crisfield where an operation was performed to relieve the pressure on the brain. When operating, it was found that several of the larger blood vessels had been broken and the young man seriously injured.[210]

---

[210] *Marylander and Herald*, "Carroll Hurley Assaulted by Negro, Schooner's Deck Hand Runs Amuck On Smith's Island," Nov. 9, 1915

Mob Law on Delmarva

Harry Paynter
Arrested April 1916 in Seaford, Delaware
The Seaford Tribune of April 22, 1916 reports,

> "While the crowd called for him to be strung up, State Detective, Oscar Thomas, hustled the prisoner into an automobile and slipping up back roads, escaped the crowd and landed his man safely in the jail at Georgetown."
>
> *April 22, 1916*
> *Seaford Tribune*

Harry Paynter, a young colored man, narrowly escaped lynching early Saturday morning when a crowd of excited farmers surrounded him after he had nearly killed Alfred P. Lingo, an aged farmer, of Indian River Hundred, and robbed him of $183. While the crowd called for him to be strung up, State Detective, Oscar Thomas, hustled the prisoner into an automobile and slipping up back roads, escaped the crowd and landed his man safely in the jail at Georgetown.

But for Thomas's quick work and the absence of a leader among the farmers, the man would have been lynched. Paynter was aware of his escape and sighed with relief when the jail doors closed behind him. Later when he realized the seriousness of his crime at the hearing before a magistrate, he expressed a wish that the crowd had lynched him and had his punishment over.

Paynter called at the Lingo home to ask for work. Lingo is more than eighty years old and lives a bachelor life on his little farm. Although he had no work for the man, he gave him his dinner. Paynter left and hid in the woods near the house until dark when he went to the door and told the aged man that someone outside wanted to speak to him. As Lingo came out, the colored man dropped him with one blow from a blackjack. Searching the unconscious man, Paynter found the $183 in a pocketbook and cooly left the old man for dead.

Later Lingo regained consciousness and dragged himself into the house where he awoke an aged brother who lives with him. The alarm was given in a short time and in an hour's time the farmers had met on horseback, fully armed and started a systematic search for the colored man.

In the meantime, the state detective in a high powered automobile was looking over the main roads and finally picked up Paynter's trail, near Springfield.

It was not until they had nearly reached Millsboro that they overhauled a strange colored man riding with a farmer in an open wagon, turning the automobile across the road, the officials jumped out and grabbed Paynter and caught him just as he was slipping the money he had stolen, under the wagon seat. The farmer explained that Paynter had been walking along the road and had asked for a ride.

Chapter 11. Eastern Shore Cases

Paynter was taken back to the Lingo home where the seriously injured man recognized him as his assailant. It was then, while the farmers were gathered around the house waiting for the old man to identify the negro that the plan was laid to hang him. The moment the crowd learned that the man was caught, and the right one, a howl went up and a rush was made to the barn for a rope while others wanted to shoot the negro. In the excitement, Thomas slipped the Negro out the back door and into the waiting automobile and before the crowd realized it, Paynter was gone.

At his hearing in Georgetown, Paynter declared that he was originally from Lewes but that he was working down on an Angola farm. He was tramping to Millsboro in search of work when he stopped at the Lingo home, seeing that both the brothers were very old he at once concocted the scheme to rob them and owned that had the brother raised any alarm after he had felled the one, that he would probably have murdered both of them.

He seemed to realize his perilous position and repeated that he wished the crowd had killed him. He is being held to await the result of Lingo's injuries and if the old man lives will have to face a charge of assault with intent to commit murder and robbery, about twenty years in the workhouse facing him.[211]

Isaiah Fountain

Executed July 1920 in Talbot County, Maryland

The case is detailed by Sherrilyn A. Ifill (2007). No spectacle lynchings have been identified for Talbot County, a fact mentioned in newspaper accounts of two identified cases of arrests. Isaiah Fountain, a notorious case of 1919 and 1920, narrowly escaped lynching, twice.

Isaiah Fountain was executed on July 23, 1920 for criminal assault in April of 1919 of Bertha Simpson, a teenager who was living at the time with her grandparents near Trappe in Talbot County. Following the alleged crime, a mob searched for Fountain believed to have headed towards St. Michaels, as described by the April 3, 1919 issue of *The Baltimore Sun*, "It is reported a large party of men in and around St. Michaels, armed with rifles, shotguns and pistols, are scouring the countryside for him and if caught it is feared he will be lynched."[212]

---

[211] *The Seaford Tribune*, Seaford, Delaware, "Negro Lynching Barely Stopped; State Detective Slips Criminal Away From Infuriated Farmers Near Georgetown; Had Attacked Aged Man," Apr. 22, 1916

[212] *The Baltimore Sun*, "Negro Assaults Girl, Posse Searching For Man Who Attacked Bertha Simpson Near Trappe, Md.," Apr. 3, 1919

Mob Law on Delmarva

Fountain was reportedly arrested in Westchester, Pennsylvania and brought to the Baltimore jail, then transported to Easton on April 19th for trial.[213] Fountain had been heavily guarded and smuggled into the Easton jail on a ruse, avoiding the crowd of over 1,000 awaiting the train station where he was expected to arrive. Fountain's defense attorneys included Eugene O'Dunne of Baltimore.[214] Fountain managed to escape following the first day of his trial. At the end of the proceedings Fountain was led outside towards the jail, as described by *The Baltimore Sun* of April 22, 1919.

> "A path was opened through the crowd from the Courthouse to the entrance to the sheriff's home. When the negro got almost to the steps of the sheriff's home the crowd closed in, shouting: 'Get him.' One man was seen to have several yards of rope and another got near enough to put his hands on the negro."
>
> *April 22, 1919*
> **The Baltimore Sun**

It was estimated that 2,000 persons were packed in the Courthouse yard following the clearing of the courtroom and it was through this mass of enraged humanity that the Sheriff and the Baltimore police led the negro on the way to the jail, which is 75 yards in the rear of the Courthouse. The negro was not handcuffed, a precaution that many thought the Sheriff and police should have taken.

A path was opened through the crowd from the Courthouse to the entrance to the sheriff's home. When the negro got almost to the steps of the sheriff's home the crowd closed in, shouting: "Get him." One man was seen to have several yards of rope and another got near enough to put his hands on the negro.

The 10 police from Baltimore held back the mob and the sheriff hustled the negro up the steps. Mrs. Stitchberry, wife of the sheriff, opened the door and the officer rushed the negro inside. The move of the sheriff was to take Fountain to the jail, the entrance to which is through the sheriff's home, but the negro saw an open window, jumped through it and darted down a road to the southwest, past what is known as the gas house, and along the road to Trappe.

The Baltimore police were still standing guard with drawn pistols at the entrance to the sheriff's home and the crowd being in front of the house did not see the negro leave. Sheriff Stitchberry fired one shot from his pistol at the fleeing negro then quickly opened the door and told the police to follow him.

---

[213] *The Baltimore Sun*, "Safe in Easton Jail, Negro Accused Of Assault On White Girl Strongly Guarded On Trip," Apr. 20, 1919
[214] *The Baltimore Sun*, "To Try Fountain Today," Apr. 21, 1919

Chapter 11. Eastern Shore Cases

Sheriff Stitchberry and the police got a good start as the mob hesitated to believe that the negro had escaped, but thought that the sheriff was trying a ruse on them. In the meantime Mrs. Stitchberry came to the door and told the crowd that it was true that the negro had escaped.

The 2,000 persons then left in the direction the negro was seen running and a man-hunt started in full swing with the sheriff and the police trying to outdo the crowd, which was bent on a lynching. Later the crowd became dissatisfied with the chase and believing that the negro was still in jail, returned and stoned the jail. They started to break down the door when Mrs. Stitchberry appeared and invited a committee of five to search the sheriff's house and the jail. ...[215]

> *"Friends of Mrs. Stitchberry quote her today as having said that she hoped that Fountain never would be returned to justice, that she would be glad if the mob 'tore him to pieces.'"*
>
> *April 23, 1919*
> *The Baltimore Sun*

The search for Fountain continued on a massive scale, encompassing several adjoining counties. Photographs of Fountain were printed in the newspaper along with news of a sizable reward which included the $5,000 provided by Judge W. H. Adkins of the Easton court for his capture. *The Baltimore Sun* reported that "Friends of Mrs. Stitchberry quote her today as having said that she hoped that Fountain never would be returned to justice, that she would be glad if the mob 'tore him to pieces.'"[216]

Fountain was captured in Delaware and returned to the Easton jail.[217] Maryland State Guard troops from Salisbury and Cambridge were brought in to protect Fountain from mob violence from an estimated four or five thousand gathered in the streets of Easton.[218] On April 24, 1919, Fountain was found guilty after about five minutes of deliberation, and given the death penalty.[219]

---

[215] *The Baltimore Sun*, "Accused Negro Gets Away; Fountain, Identified As Girl's Assailant, Jumps Through Window; Mob of 2,000, Bent On Lynching, Is Seeking Fugitive," Apr. 22, 1919

[216] *The Baltimore Sun*, "All Talbot in Man Hunt; Search For Fountain Extends To Adjoining Counties; Roads and Bridges Held by Armed Men; Rewards Aggregate $5,500," Apr. 23, 1919

[217] *The Daily Banner*, Cambridge, MD, "Fountain is Lodged Safely in Easton Jail," Apr. 24, 1919

[218] *The Baltimore Sun*, "Troops Guard Accused Negro, Two Companies Rushed To Easton To Prevent Lynching Of Fountain," Apr. 24, 1919

[219] *The Baltimore Sun*, "Death Decree for Fountain," Apr. 25, 1919

Fountain's case was appealed and the second trial began in May of 1920 at Towson where he was again convicted and sentenced to hang.[220] On June 16, 1920, Fountain made a second escape, this time from the Easton jail as he again awaited execution, initiating another massive man-hunt.[221] He was captured on June 23rd near Queen Anne, about 14 miles away and returned to Easton.[222]

Fountain was executed in Easton on July 23, 1920. The execution was held inside of the jail to about 20 witnesses. Fountain was reportedly buried on his farm near Trappe.[223]

> *"Those who brought suit are Fountain's mother and two brothers, Fannie, George and William Fountain; Annie May Ross, Eliza Slaughter and Isabella Brooks. All allege they were assaulted in their homes and made to spend 'a black night of fear.'"*
>
> October 1, 1920
> The Baltimore Sun

The Baltimore Sun of October 1, 1920 reports,

> Six negroes, arrested and taken to Easton jail after the escape of Isaiah Fountain, colored, from that prison last June instituted suits for $25,000 each in City Court yesterday against Sheriff Charles M. T. Soulsby, of Talbot county. Fountain was under sentence of death when he escaped and other arrests were made in the hope of obtaining information as to his whereabouts.
>
> Those who brought suit are Fountain's mother and two brothers, Fannie, George and William Fountain; Annie May Ross, Eliza Slaughter and Isabella Brooks. All allege they were assaulted in their homes and made to spend "a black night of fear." Two of the women allege they were suspended by ropes in the jail and were swung to and fro like the pendulum of a clock; and George Fountain says he lost 66 turkeys. Most of them say they were kept in jail 10 days, although none had committed any offense. G. L. Pendleton, colored, is their attorney.[224]

---

[220] *The Baltimore Sun*, "Fountain Convicted; Is Sentenced to Hang," May 9, 1920
[221] *The Baltimore Sun*, "Fountain Again Escapes From Easton Jail," Jun. 16, 1920
[222] *The Baltimore Sun*, "Fountain is Captured 14 Miles from Easton; Safely Landed in Jail," Jun. 23, 1920
[223] *The Baltimore Sun*, "Denying Guilt, Fountain Goes to his Death," Jul. 23, 1920
[224] *The Baltimore Sun*, "Six Negroes Sue Sheriff, Demand $25,000 Each For Arrest In Fountain Case," Oct. 1, 1920

Chapter 11. Eastern Shore Cases

George Chelton

Executed June 1923 in Baltimore for crime in Somerset County, Maryland

George Chelton was the first person executed under the new laws requiring executions be held at the Maryland Penitentiary in Baltimore rather in local municipalities as was the previous practice. Chelton was convicted of assault on a young white girl.

The January 20, 1923 edition of *The Crisfield Times* includes fears of lynching.

> *"The negro was removed from the County jail Monday night and taken to Baltimore by Sheriff Chas. S. Dryden. Shortly after his removal, a mob of lynchers recruited from different parts of the county, is alleged to have visited the jail in an effort to get the negro."*
>
> *January 20, 1923*
> *The Baltimore Sun*

Fearing that lynchers would administer a swift justice upon George Sheldon [sic], colored, confined in the county jail at Princess Anne charged with committing a felonious assault on a white girl, Somerset County officials had the accused man removed to the Baltimore City Jail for safekeeping.

The negro was removed from the County jail Monday night and taken to Baltimore by Sheriff Chas. S. Dryden. Shortly after his removal, a mob of lynchers recruited from different parts of the county, is alleged to have visited the jail in an effort to get the negro. When informed that the man they wanted had been removed from the jail, the lynchers were alleged to have demanded the jailers keys after which they made a search of the building. Upon being convinced that Sheldon was not in the jail, the mob dispersed without demonstration.

Sheldon was arrested at a late hour Sunday night by Sheriff Dryden and Deputy Fred Culver, charged with committing an assault on Thelma Hughlett, a white girl aged 14 years, a short distance from Princess Anne about 9 o'clock Saturday night. The negro was found at his home near the county seat, and offered no resistance when confronted by the officers, but denied any knowledge of the crime and protested that he was innocent.

According to the girl's story, she was returning to her home in a one-horse wagon from a country store, accompanied by her brother, 5 years old. The Hughlett family, who are newcomers in the neighborhood, live about five miles from Princess Anne. The girl states that the negro, who was known to her, asked for a ride and, when she assented, he jumped into the rear of the wagon and rode until she turned into what is known as the back road leading to her home. Sheldon then got out and started in the direction of his home.

> When Thelma had gone about 300 yards down the road, she states, the negro appeared from some woods with an open knife in his hand and commanded her not to make any outcry he would kill them both.[225]

The article further reports that he jumped into the wagon and committed the assault. She made her way to home and told her parents, and a neighbor notified the Sheriff. Dr. J. T. Smith, of Princess Anne was reportedly summoned to check on her condition. "Sheldon is known to have had a criminal record, having served different terms in the Maryland penitentiary for various offenses. He was released from the State prison some months ago, following the completion of a sentence which he served for forgery in this county."

Chelton had elected a court trial, which was presided by Chief Judge John R. Pattison, and Judges Robert F. Duer and Joseph L. Bailey.

The June 8, 1923 issue of *The Baltimore Sun* reports,

> Marking the first hanging in the Maryland Penitentiary and marking a departure from the usual custom of hanging convicted men at daybreak, George Chelton, colored, convicted assailant of a young white girl last year in Somerset county, was hanged at 12:39 o'clock this morning.
>
> His execution took place in the newly erected "death house" at the Maryland Penitentiary, built recently by order of the last Legislature. During the last General Assembly a bill was passed abolishing hangings in the counties of Maryland, and making it obligatory upon the State Government to provide a centralized place for this purpose.
>
> Colonel Sweezey himself did not spring the trap, however, but two Penitentiary officers attended to the details of the execution. There were few persons present, only the maximum of 12 witnesses required by law, two physicians, Colonel Sweezey and the executioners.
>
> Chelton was pronounced dead by Dr. William F. Schwarz, of the Penitentiary, and Dr. Frank Powers, of the City Jail, 10 minutes after the trap had been sprung.[226]

In April, George Chelton was transported from Baltimore to Salisbury where he was held until his trial. At least seven law enforcement officials guarded the prisoner as he was transported to the courthouse in Princess Anne on Tuesday, April 17, 1923, where he was tried and sentenced to be

---

[225] *The Crisfield Times*, "Negro Accused of Rape Removed From County Jail; Officers Feared Lynching," Jan. 20, 1923
[226] *The Baltimore Sun*, "First Hanging Is Held In State Penitentiary; George Chelton, Colored, Executed At 12:39 A.M. For Assault On Girl," Jun. 8, 1923

executed. *The Crisfield Times* reported on the trial but described no mob. On April 24th the same contingent of guards delivered the prisoner to Baltimore for the execution in the new death house constructed for the purpose. He was hanged on June 8th; there were few witnesses due to the required maximum of 12 to witness the execution under the new law.

There is no available printed description of local reaction in Princess Anne, but *The Crisfield Times* reported on the execution on the front page of its June 9th edition. As an aside, next to the article was the story of a raid in Crisfield by members of the Ku Klux Klan, dressed in full regalia, locating an African American named Jack Hall and turning him over to the Chief of Police, for the charge of selling liquor. Their vigilantism was not limited by race, however, as Wells Bond, white, was also later picked up by on similar charges filed by members of the Ku Klux Klan.

Howard, Gunby, Mills, Wise, and Cutler
Arrested 1924 for arson in Worcester County, Maryland

The November 22, 1924 edition of *The Baltimore Sun* reports the following about a Worcester County fire of which there were white and black suspects.

> Snow Hill, Md., Nov. 21 -- Implicating as principals Andrew Bevans and Luther Bevans and three negroes of Pocomoke, Alonza Taylor, alias Gumby, and Richard Howard, alias Slim, both negroes, have confessed that they assisted in the burning of the Webb house at Mattaponi Landing on the Pocomoke River November 8.
>
> The house was occupied by Levin Burke and his family.
>
> The confession of Howard tells of their movements from the time they left Pocomoke until they returned the following morning. He said that he first met Andrew Bevans in Baltimore jail. Bevans asked him to come to Worcester county to make whiskey, promising him $1 a gallon.
>
> Howard said he came to Worcester upon his release from jail to work on the Bevans farm in Pocomoke and began to make whiskey in the still with Andrew and Luther Bevans and Sidney Mills. "One morning Luther Bevans told me to go to the still and light the fires," Howard said, "and when I reached there the still was burned. I fired a rifle three times to call them. Luther came down and we began to search for the one who fired the building.
>
> "On the night of November 7 Andrew and Luther Bevans, with Sidney Mills, two strange negroes and myself, left Pocomoke at midnight and drove to the Webb house. They had three cans of gasoline and at the

Mob Law on Delmarva

Bevans farmhouse Andrew Bevans awakened Alonza Taylor and forced him to come along.

> *"The three negroes have changed prisons four times since they were taken from the Snow Hill jail after midnight Tuesday. Several threats to break into the jails where the negroes have been incarcerated and lynch the prisoners have been repeated to the police and each time they were removed under protection of guards to another institution."*
>
> *December 6, 1924*
> *The Baltimore Sun*

"The car was parked near the church, and Alonza Taylor carried one can of gasoline in a bag and two other negroes with myself carried the other can. Andrew Bevans then told us what to do. He said, 'you know, if I could pull off a job in town I could do it in the country. I burned the preacher's house because he made my father pay $1,000.'

"We threw a can in the window and lighted the can with a match. Andrew attempted to fire the stove, but his matches were not dry.

"We returned to Andrew's house in Pocomoke. He gave us a quart of whiskey and then threatened us with death if we told anything."

The confession, State's Attorney Edward H. Johnson says, is substantiated by other evidence, and he will go to Salisbury tomorrow morning to confer with Judge Bailey as to the advisability of calling a special session of the grand jury to consider the case. Johnson stated today that he believed Andrew Bevans had attempted to get poisoned sandwiches to Alonza in jail and sent them by a trusty. The sandwiches had been analyzed by Baltimore chemists and found to contain poison, it was said.

Efforts to find the Bevans have not been successful and officers think they have left the section or are hidden away in the Pocomoke swamp.[227]

The December 6, 1924 edition of *The Evening Times*, Salisbury, describes the removal of three prisoners, accused of arson, and threats of lynching. The article indicated that some of the fervor might be the result of raids of stills.

> Richard Howard, Alonzo Gunby and Sidney Mills, Worcester County negroes who in confession to arson last week implicated other persons, are today resting in some prison in location of which is known only in highest police circles.
>
> The three negroes have changed prisons four times since they were taken from the Snow Hill jail after midnight Tuesday. Several threats to

---

[227] *The Baltimore Sun*, "Two Confess Part in Worcester Fire, White Men and Negroes Named by Imprisoned Pair, Followed Still Burning," Nov. 22, 1924

Chapter 11. Eastern Shore Cases

break into the jails where the negroes have been incarcerated and lynch the prisoners have been repeated to the police and each time they were removed under protection of guards to another institution.

They were taken from the Snow Hill jail late Tuesday night and brought to Salisbury when threats to blow up the jail were heard by authorities. Wednesday afternoon they were returned to Snow Hill but later brought back here. Shortly after six o'clock last night, officers left in an automobile with the three prisoners for "destination unknown."

The latest move was prompted by the report that a mob was forming in Worcester County with the announced purpose of storming the Salisbury jail and lynch the negroes. The wind and rain storm, and the 42 mile journey, is thought to have prevented consummation of the plans.

The renewed threats of lynching, authorities say, have resulted from raids in Pocomoke swamp on Wednesday and Thursday by Federal Prohibition agents and nearly a score of county officers and deputies. The hostile attitude is said to have been prompted by the belief that the negroes disclosed to the officers the location of the stills.

Seven persons arrested in the raid through the swamp will be arraigned before U.S. Commissioner Louder T. Hearne, this afternoon.[228]

The Bevans were apparently apprehended, as reported in the May 5, 1925 edition of *The Baltimore Sun*.

> Cambridge, Md., May 4 – Andrew Bevans and Luther Bevans were placed on trial here today charged with arson in the burning of the home of Mrs. Cordelia West, at Mattaponi, Worcester county, on November 6, 1924.
>
> Indicted with the two Bevanses are five negroes – Sidney Mills, Wilbur Wise, Joseph Cutler, Richard Howard and Alonzo Taylor. The negroes have been granted a severance and turned State's evidence.
>
> The trial of the Bevanses was removed from Worcester to Dorchester and is being heard by Judges Pattison, Bailey and Duer and a Dorchester court jury.[229]

---

[228] *The Evening Times*, Salisbury, Maryland, "Mob Again Threatens Lynching; Negroes are Removed for Fourth Time; Worcester Prisoners Taken From Salisbury Jail Second Time for 'Unknown Prison," Dec. 6, 1924

[229] *The Baltimore Sun*, "Bevanses in Court on Arson Charge, Brothers Forced Crime, Alleged Accomplices Declare For State," May 5, 1925

Mob Law on Delmarva

Carroll Gibson

Executed February 1925 for crime in Talbot County, Maryland

In August of 1924, Carroll Gibson, 19 years old, was arrested for assault. The August 28, 1924 article from *The Baltimore Sun* describes the following.

> "Another member of the searching party is said to have shouted: "Let's lynch him!""
>
> *August 28, 1924*
> *The Baltimore Sun*

Easton, Aug. 27 (Special) – Threats of lynching were silenced tonight by Frank ("Home Run") Baker, manager of the Easton baseball team, when he captured a negro who is charged with assaulting Mrs. Norman Baker, the baseball manager's sister-in-law.

Shortly before midnight the negro, Carroll Gibson, was locked up in the Talbot County Jail in Easton. His capture followed an organized search for him by a posse which included more than 100 men. In the group were William Hopkins, Sheriff of the county, deputy sheriffs, citizens, members of the Easton baseball team and a part of headquarters company, First Regiment, Maryland National Guard.

According to a report made to the Sheriff, Mrs. Baker was attacked in her home, three miles south of Trappe, shortly after she had retired for the night. The negro, who is a laborer on the Baker farm, was captured about two hours later at a negro festival, one mile north of Trappe.

Harry Schuyler, a resident of Trappe, recognized Gibson in the group at the festival. He called to Frank Baker, who was standing near by, and the latter grabbed him by the arm with the command, "Come and go with me."

Another member of the searching party is said to have shouted: "Let's lynch him!"

Baker silenced the threat and started away with his prisoner. Gibson offered no resistance and asked no questions as to his capture. County officials said there seemed to be no question but that Gibson was the guilty man. He was turned over to E. W. Bartlett, constable, and taken to the jail in Easton.

According to the report of the attack made to the Sheriff, Gibson went to Trappe early this evening with his employer, Norman Baker. A little later he was said to have borrowed a bicycle from another negro and to have returned to the Gibson home.

News of the attack prompted the immediate organization of a searching party. The Sheriff and his deputies were joined by members of the Easton baseball team, who had just returned from Crisfield, and by a

Chapter 11. Eastern Shore Cases

number of National Guardsmen who had been drilling in the armory at Easton.[230]

Shortly after his arrest, Gibson was secretly transported to Baltimore for safekeeping. The evening of the day of the removal, a mob of about 500, according to accounts, "surrounded the jail and tore down the doors in their attempt to seize the negro and lynch him, it is said." Told that Gibson was not in Easton, the mob was allowed to search the premises.[231]

The August 30, 1924 edition of *The Baltimore Sun* reports,

> Carroll Gibson, 19-year-old negro, charged with assaulting Mrs. Norman Baker last Wednesday night at her home near Trappe, Md., was brought to the Baltimore City Jail early this morning for safekeeping.
>
> He was removed from the jail in Easton early last night and brought to this city in an automobile by W. H. Hopkins, Sheriff of Talbot county, and deputy sheriffs.
>
> Fear of a repetition of efforts by a mob to storm the Easton jail Thursday night prompted the removal of the prisoner to this city. The mob was repulsed by the Sheriff when an attempt was made to get his keys and gain entrance to the negro's quarters.
>
> Gibson was taken from the Talbot county jail secretly while members of the local Ku Klux Klan organization were assembling in a hall directly across the street.[232]

On November 22, 1924, in Easton, Carroll Gibson was sentenced to be executed by hanging for attacking Mrs. Clara Baker, wife of Norman Baker, at her farm three miles south of Trappe in Dorchester County. Further documentation is needed to determine if the execution took place and for information about the execution. According to newspaper accounts, Mrs. Baker let out a scream after Deputy Sheriff Howard Kinnamon presented Gibson's confession to the court, and her husband tried to get at the prisoner but was prevented by court attendants.[233]

On February 13, 1925, Gibson was executed by hanging at the Maryland Penitentiary.[234]

---

[230] *The Baltimore Sun*, "Talbot Negro Held on Assault Charge; Seized by "Home-Run" Baker after Alleged Attack on Ballplayer's Sister-in-Law," Aug. 28, 1924
[231] *The Evening Times*, Salisbury, Maryland, "Angry Mob Storm Jail to Lynch Negro; Easton People Surround Jail and Tear Down Doors to Find Negro," Aug. 30, 1924
[232] *The Baltimore Sun*, "Negro in Assault Case in City Jail," Aug. 30, 1924
[233] *The Baltimore Sun*, "Maryland Woman's Assailant To Hang; Negro Sentenced After Trial In Easton – Victim Becomes Hysterical In Court," Nov. 23, 1924
[234] *The Baltimore Sun*, "Negro Pays Death Penalty For Assaulting Woman," Feb. 13, 1925

Mob Law on Delmarva

Harry Merrill

Sentenced February 25, 1925 for crime in Somerset County, Maryland

On Saturday morning about eleven o'clock, December 13, 1924, Deputy Sheriff Louis (sometimes spelled Lewis) L. Dryden was found murdered and policeman Orrie J. Carey seriously wounded in the Wellington neighborhood of Somerset County, about four miles from Princess Anne, and a manhunt went out for the accused, Harry Merrill, aged either 21 or 22 depending on accounts.

Dryden was found dead about six miles from Princess Anne and Princess Anne Officer Orrie Carey was taken to the hospital in Salisbury with wounds to his back and leg. A posse of over 200 searched the woods for Harry Merrill. The December 13, 1924 edition of *The Evening Times* of Salisbury includes the following.

> *"A lynching is predicted if the fugitive is captured."*
>
> *December 13, 1924*
> The Evening Times, Salisbury

A lynching is predicted if the fugitive is captured. The wanted negro is 22 years old, 6 ft. tall, and weighs 165 lbs, has black mustache and was wearing blue overalls and jumper at the time of his escape.

Another negro, a companion of Merrill, was seriously shot by Officer Carey in the exchange of firing. Though dangerously wounded and bleeding profusely, Officer Carey drove his Ford car to Princess Anne and gave the alarm. The killing occurred about one o'clock when Warden Dryden, together with the Princess Anne policeman drove into the country to arrest Merrill for whom they held a warrant for shooting another negro. Arriving at the home of the negro, it is said that Dryden accosted his quarry and told him to accompany the officers back to town. Without warning, Merrill is alleged to have seized his captor's revolver and emptied its chambers in the direction of both white men. Dryden dropped instantly and Carey wounded, snatched his gun from the holster and fired at the fleeing negroes. Merrill escaped, but his partner fell to the ground.

The residents of the township formed a posse immediately upon hearing the news of the fracas and with local officers are searching the section for the alleged murderer. State police have been called upon to guard every outlet on the county and state highways leading from the place.[235]

---

[235] *The Evening Times*, Salisbury, Maryland, "Jail Warden Dryden Dead Posse Formed; Policeman Carey Probably Fatally Wounded – Another Negro Also Shot; Prisoner Seizes Gun and Turns on Captors; Somerset Citizens 200 Strong Scour Countryside For Fugitive – Lynching Predicted," Dec. 13, 1924

Chapter 11. Eastern Shore Cases

Merrill was captured and on December 15th and arrested at 11:45 a.m. by Deputy Sheriff James B. Sterling and Charles F. Dryden, the former Sheriff. It took about an hour for the news to reach Princess Anne; and upon hearing the news, talk of lynching increased. The December 15, 1924 edition of *The Evening Times* includes,

> Surrounding Sheriff Luther Daugherty about 1:30 the mob demanded to know where the prisoner had been taken. When informed that he was in the Salisbury jail, they demanded that he be brought back to Princess Anne. Sheriff Daugherty, according to reports, promised that the prisoner would be taken from the Salisbury jail at 2 o'clock and carried back there.
>
> Meanwhile several carloads of armed citizens left Princess Anne for Salisbury with the announced purpose of seeing the sheriff's promise executed.[236]

The *Marylander and Herald* provided more detail about Merrill's arrest and that he was transferred to the Salisbury jail. The newspaper describes the following.

> About three o'clock an automobile containing Sheriff Luther Daugherty, Deputy Sheriff Sterling and State's Attorney Harry C. Dashiell went to Salisbury, and when they arrived there immediately consulted with Judge Joseph L. Bailey, where they found that the judge had made all arrangements to have the prisoner transferred to the Baltimore City jail, and even while the conference was going on between the Sheriff's party and Judge Bailey, a Nash automobile, containing the two members of the Maryland State Police, slid up in front of the jail, and rushing Merrill into the car, darted away on its trip to Baltimore, where it arrived Monday night, and Merrill was lodged in the jail there.

On January 12, 1925, Merrill was indicted on three counts: once for the murder of Dryden, the second for assault with intent to kill Carey, and the third for intent to kill Clarence Hitch. Merrill remained held in the Baltimore jail during the Princess Anne proceedings. Judge Duer appointed Gordon Tull as Merrill's attorney. As reported in the January 17, 1925 edition of The *Maryland and Herald*, it was expected that Tull would seek a change of venue.

> State's Attorney Harry C. Dashiell said on Thursday that he had used every means in his power to have the case tried in Princess Anne, believing that our own courts were capable of taking care of our local cases, and also in an effort to save as much as possible in the costs of trying and convicting the negro. Mr. Dashiell further stated that he was confident that the negro would be just as safe in Princess Anne as he is

---

[236] *The Evening Times*, Salisbury, Maryland, "Negro Slayer Somerset Officer Is Captured In Swamp At 11:45 Today; Somerset Citizens Demand Prisoner Be Returned; Mob Rushes To This City Where Negro Was Taken; Their Plans Frustrated," Dec. 15, 1924

Mob Law on Delmarva

> in Baltimore, as far as any attempt being made by our citizens to take the law into their own hands, and that a considerable saving would have been made to the taxpayers of the county, as if the case is carried to Baltimore City, all the witnesses will have to be carried there at the time of the trial, together with other large items of expense in conducting the trial.[237]

The trial was transferred to Dorchester County, with Merrill's attorney asking for a court trial.[238] On February 25, 1925, Harry Merrill was found guilty and sentenced to life imprisonment. The February 28, 1925 edition of the *Maryland and Herald* reported the results of the trial and printed the statements of Merrill and of witnesses Orrie Carey, Clarence Hitch, Earle Ballard (son of John and Kate Ballard and a cousin of Merrill), and Kate Ballard. The newspaper's description of the rendering of the sentencing is as follows.

> Judge Patterson, in announcing the findings of the Court, stated that it was unanimous, but was rendered only after several hours of deliberation by the three judges. It is understood that there was some disagreement as to the infliction of capital punishment and an unanimous verdict was only reached by agreement upon life imprisonment.[239]

At the end of 1931 and beginning of 1932, Merrill was declared insane and removed to the "Hospital for colored insane" in Crownsville, Maryland.

> As he was escorted from his cell to be taken to the above institution, Merrill, who was suffering from a delusion that someone was trying to get him, drew a long knife from under his coat, plunged it into the abdomen of guard Samuel J. Bateman and rushed back to his cell.
>
> Warden Patrick J. Brady, accompanied by several guards followed the crazed negro to his cell and discharged a tear gas bomb through the bars at the same time demanding that Merrill give up the knife. The negro passed the knife through the bars and calmly came out and surrendered to one of the guards, who placed handcuffs on his wrists. He was then removed to the Hospital for the Insane without any further trouble."[240]

---

[237] *Marylander and Herald*, "Jury Finds Six Indictments, Merrill Is Charged With Murder of Louis L. Dryden," Jan. 17, 1925
[238] *Marylander and Herald*, "Merrill To Be Tried In Dorchester," Jan. 31, 1925
[239] *Marylander and Herald*, "Murder In First Degree, Verdict, Court Finds Harry Merrill Guilty and Sentences Him To Life Imprisonment In The Maryland Penitentiary," Feb. 28, 1925
[240] *The Crisfield Times*, "Somerset County Negro Serving Life Sentence Severely Wounds Guard, Plunges Knife into Abdomen of Penitentiary Official," January 9, 1932

Chapter 11. Eastern Shore Cases

Wilbur Barnes

Arrested November 1925 in Chestertown, Maryland

The Baltimore Sun of December 1, 1925 reports,

> Chestertown, Md., Nov. 30 (Special) – Quiet prevails tonight in the streets surrounding the Chestertown Jail, where Wilbur Barnes, Negro, 17, is being held for a hearing on a charge of an attack on a 9-year-old white girl. The danger of mob violence which threatened last night, when about twenty-five men congregated in front of the jail, now is past, in the opinion of Sheriff Goodman, but on the return from New York tonight of State's Attorney Beck it was deemed safer to take Barnes away, and he was sent to the Baltimore Jail.
>
> The attempted assaults with which Barnes is charged occurred yesterday on the farm of Barnes' employer at Quaker Neck, about seven miles from Chestertown. The victim was the farmer's daughter. She was slightly bruised and scratched.
>
> News of the alleged attack spread quickly through the countryside, and about 10 o'clock last night men began gathering in front of the jail and an attempt at lynching was feared. After conversing in low tones for a time the men dispersed quietly. There has been no evidence of contemplated violence today.[241]

The Baltimore Afro-American of December 5, 1925 reports, "Following the gathering of a mob in front of the Chestertown jail Sunday night, Wilbur Barnes, 17, accused of an attempted assault on a nine year old white girl, was brought here for safe keeping Monday."[242]

---

[241] *The Baltimore Sun*, "Accused Kent Negro Sent to Baltimore Jail," Dec. 1, 1925
[242] *The Baltimore Afro-American*, Baltimore, MD, "Lad Brought Here To Avoid Lynching," Dec. 5, 1925

Joshua Tiller

Sentenced January 1926 for crime near Millington, Maryland

The November 17, 1925, *The Baltimore Sun* reports that attempted lynching.

> *"A mob of between 200 and 300 men, who stormed the Centreville Jail tonight, forced its way into the residential section occupied by Sheriff T. Frank Seward in an attempt to lynch Joshua Tiller..."*
>
> November 17, 1925
> The Baltimore Sun

A mob of between 200 and 300 men, who stormed the Centreville Jail tonight, forced its way into the residential section occupied by Sheriff T. Frank Seward in an attempt to lynch Joshua Tiller, a Negro charged with attempting criminally to assault the 4-year-old daughter of a farmer who lives near Millington.

At midnight the crowd had dispersed, without accomplishing its object, except for several small groups of idlers who lounged on corners adjacent to the jail.

The jail was stormed after the mob had extinguished all the lights in courthouse square and had fired several shots into the air. When the mob advanced toward the jail door under cover of darkness, Madison Brown, State's attorney, pleaded with them to disperse, assuring them that speedy justice would be done.

Ignoring Mr. Brown's appeal, the mob surged on to the door leading into the section occupied by the sheriff. At this door were Sheriff Seward, Constables John P. Williamson and Louis B. Perkins, and Justice of the Peace Robert Coursey. None of these drew weapons nor attempted to resist forcibly the mob, which pushed them aside and went on through the door.

The mob was halted by five heavy steel-barred doors which separate the Sheriff's section of the building from the cells. Sheriff Seward had the keys to the doors, but the mob made no demand for them. The Sheriff's section is comparatively small, and after about seventy-five of the mob had crowded inside there was no room for more.

Those inside appeared to lack leadership and had brought no implements for cutting the bars. No rope was carried by any of them, so far as could be learned.[243]

Governor Ritchie was contacted and was assured by Mr. Brown, "who told him the crowd was dispersing after the child's father had pleaded

---

[243] *The Baltimore Sun*, "Mob of 200 Storms Centreville Jail—Attempt to Lynch Negro Accused of Assaulting Child Fails—Barred By Steel Doors—Crowd Disperses After Appeal By Victim's Father—Ritchie Sends State Police To Scene," Nov. 17, 1925

Chapter 11. Eastern Shore Cases

with them 'to go home and think it over.'" The Governor ordered extra protection for Tiller for the following day.

Tiller had been arrested November 16th at his home near Millington in Queen Anne's County and brought to the Centreville jail.[244]

The Baltimore Sun of January 5, 1926 reports the sentencing on January 4, 1926 of Joshua Tiller, tried in Elkton for the crime of attacking a 4-year-old daughter of a farmer near Millington. Tiller had been brought to Elkton from Baltimore for the trial. He was sentenced to fifteen years in the Maryland Penitentiary. Tiller had been taken to the Baltimore jail following threats after his arrest at Centreville.[245]

---

[244] *The Baltimore Sun*, "Child 4, Accuses Negro of Assault—Joshua Tiller Held in Centreville Jail For Alleged Crime—Girl Identifies Him—Victim is Daughter of Farmer For Whom Arrested Man Worked," Nov. 16, 1925
[245] *The Baltimore Sun*, "Fifteen Years For Assault On Child Near Millington," Jan. 5, 1926

Mob Law on Delmarva

Henry Butler
Executed February 1926 in Wilmington, Delaware
The following excerpt is from *The Baltimore Sun* February 6, 1926 edition.

> *"It was learned tonight that a meeting was held in Bridgeville last night and 500 men offered to go to Georgetown on Monday and remain during the trial of Butler. It was expressly stated that they would make no demonstration at the trial, but that if the Negro was not sentenced to be hanged there would be trouble. This was said to have been the final factor influencing the Governor to call out the troops."*
>
> *February 6, 1926*
> *The Baltimore Sun*

Wilmington, Del., Feb. 5 – To protect Henry Butler, Negro, who will be placed on trial in Georgetown on Monday, from mob violence, several batteries of the Delaware National Guard will be sent to the Sussex county seat on Sunday morning.

Butler is charged with feloniously assaulting a 12-year-old girl near Bridgeville January 21. The order for the guard mobilization was issued by Gov. Robert P. Robinson today from the room to which he has been confined by a serious illness for several weeks. His proclamation called upon all citizens to assist the military authorities of the State in preserving the public peace by refraining from loitering in the vicinity of Sussex County Courthouse in Georgetown.

Governor Robinson said it was not advisable to tell when Butler would be taken from the workhouse at Greenbank, near here. It was understood, however, that he would leave for Georgetown early Sunday morning, guarded by highway policemen, detectives and members of the militia.

This is the first time that the Delaware National Guard has been called out to protect a defendant on trial, but Governor Robinson thought it was necessary after the demonstration made by the mob at the Georgetown Jail when Butler was arrested and hurried to Greenbank for safekeeping.

It was learned tonight that a meeting was held in Bridgeville last night and 500 men offered to go to Georgetown on Monday and remain during the trial of Butler. It was expressly stated that they would make no demonstration at the trial, but that if the Negro was not sentenced to be hanged there would be trouble. This was said to have been the final factor influencing the Governor to call out the troops.

The last lynching in Delaware took place June 26, 1903, when George White, Negro, was taken from the Courthouse at Greenbank and burned

Chapter 11. Eastern Shore Cases

at the stake. He was waiting trial on a charge of feloniously assaulting a white schoolgirl.[246]

The February 27, 1926 edition of *The Baltimore Sun* reports,

> Georgetown, Del., Feb. 25 (Special). [note: the newspaper says the 25th and is likely an error; the execution was scheduled for the 26th] While upward of 8,000 men, women and children filed past the open gateway of the Sussex County Jail here this morning, the body of Harry Butler, 21-year-old Negro executed for an assault on Elnora Steinmetz, 12-year-old white girl, swung from the end of a heavy rope. The body was suspended for a few minutes less than two hours. It was then cut down, placed in a coffin and sent to the home of the youth's parents, at Cannons Crossing, near Bridgeville. ...
>
> A few seconds later the gate of the jail was opened and the one hundred witnesses, including newspaper men, official jury, physicians and officials departed.
>
> The immense crowd which surrounded the jail was then permitted to pass by the gate in single file to look at the hanging body. At 12.10 o'clock the gate was closed and the body cut down.
>
> The hanging of Butler was the first held in this county in twenty-nine years.
>
> Before he was led to the scaffold he gave the following message to the Rev. Henry Y. Arnett, colored, of Wilmington, to carry to his mother and wife: "Tell them good-by. I'm going to Heaven. The spirits tell me everything's all right."
>
> It was learned for the first time this morning that Butler is married. He said he married Amanda Brown, who lives near his home, six months ago.
>
> Butler will be buried tomorrow afternoon in Bethel, Md.[247]

---

[246] *The Baltimore Sun*, "Delaware Militia for Negro's Trial; Governor Orders Guardsmen Out To Protect Butler; Case Up Monday; Soldiers Report Today; Man Accused of Assaulting Girl Expected To Be Moved To Georgetown Tomorrow," Feb. 6, 1926
[247] *The Baltimore Sun*, "8,000 Gaze on Body of Hanged Negro, File By Gate Of Jail At Georgetown, Del., To View Harry Butler," Feb. 27, 1926

Mob Law on Delmarva

Unidentified Man

Lynched late 1920's in Queen Anne's County, Maryland

Cal Skinner was told by his father of his witnessing a lynching as a child, north of Centreville in Queen Anne's County, believed to have been on White Marsh Road where his father lived at that time. Skinner had contacted the Maryland Archives but there was no evidence of a lynching recorded. (2011).

Cal Skinner wrote,
"While my mother's family owned land, my father's did not. Roy Skinner was a carpenter and handyman of many skills, if his tools (including a cove molding device) in the basement are any indication, but often a farmer. One of the family's tenant farms (in high school) was next to my mothers.

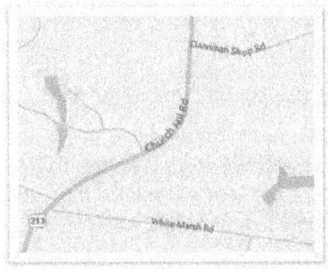

"Somewhere on White Marsh Road my father saw a lynching in the late 1920's. When my father was undergoing lung cancer treatment in Washington, we drove over to the Eastern Shore. As we went past one road at a bend in the highway between Centerville and Church Hill with a rundown building that appeared to have been a store on the west side of the intersection, Dad told me he used to live down it. It is south of Clanahan Shop (I think) Road. Dad said he knew Mr. Clanahan for whom it was named after. I see from the map it is White Marsh Road.

"He told of walking down the dirt road with his father. I gathered he was over ten but not in high school yet. That would have put it in the late 1920's, since he was born in 1916. 'What's that?' he asked, as he saw a crowd of men up ahead. 'Don't look at them. Just keep on walking,' his father said. It was a lynching. The road on which my father lived had both whites and blacks." (2011).

From the description, it is not surprising there was no information available from other sources, nor could I locate such a description for the time period and location described. If a person was never arrested or brought to town and jailed, newspapers would not be made aware of the case or the lynching.

Chapter 11. Eastern Shore Cases

George Davis
January 1932 for crime near Kennedyville, Maryland
More detailed information is detailed by Sherrilyn A. Ifill (2007).

> *"So insistent were numbers of those in the crowd that the Negro was in the jail that Sheriff John T. Vickers finally conducted a delegation of them through the jail doors and permitted them to make a thorough search of the cells before they were satisfied.*
>
> *"One man, identified as a prominent farmer of Cecil county, carried a long rope in his hand."*
>
> November 24, 1931
> The Baltimore Sun

George Davis was convicted of attempted assault on Elizabeth Lusby, 25, near Kennedyville several weeks earlier and sentenced to sixteen years imprisonment. There had been several unsuccessful attempts by mobs to lynch Davis, the events occurring during the time of mob violence towards Euel Lee and Matthew Williams.

As reported by *The Baltimore Sun* on November 22, 1931, a posse formed to search the area for George Davis, a farmhand alleged to have attacked Mrs. Edgar Lusby near Kennedyville. Davis' home was reported to be at Daois Hill, between Kennedyville and Galena.[248] *The Baltimore Sun* of November 24th reports

Chestertown, Md., Nov. 23 – A mob of 500 persons, among whom were some of the most prominent residents of Kent, Queen Anne's and Cecil counties, stormed the Kent county jail here tonight in an attempt to wreak vengeance upon George Davis, 28-year-old Negro, arrested today in Wilmington for an alleged attempt to attack Mrs. Elizabeth Lusby, who lives in the vicinity of Kennedysville, early Saturday morning. ...

So insistent were numbers of those in the crowd that the Negro was in the jail that Sheriff John T. Vickers finally conducted a delegation of them through the jail doors and permitted them to make a thorough search of the cells before they were satisfied.

One man, identified as a prominent farmer of Cecil county, carried a long rope in his hand.[249]

---

[248] *The Baltimore Sun*, "Shore Posse Seeks Woman's Attacker; George Davis Accused By Mrs. Edgar Lusby, Of Near Kennedyville," Nov. 22, 1931
[249] *The Baltimore Sun*, "Mob Storms Shore Jail Seeking Negro; 500 Stage Attempt To Wreak Vengeance On Alleged Attacker Of Woman," Nov. 24, 1931

Mob Law on Delmarva

The trial had been moved from Chestertown to Elkton, Maryland. The following is from the January 5, 1932 edition of *The Daily Banner*, Cambridge, Maryland, which reports on the beginning of the trial at Elkton.

> Elkton, Md., Jan. 5 – Heavily guarded by State and Baltimore City police riot squads, George Davis, 28 year old negro was placed on trial in Circuit Court here today, charged with an attempted attack on a Kent County white woman, wife of a Kennedyville farmer.
>
> The negro, who, according to officials confessed the attempted attack, entered a plea of not guilty before the three Judges of the Court, sitting without a jury. Davis, through his attorneys, had asked a trial without a jury at the time the case was brought here from Chestertown on a change of venue.
>
> Davis, held in the Baltimore City Jail since mob threats against him at Chestertown, Easton, and Elkton, was brought here by the State and City Police detail, heavily armed with riot guns and tear gas bombs.
>
> A crowd of several hundred persons milled around the courthouse as State's Attorney Stephen R. Collins of Kent County opened the case with a recital of the alleged attack. The crowd was orderly, and no demonstration was staged against the accused man.
>
> The change of venue for Davis was granted after the mob at Chestertown had searched the jail there and at Easton the night he was brought here from Wilmington where he was captured two days after the alleged attack.
>
> Davis' counsel were R. Hinson Rogers, of Kent County, and J.H.C. Legg, of Centreville.[250]

On January 6, 1932, Davis was sentenced to sixteen years. The January 6th edition of *The Daily Banner* reports on the sentencing and included the following.

> "This court doesn't agree with counsel for the state, that an attempt should punish ordinarily the same as a crime," Judge Adkins said in pronouncing sentence.
>
> "If that view was correct, we have been wrong all of these years in distinguishing between assault with intent to kill and murder. We realize that under the statutes the death penalty may be imposed, but we fell in the absence of fiendishness and brutally [sic] it should not be imposed in this case."

---

[250] *The Daily Banner*, Cambridge, MD, "George Davis Placed on Trial; George Davis, Negro, Was Placed On Trial In Circuit Court In Elkton Today, Charged With As Attempted Attack On Kent County Woman," Jan. 5, 1932

Chapter 11. Eastern Shore Cases

Judge Keating announced he did not agree with Judge Adkins and Judge Lewin Wicks.[251]

Ifill writes that prosecutors took "the extreme step of seeking the death penalty" for an attempted rape case although there was no evidence of physical harm. The prominence of the defense attorneys, the absence of jury trial, and division among the judges upon sentencing saved Davis' life. Ifill reports that the last penitentiary record showed that Davis was transferred to a prison farm at Hagerstown in 1942.

---

[251] *The Daily Banner*, Cambridge, MD, "Negro Sentenced to Sixteen Years; George Davis, Negro, Was Convicted of Attempted Assault On A Kent County Woman, And Began Serving A Sixteen Year Sentence Today," Jan. 6, 1932

Euel Lee, Matthew Williams and George Armwood
Williams lynched 1931; Armwood lynched and Lee executed in 1933

Euel Lee

The Euel Lee case spanned two years. He was arrested in Worcester County, Maryland, in October of 1931, and executed in November of 1933. During that time span, two lynchings occurred in nearby counties. Because of the timing and proximity of the events, and historical connections, the three cases are often linked or described in published histories. Other cases occupied the news during that time, such as the aforementioned George Davis case of Kent County, as well as lesser known cases of violence.

The cases have been researched by other historians, including authors Sherrilyn A. Ifill (2007), Joseph E. Moore (2006), Jack R. Wennersten (1992), C. Fraser Smith (2008), and Meredith Ramsay (2013 Revised Edition), and as individual cases detailed by others.

On October 12, 1931, Green K. Davis, his wife and two daughters were found dead in their home located near Taylorville. Davis operated a produce stand at their home on the road between Berlin and Ocean City. The next day Lee, known to work for Davis, was arrested where he rented a room in Ocean City. He was taken first to Berlin, then to the jail in Snow Hill where statements were taken from him after hours of interrogation, then removed to Baltimore, narrowly avoiding mobs. The October 31, 1931 issue of the *Baltimore Afro-American* reports,

> A mob, estimated as between 300 and 500 men, gathered about the Snow Hill jail, and left only after Warden Ernest West had allowed them to search the jail for their intended victim. A number of them then proceeded to Pocomoke City and demanded that they be told the whereabouts of the accused man.[252]

> *"It was also reported that a mob of whites stoned Earle Douglass as he was on the way to secure a doctor for his sick wife. Many other citizens, who were caught on the street, it was said, had to flee into stores to avoid the attack of the whites who were milling about the streets in an angry mood..."*
>
> October 24, 1931
> Baltimore Afro-American

---

[252] *Baltimore Afro-American*, "Sho' Mob Waits for Accused Orphan Jones," Oct. 31, 1931

Chapter 11. Eastern Shore Cases

The *Baltimore Afro-American* of October 24, 1931 includes the following about violence in Berlin.

> Berlin, Md. – Reports that many whites on the Eastern Shore in the vicinity of the murder of Green Davis and his family, are terrorizing colored citizens, were denied by Mayor Quillen of this town, to a representative of the Afro-American, Monday.
>
> Citizens here, however, told the Afro-American that all colored citizens were warned to stay off the streets Saturday night after more than 50 whites had attacked Purnell Leonard, 30, and his wife, Mrs. Mattie Leonard, 24, on the streets of the city.
>
> It was also reported that a mob of whites stoned Earle Douglass as he was on the way to secure a doctor for his sick wife. Many other citizens, who were caught on the street, it was said, had to flee into stores to avoid the attack of the whites who were milling about the streets in an angry mood. ...
>
> Although Mayor Quillen denied the riot story, the Afro-American learned that a number of white citizens had been sworn in for special police duty.
>
> Ben Parsons, white, charged with leading the mob which attacked Leonard and his wife, has been arrested, according to the Mayor, and will be tried this week.[253]

Another mob again gathered in Snow Hill, at the courthouse on November 4th, as reported by *The Baltimore Sun*.

> A Worcester county mob, thwarted in three attempts to gain possession of Yuel [sic] Lee, ... turned on Bernard Ades, of Baltimore, attorney for the International Labor Defense League and voluntary counsel for Lee.
>
> Twice during the day, Ades and two companions, one a woman "protector," were attacked by the mob. After the second attack, Ades and his companions left Snow Hill for Baltimore, promising never to return.
>
> The second and more serious demonstration came as Ades, with Miss Helen Mays and Oscar Rabowsky, attempted to leave the courthouse when Circuit Court was adjourned. The mob attacked the trio and beat them severely before they were rescued by Judge Joseph Bailey of Circuit Court.
>
> Earlier in the day Ades and Miss Mays were accosted by part of the mob in a lunchroom and ordered to leave town. They were rescued by officials of the Sheriff's office....[254]

---

[253] *Baltimore Afro-American*, "Berlin Mayor Denies Riot Stories," October 24, 1931
[254] *The Baltimore Sun*, "Snow Hill Mob Beats Lawyer Aiding Negro," Nov. 5, 1931

Mob Law on Delmarva

The case was controversial not only for the inflammatory nature of the crime and the missed opportunities to lynch Lee, but also for the outside influence of the International Defense League, a communist organization providing defense services including defense of the nationally-reported case of the Scottsboro trials which began after the arrests of several African American youths in Alabama earlier in the year. Bernard Ades, who worked out of the Baltimore branch of the ILD, sought to be Lee's counsel.

Another mob formed in Snow Hill on November 5th, as reported by *The Baltimore Sun*.

> As a crowd of between 200 and 300 men gathered on the lawn in front of the courthouse and in nearby streets late tonight, Sheriff Randolph Purnell posted armed guards to prevent disorder.
>
> A rumor was current in the town that Yuel [*sic*] Lee...would be in court at 9 o'clock tomorrow morning, though there was no official confirmation... Describing the crowd tonight as made up of local men, officers on duty pointed to an absence of automobiles on the streets.[255]

After becoming Lee's counsel, Ades worked to get a change of venue for the case. Failing to get the trial removed off of the Eastern Shore, Lee's trial was set to be held in Cambridge on Tuesday, December 8, 1931.[256] But something unexpected happened, on December 4, the lynching of Matthew Williams in Salisbury, Maryland.

Matthew Williams

The December 4, 1931 lynching of Matthew Williams in Salisbury delayed the scheduled Lee trial, further strengthening Ade's case for removal of the trial off of the Eastern Shore. Interestingly, the newspaper accounts and legal decisions reported after the December 4th lynching came to a consensus of opinion for the removal of the Lee case off of Delmarva without pointing to the lynching as the impetus or cause for the decision, or even a significance influence. It's as if the elephant in the room was not seen to be the cause for the need for more space. Even the Salisbury newspaper reversed its position on the location of the Lee trial, stating,

---

[255] *The Baltimore Sun*, "Snow Hill Mob Forms; Armed Guard Posted," Nov. 6, 1931
[256] *The Baltimore Sun*, "Plans for Lee Trial Tuesday Progressing, Ades Gets No Reply To His Efforts To Halt Proceedings," Dec. 4, 1931

Chapter 11. Eastern Shore Cases

"In asking for removal we reverse the stand we took a few weeks ago in advocating the trial be held in the First Judicial circuit...."[257]

A "few weeks ago" Matthew Williams of Salisbury was still alive.

> *"Ain't that a damn shame that nigger died so soon. There was going to be some fun here tonight."*
>
> [quote from a bystander when it was first erroneously reported that Williams had died from his wounds]
>
> *December 12, 1931*
> Baltimore Afro-American

Figure 30 Matthew Williams
The Baltimore Afro-American, December 12, 1931

Matthew Williams, 23, was born in Norfolk in 1908, to Annie and Harry Williams. His mother died when Matthew was four years old, after which he and his sister Olivia were sent to Salisbury to live with their maternal grandmother, Mrs. Mary Handy. A year after starting school, Matthew's father died. Matthew stopped attending school when he was fourteen in order to help support the family. By December of 1931, he was living on Isabella Avenue with his aunt, Mrs. Addie Black. "Buddie," she called him, took a job at the box and crate factory owned by Daniel Elliott.

What happened that Friday afternoon, December 4th, became the subject of speculation and rumor. What is known for sure is that Williams was at the box and crate business of Daniel J. Elliott, aged 67, located on Lake Street, not far from William's home. Williams would be accused of murdering his employer, but other reports indicate that the elder Elliot was shot by his son (A. Smith, 116-125). What is known is that Williams was wounded by gun fire and taken to the hospital from which he was dragged and lynched.

---

[257] *The Baltimore Sun*, "Shore Paper Asks Removal of Lee Trial, Salisbury Times Says Justice Would Be Served Best on Western Side," Jan. 1, 1932

Mob Law on Delmarva

The *Baltimore Afro-American* reported on the statement of an eyewitness, Howard A. Nelson, of South Philadelphia, of his experience following the killing of Elliott. Nelson was described as having light skin, light enough to pass or be thought of as white. Nelson's statement as reported by the newspaper is as follows.[258]

> *"Two types of mobs participated in the hanging and burning – one a serious and silent group intent only on murder, 'and the other a group of youngsters out for an orgy of brutality on a veritable Roman holiday.'"*
>
> *December 5, 1931*
> **The Baltimore Post**

I arrived at Salisbury Thursday afternoon on a business trip. Early Friday I went to Princess Anne and returned late in the afternoon. I was standing talking to an acquaintance on Main Street about the killing of that man Elliott, when I noticed a group of men milling about the front of the town paper, the Salisbury Times. When I had finished my conversation, I went over to read the bulletin.

I read the bulletin that was posted on the front of the building. It read: "Nigger is Dead. The nigger who murdered Mr. Elliott, a prominent citizen, has been reported as being dead."

While I was reading this, a white man who was standing by mistook me for one of them and said, "Ain't that a damn shame that nigger died so soon. There was going to be some fun here tonight." Just about that time another bulletin was posted. It read: "The statement made by officials that the Negro was dead is false. A message just received says that he is improving."

The men stood there for about five minutes. They stood talking in groups; more persons read that bulletin, and the crowd grew ever so thick. Almost like an explosion, some one yelled, "Let's go to the hospital and get this nigger and lynch him."

Almost as though it was a military command, the crowd started toward the hospital. I followed along to see what was going to happen.

The white man who was walking along side of me said: "It's going to be good to see that nigger swing."

When we arrived at the hospital, there was some man who asked the mob not to bother Williams. The crowd started to curse and swear and then a man said to be Dr. Dix [sic] came outside and asked the men to be quiet as there were many dangerously ill persons in the hospital. By that time a group of men – just how many I don't know – had gotten in the hospital and seized Williams. The colored ward is on the first floor towards the rear of the building.

---

[258] *The Baltimore Afro-American*, Baltimore, MD, "Eye Witness to Lynching Tells How Mob Acted," Dec. 12, 1931

Chapter 11. Eastern Shore Cases

> Instead of carrying his body through the door, the men threw him out of the first floor window to a large group of men. Williams had on the regulation hospital gown and his head was swathed in bandages which covered his eyes and his feet were bare.
>
> Seemingly in a semi-conscious condition, the fellow was dragged to the court house lawn...[258]

The December 5th edition of *The Baltimore Post* includes photographs of the courthouse and the site of where the body was burned. The *Post* includes the following description.

> The Negro was dragged from a hospital cot about 8 p.m. and hanged to a limb of a tree in the Courthouse square by a mob of more than 2,000 persons.
>
> Later the body was dragged a quarter of a mile through the business section to a Negro subdivision, saturated with 40 gallons of gasoline and burned.
>
> Two types of mobs participated in the hanging and burning – one a serious and silent group intent only on murder, "and the other a group of youngsters out for an orgy of brutality on a veritable Roman holiday." [no source attributed to the specific quote]
>
> The lynching took place in the very shadow of a large Salisbury Community Fund banner, bearing the picture of Jesus Christ with arms appealingly outstretched. The banner, draped across the Courthouse square, carries the plea:
>
> "He Who Gives All Feeds Three – Himself, His Hungry Neighbor and Me."[259]

The Baltimore Sun includes a description by Sheriff Phillips, "After the mob had cut the Negro down after the lynching I attempted to recover the body, but the mob over-powered me, retrieved the Negro and carried him a few blocks distant, where the cremation took place."[260]

The Baltimore Afro-American reported that at the vacant lot where the body was burned, mob members took 45 gallons of gas from a nearby garage for the burning.[261]

---

[259] *The Baltimore Post*, Dec. 5, 1931
[260] *The Baltimore Sun*, "'Shore Mob Lynches Negro," Dec. 5, 1931
[261] *The Baltimore Afro-American*, from the caption of photographs, Dec. 12, 1931

Mob Law on Delmarva

Figure 31 Image of Salisbury courthouse and sign near site of lynching

Taken of the courthouse in Salisbury following the lynching of Matthew Williams. The lynching tree was to the right, out of view of the photograph, *Baltimore Post*, December 5, 1931

The Baltimore Sun further describes,

> More than 2,000 persons, most of them members of the mob which had witnessed the hanging, but many new recruits, grouped around the pyre. They did not disperse until the last flame had flickered out.

The Baltimore Afro-American of December 12th reports that after the burning, the body was dragged through town to a lamppost. The newspaper reporter described the charred body, reporting, "With this hideous form the mob leaders toyed and made sport like a cat with a mouse for about five hours."[262]

---

[262] *The Baltimore Afro-American*, "Salisbury Mob Played 5 Hours," Dec. 12, 1931

Chapter 11. Eastern Shore Cases

The Baltimore Afro-American of March 12, 1932, includes an account from an unidentified eyewitness in a letter obtained by the Crusader News Agency. The following is from that account.

> "First they dragged him to the court house square and hanged him, then they cut him down, tied the rope to the back of an auto, and dragged him to the Negro section of the town. They then got about 40 or 50 gallons of gasoline, but before they threw this gas over him, they cut off his fingers and oes, threw them on the porches and in the yards of the colored people's homes, shouting these remarks, that they (the colored people) could make 'nigger' sandwiches out of them. Then they threw the gas over him, set a match to him, and while the human tourch burned, they passed booze around, drinking and shouting...."[263]

Unidentified Murder Victim

A lesser-known murder occurred the day after the lynching of Matthew Williams. If it had not been for the *Baltimore Afro-American*, the second murder might never have been known or reported, even though the victim had been buried in Salisbury's Potters Field. To date, the murdered man is publically unidentified. The following is from *The Baltimore Afro-American*, December 12, 1931.

> With the lust for blood still running high in this mob-ridden community, the dead body of an unidentified man was found badly mutilated and slashed early Sunday morning.
>
> There are many mysterious elements surrounding the man's death. The identity and finding of the man's body at College Avenue and Railroad Streets has caused beliefs and rumors that the man was attacked and fatally injured by a group of blood-thirsty whites who were out to get any unprotected colored person seen on the streets Saturday night.
>
> It was learned that a telephone call was sent to police officials early Sunday morning stating that the body of a man could be found at the location which is near the dividing lines of the white and colored residential sections. The sender of the call refused to disclose his identity.
>
> Examination of the body by Afro-American reporters showed that the man's skull was fractured on the right side and the entire left side of his face was also crushed. On the right side there was a long, deep gash along the templar region, similar to a wound inflicted by a heavy sharp instrument. Rigor mortis had set in, with the man's arms lifted as though to ward off a blow.

---

[263] *The Baltimore Afro-American*, "Lynched Man's Fingers, Toes, Used to Make 'Nigger Sandwich,'" Mar. 12, 1932

No bullet wounds could be found on the body nor the head, which was covered with blood. The wound on the head was two inches deep and about six inches long.

Near the body was a half of a ham which was wrapped in brown paper, and a piece of bacon. It is believe that the man went to a store Saturday night after officials of the city had advised all colored citizens to stay off the street. It is believed that while he was marketing, he was set upon by a group of the whites who badly wounded him and carried him to the spot where he was found. No witnesses to the crime could be found.

According to information, there was little blood at the intersection where he was found, which is a short distance from the N.Y. and P. and A. railroad, although the man's face and clothing showed that he bled freely.

The man is about 35 years of age, 5 feet 7 inches tall, 160 pounds in weight, dark brown skin. He was dressed in overalls, jumper and a brown khaki shirt, with badly worn army shoes.

Officials made an attempt to keep the finding of the man's body a secret. Later Sunday afternoon, three white men riding in a taxicab made inquiries as to whether the body had been found or not.

They approached a group of colored citizens at a corner adjacent to where the man's body was awaiting a coroner's inquest at the establishment of James Stewart. After questioning members of the group, the men got back into their taxicab and hurried away. They made no attempt to visit the undertaking establishment or make inquiries of Mr. Stewart.[264]

The death certificate for this victim lists the man as unidentified and was buried in the City Cemetery, often referred to as the Potter's Field.

Euel Lee

The trial for Euel Lee was held in Towson, Maryland, in January of 1932. In that month, Lee was found guilty[265] and sentenced to hang.[266] The trial was followed by appeals and the status of the appeals were reported locally for months. Euel Lee was still alive at the time of the Eastern Shore's next lynching, of George Armwood on October 18, 1933 in Princess Anne, Maryland.

---

[264] *The Baltimore Afro-American*, "Mystery Death Believed to be Second Mob Victim, Shore Lynchers May have had Second Victim, Man Found with Skull Broken After Demonstration," Dec. 12, 1931
[265] *The Baltimore Sun*, "Euel Lee Found Guilty of Killing Davis, Pleads Next Week for New Trial," Jan. 21, 1932
[266] *The Baltimore Sun*, "ToAppeal Death Penalty for Lee," Jan. 29, 1932

Chapter 11. Eastern Shore Cases

George Armwood

On Monday, October 16, 1933, George Armwood was arrested for the crime of sexual assault of Mary Denston near Manokin in Somerset County. He had been located in Worcester County, near Pocomoke. *The Baltimore Sun* of October 18th reports,

> Lieutenant Ridgely placed Armwood in a State Police automobile and eluded the aroused residents of the countryside by taking the prisoner to the Salisbury Jail by way of Snow Hill. The party had been at the jail only a few minutes, however, when a crowd formed around the door.
>
> The police again placed their prisoner in a machine and set out for Baltimore....[267]

Following the arrest of George Armwood, he was transported to Baltimore for safekeeping, stopping first in Salisbury where he was photographed. Shown left to right are Lieut. James Itzel, George Armwood, and Lieut. Ruxton Ridgely.[268]

Figure 32 George Armwood being transported following arrest

From *The Baltimore Afro-American* dated October 21, 1933. Portion of caption reads, "Exactly in the same spot where Matthew Williams was lynched two years ago, this man, manacled helplessly, missed the same fate by the skin of his teeth last Monday night when a mob in Salisbury grabbed at him as state cops snatched him in their auto and made a flying trip to Baltimore. Left to right: Lieut. James Itzel, George Armwood...."

---

[267] *The Baltimore Sun*, "Police Squads Escort Negro Back to Shore," Oct. 18, 1933
[268] *The Baltimore Afro-American*, "Maryland Prisoner Snatched from Ready Eastern Shore Mob," Oct. 21, 1933

Mob Law on Delmarva

The Baltimore Sun of October 18th also reports that late Tuesday evening, Armwood was transferred from the Baltimore city jail back to Princess Anne, in an entourage of five automobiles which included state policemen and Somerset County Sheriff Luther Daugherty.

Armwood was delivered to the jail in Princess Anne in the early hours of Wednesday October 18, before sun-up.

Eldon Hayman's sister, Carlyn Juanita Hayman-Bingham (1916-2003), a young student at that time, described the day of Armwood's arrival as one of unusual activity. After lunch her teacher dismissed class early, and gave specific instructions for how and what routes students were to walk home. In a description she later wrote about the day, she described that the fire siren "shrieked and wailed." The siren blew much of the day and a bullhorn could be heard blaring announcements. Her father had spent the night inside of the courthouse and later described from his vantage in town, that the bullhorn announcer had been announcing, "All niggers clear the streets. All niggers clear the streets. Get out of town right away." In her narrative about that time, she describes the mob.

> They stampeded the streets. Ran wild! They forced Negroes who lived near the jail to leave their homes. They broke down the doors on one of these houses and made it their headquarters for serving donuts and coffee to the mob.[269]

The Baltimore Afro-American reports, "Some of the residents in the town proper declared that they saw the body as it was being dragged through the streets while the lynchers marched to the tune of a popular song."[270] The title of that song was not identified.

Armwood was dragged or marched through the main street along the two or three blocks of the downtown, then through part of the residential where he was hanged from a tree. His body was cut down and dragged back into the center of town where his body was set on fire at the intersection of Main and Prince Williams streets, near the county courthouse and downtown businesses.

The October 28th issue of *The Baltimore Afro-American* reports,

> Princess Anne, Md. – The town took on a festive atmosphere when a mob, estimated at 2,000, participated in the lynching of George Armwood, Wednesday night. …..

---

[269] Carlyn Juanita Hayman-Bingham, "That Awful Day," date not specified
[270] *The Baltimore Afro-American*, Baltimore, MD, "AFRO First on Lynch Scene," Oct. 28, 1933

Chapter 11. Eastern Shore Cases

> After they succeeded in taking the prisoner from the jail, many of them went home for small children and brought them to view the scene.
>
> A little girl who protested against watching was [scolded] by her mother and told to come and "watch the N----- being barbecued."
>
> Another man, when asked by his small son what was a lynching, was about to reply when he discovered the house near which he was passing had colored residents and were listening so he refrained.
>
> All in all, it had the general atmosphere of a bloody carnival. Boys just out of their teens were seen to help in wielding the battering ram which demolished the door of the jail.
>
> A student who lives nearby declared that he heard an anguished cry of "My God, it ain't me!" when attackers went in search of the victim and got into the wrong cell. ....[271]

The Baltimore Sun of October 19, 1933, provides the following description.

> With battering rams they beat in the doors, broke into the Negro's cell and, after slipping a noose around his neck, dragged him for a mile through the town at the end of a fifty-foot length of rope.
>
> The State police, their force of twenty officers reduced to a handful of injuries sustained in defense of the jail, were powerless to stop the surging mass that swept down the main street to the home of Judge Robert F. Duer, associate judge of the First judicial circuit.
>
> There they debated whether to hang the Negro on the jurist's front lawn, decided against it, and continued to the lawn of another home, threw the end of the rope over a high limb and pulled the body from the ground. It was limp.
>
> An attempt was made to burn the body, but failed, and it was lowered and the procession doubled back on the path passing again through the business section of the town. The march ended, gasoline was poured over the body, from which all of vestige of clothing had been stripped, and a match was applied amid the frenzied shouts of the mob.
>
> The rope was measured off into five-inch lengths and distributed to members of the mob as souvenirs. A young boy darted about wildly waving a severed ear of the lynch victim.[272]

After about three hours, Armwood's body was removed and dumped in a lumber yard a block away. The day after the lynching, *Baltimore Afro-American* reporters photographed the body; the photograph appeared on the front page of the October 28th edition of the newspaper. The caption

---

[271] *The Baltimore Afro-American*, Baltimore, MD, "Roman Holiday as Armwood is Hanged, Burned," Oct. 28, 1933

[272] *The Baltimore Sun*, "Shore Mob Lynches Negro: Drags Him to His Death From Princess Anne Jail," Oct. 19, 1933

Mob Law on Delmarva

of the photograph: "George Armwood 'a la Maryland.' His body was found by AFRO reporters at 6:30 Thursday morning in a lumber yard in Princess Anne, Md., after 2,000 of Maryland's 'best' staged their 'barbecue' in front of the courthouse. He had been hanged to a telegraph wire and burned in gasoline. White spots show huge blisters raised by the fire. Women and children, modest under normal circumstances, pressed to gaze at a naked, tortured body."

Figure 33 Body of George Armwood at lumber yard
From *The Baltimore Afro-American* of October 28, 1933.

Chapter 11. Eastern Shore Cases

Euel Lee

The day after George Armwood was lynched in Princess Anne, Governor Ritchie signed the death warrant for Euel Lee who was executed at the Maryland Penitentiary in Baltimore. Clarence Mitchell, then a reporter for the *Baltimore Afro-American* newspaper and who only days before had traveled to Princess Anne to report on the aftermath of the lynching, was in Baltimore and reported on Lee's execution. In the November 4, 1933 edition of the *Baltimore Afro-American* with the heading "Crowd Outside Makes Merry as Lee Dies," Mitchell reported on Lee's last day.[273]

In this Saturday edition of newspaper, Mitchell describes the crowd on the Friday of Lee's execution, noting, "Hard-faced men from the Eastern Shore and Baltimoreans, one by one, entered the iron gateway which closed behind each man to prevent any sudden or intrusive arrivals." Mitchell further noted,

> Only here and there comments dropped about Euel Lee, while the recent lynching of George Armwood figured largely in the current conversation. "Well," said an Irishman who was chewing on some unknown substance, "they sure did that fellow up bad the other day down at Princess Anne." His companion answered, "Not half as bad as--" and as an AFRO reporter moved a little closer, he failed to finish the statement.

George Armwood

The lynching of George Armwood did not end the mob threat. On November 28, 1933, four men were arrested for lynching of Armwood and delivered first to Salisbury and then to the Baltimore jail. In Salisbury, the prisoners were held in the Armory where they were being guarded before transporting to Baltimore. *The Baltimore Sun* of November 29, 1933 reports,

> Quiet was restored here tonight after a mob of several thousand Eastern Shoremen earlier in the day had engaged a force of 300 National Guardsmen in a pitched battle to prevent the delivery of four men held prisoners in the Salisbury Armory as suspects in the George Armwood lynching.
>
> After battling the mob for more than hour in the streets about the building, the troops, with tear-gas bombs and fixed bayonets, managed to repulse the crowds sufficiently to move the prisoners out in busses toward Baltimore.
>
> The crowds hurled showers of brick-bats at the soldiers, blocked the busses for a time with a fire engine, turned fire hoses on the picket lines

---

[273] *Baltimore Afro-American*, "Crowd Outside Makes Merry as Lee Dies," Nov. 4, 1933

> about the armory and later attacked out-of-town newspaper reporters and photographers, smashing their cameras, beating several men and overturning automobiles.
>
> As Attorney-General William Preston Lane, Jr., was driving away from the Armory his car was stoned and he narrowly missed being struck by a large rock that almost crashed through the top of the machine.
>
> Burning wads of waste were thrown on the roof of a low building alongside the hotel where some newspaper men took refuge, but the flames were extinguished before they spread.
>
> After the guardsmen from nearby towns—the fight reached its climax. Members of the mob attempted to close in on the soldiers despite the bayonets that gleamed in their faces.
>
> Realizing that a crisis had been reached, Brig. Gen. Milton A. Reckord, Adjutant-General of Maryland, issued his final order of the engagement:
>
> "We will keep our prisoners if we have to shoot somebody." ...[274]

The crisis soon passed without firing on the crowd. The suspects were loaded onto a bus around which safety had been secured. However, as *The Baltimore Sun* reports, "In the street toward which the busses were headed, however, and upon which the armory faces, there was a surging crowd of Shoremen—some displaying pistols and one a sawed-off shotgun." National Guardsmen protected the bus against assault and used more tear-gas.

As described by *The Baltimore Sun*,

> There had been threats all day against newspaper men in general, and there had been efforts to take away the photographers' cameras during the morning. As feeling grew stronger and the difficulties of the guardsmen increased, some anxiety began to develop around noon for the safety of the press group in the hotel.
>
> Then a crowd of about 100 Shoremen entered the lobby—bent on finding the Attorney-General. After they had required the hotel manager, O. G. Clements, to take oath that Mr. Lane wasn't there, they demanded to be allowed to search the building. Inspecting the register, they also demanded to know what persons were in town from Baltimore.
>
> They were persuaded not to carry out the search and the cards showing no registrations from Baltimore. After they had left the management escorted the newspaper men to the seventh floor of the hotel and concealed them.
>
> They remained at the hotel for a long time until the ranks of the mob had thinned, and finally left the hotel one by one through various doors.

---

[274] *The Baltimore Sun*, "Shore Mob Attacks Lane After Battle With Troops," Nov. 29, 1933

Chapter 11. Eastern Shore Cases

Meanwhile on the street the crowds spotted an automobile bearing District of Columbia tags. They overturned the machine and set it afire. With the engine house only about a block away, the car was allowed to burn and it was reported ruined. Later another car, also from Washington and containing newspaper equipment, was set afire on Main street and the mob watched it burn.

Another car, owned by Henry T. Ward, of Baltimore, who rented five machines to the advance guard for the trip to Salisbury Monday night, was ignited by a tear-gas bomb and considerably damaged.

Sam Jones

Acquitted February 1934 for crime in Somerset County, Maryland

Little over two months after the lynching of George Armwood in Somerset County, Mrs. Margaret Brumbley was found murdered in her home at Marion Station, on New Year's Eve. Three men were questioned, including Brumbley's husband Fred Brumbley, and two black men, Sam and his son James Jones who lived nearby.[275][276]

The *Marylander and Herald* of January 19, 1934 reports,

> Mrs. Margaret Brumbley took place at the Brumbley home near Marion Station on the night of December 31st, the body being discovered by her husband, Fred Brumbley, upon his return home from Crisfield.
>
> Authorities investigating the crime, arrested Sam Jones and his son, James, and carried them to Crisfield for questioning. Subsequently they were released, and Baltimore detectives called in to aid in the investigation, and evidence turned up by these men led to the re-arrest of Sam Jones, charged with the murder.
>
> Jones was taken to the Baltimore City Jail by Sheriff Luther Daugherty, where he is confined at present....[277]

---

[275] *The Baltimore Sun*, "Arrest Deferred In Shore Murder. Officers Expect Developments In Brumbley Investigation Today. Detectives On Scene. Three Persons Questioned In Check On Husband's Account Of Finding Body," Jan. 4, 1934
[276] *The Baltimore Sun*, "Shore Murder Probe Delayed By Fear of Mob," Jan. 5, 1934
[277] *Marylander and Herald*, Princess Anne, MD, "Grand Jury Ends Probe of Armwood Lynching Here On Tuesday, Jan. 23; Brumbley Murder Investigation Consumes Entire Day Wednesday," Jan. 19, 1934

Mob Law on Delmarva

In the aftermath of the Armwood lynching of October 1933 the Brumbley murder and Jones' arrest shared the headlines with accounts of the Armwood case. The grand jury probe investigating the Armwood lynching occupied much of January of 1934. On Wednesday, January 17th the grand jury probe of the Brumbley murder began but was partially delayed by the Armwood grand jury hearings. The Brumbley hearings with the hearings continued after the Armwood hearings ended on January 23, 1934.

The Baltimore Sun of February 4, 1934 reports,

> Princess Anne, Md., Feb. 3 – Declaring he felt no uneasiness for the safety of his client, State Senator L. Creston Beauchamp, attorney for Sam Jones, Negro, charged with the murder of Mrs. Margaret Brumbley, today announced that Jones will be brought to Princess Anne next week for trial."[278]

On February 4th, Jones was transported to Princess Anne for trial, lodged in the jail from which George Armwood had been dragged little over three months earlier. Referring to Jones being held in Baltimore prior to trial, *The Baltimore Sun* of February 5th reports that Jones "was hurried to Baltimore when Somerset county officers heard rumors of the formation at Marion Station, where Mrs. Brumbley lived, of a mob of some 500 person." Still, according to the newspaper, Jones' attorney "felt no uneasiness for Jones' safety."[279]

Jones was acquitted of the charge on February 6, 1934. *The Baltimore Sun* of February 7th reports,

> Princess Anne, Md., Feb. 6 – Sam Jones, 55-year-old Negro, was acquitted in Somerset County Circuit Court early tonight of a charge of murdering Mrs. Margaret Brumbley at Marion Station last New Year's Eve.
>
> Jones appeared dazed when the verdict was returned. He had to be told twice that he was free.
>
> There was only a slight rustle among the spectators in the courtroom as the decision of the jury was announced...
>
> From the witness stand this morning Jones had denied any knowledge of the murder and presented an alibi showing he was at the home of Frank Borden, who lives near the Brumbley home, at the time doctors estimated Mrs. Brumbley was killed.[280]

---

[278] *The Baltimore Sun*, "Asserts Negro Will Be Tried in Somerset," Feb. 4, 1934
[279] *The Baltimore Sun*, "Negro Taken Back to Shore for Trial," Feb. 5, 1934
[280] *The Baltimore Sun*, "Shore Negro Freed by Jury in Murder Case," Feb. 7, 1934

Chapter 11. Eastern Shore Cases

The Baltimore Afro-American of February 17, 1934 reports,

> Princess Anne, Md. – After the sheriff testified that bloody clothing found in the home of Sam Jones, 55, suspected of the murder of Mrs. Margaret Brumbley, white farm wife, New Year's Eve, had evidently been planted there, the suspect was freed by a jury of white men here, February 6.
>
> The sheriff told the court that on two previous searches of Jones's home, the clothing had not been present. It was found there upon the third search.
>
> Charles H. Houston, Howard law school dean and NAACP legal staff member, conferred on the case with Jones's attorney, State Senator L. Preston Beauchamp.
>
> The fact that the acquittal was made on the spot where a lynching had taken place 100 days ago (George Armwood) has caused considerable comment.[281]

---

[281] *The Baltimore Afro-American*, "Bloody Clothes are Planted in Jones's Home," Feb. 17, 1934

Mob Law on Delmarva

Howard McClendon, alias Harry Flemming

Sentenced July 1934 for crime in Crisfield, Maryland

In Somerset County, on the heels of the Armwood and Brumbley cases, Patrolman Harry Daugherty was killed.

Upon arrest, the accused's name was reported as Harry Flemming, but later reported as Howard McClelland, then finally as Howard McClendon. The last account located in *The Baltimore Sun*, dated Jul. 21, of either name is that McClelland was charged in Princess Anne, with the murder of Patrolman Harry Daugherty at Crisfield on Apr. 28, 1934.[282]

The Baltimore Sun of April 30, 1934 reports,

> Crisfield, Md., Monday, April 30 – As a posse of from 500 to 1,000 men searched the woods for Harry Flemming, Negro accused of shooting Patrolman Harry Daugherty here last night, officers were advised to guard against violence should the Negro be caught. ...
>
> Feeling ran high as men assembled from miles around and beat the swamps for the fugitive. He was thought to be surrounded in a wooded section early this morning.
>
> "I don't think there will be any lynching," Mayor William H. Bradshaw said as he surveyed the crowd. "I told the officers to do all they can to prevent any trouble," he added.
>
> The Mayor said he had advised Sheriff Luther Daugherty "not to stop until you get to Baltimore" if officers found the Negro.
>
> Crisfield is in Somerset county, sixteen miles from Princess Anne, where a Negro was lynched last October.
>
> Search parties assembled rapidly after Daugherty was found lying unconscious in the Negro's house, where he had gone to arrest Flemming.[283]

Patrolman Harry Daugherty died in a hospital on May 1st without gaining consciousness; he had been fatally stabbed in the head with a chisel.[284]

The Baltimore Afro-American of May 5, 1934 reported on the case. A reporter for the newspaper tried and failed to gain access to McClendon for an interview. The newspaper reported that McClendon lived in Crisfield on Seventh Street with his wife, and that he "weighs 133 pounds,

---

[282] *The Baltimore Sun*, "News From Maryland Told In Brief," Jul. 21, 1934
[283] *The Baltimore Sun*, "Shore Posses Scour Swamp After Negro. Fugitive Wanted For Shooting Of Crisfield Night Policeman. Quarry Believed Trapped In Woods," Apr. 30, 1934
[284] *The Baltimore Sun*, "Finds Negro Killed Shore Policeman," May 3, 1934

Chapter 11. Eastern Shore Cases

is 5 feet 5 inches tall, and was born in Knoxville, Tenn."[285] The article further includes the following,

> The slain policeman was the fourth of his family to be attacked by colored men, investigations disclose.
>
> John H. Daugherty, also a policeman, was shot and killed [in Crisfield] in 1906. His alleged slayer [James Reed] was lynched by a mob shortly after, his body being burned in a swamp near [Crisfield].
>
> The father of the officer slain Sunday night was beaten in 1926 and left lying in a semi-conscious condition in a ditch. His attacker was sentenced to ten years in the house of correction.
>
> In 1932, the slain patrolman's uncle by marriage, David Evans, was beaten by three men, in his store at Daughertytown. The three were sentenced to prison terms.

The details about the 1926 and 1932 cases are not provided here.

The Crisfield Times reported on July 27th that Howard McClendon was convicted on July 25, 1934 and sentenced to life in prison for slaying Harry Daugherty. McClendon was sentenced in Cambridge following a two-day trial, and was transported afterwards to Baltimore. The newspaper reports the following background.

> Daugherty was stabbed with a chisel on the night of April 28th, in a struggle with McClendon when he attempted to place him under arrest. McClendon admitted to fighting with the officer and said he remembered having a chisel in his hand during the struggle, but did not remember stabbing him.
>
> Many witnesses testified for the State how McClendon fled from one Negro home to another seeking shelter from a posse seeking to apprehend him. He was arrested early the following morning near Westover by Sheriff Daugherty, and was taken to Baltimore by State Police, where he had remained until brought to Cambridge for trial.[286]

James E. Bowland
Princess Anne, Maryland, 1934, sentenced to 20 years,
(See page 106 for description of case and alleged rioting.)

---

[285] *The Baltimore Afro-American*, "Alleged Slayer of White Cop Is Snatched From Shore Mob," May 5, 1934
[286] *The Crisfield Times*, "Slayer of Crisfield Policeman Convicted First Degree Murder—Trial of Howard McClendon Held At Cambridge—Gets Sentence of Life Imprisonment," July 27, 1934

Mob Law on Delmarva

William Holland

Sentenced October 1934 for crime in Worcester County, Maryland

Only one newspaper article was located, that of the Friday, October 19, 1934, edition of the *Marylander and Herald*, so it is not known the circumstances of the reported confession or if there had been attempts of violence on Holland, particularly by "the crowd" that was searching for him. The article includes the following description.

> Twelve years imprisonment in the Maryland Penitentiary was the sentence meted out to William Holland negro following his conviction Thursday morning in Worcester County Circuit Court, on indictments charging him with assault with intent to kill former Senator James M. Crockett, and with assault with intent to rob and assault J. Wesley Burton, both residents of Pocomoke City.
>
> The negro plead guilty to both charges, was found guilty by the court and given six years imprisonment on each count, a total of twelve years.
>
> Testimony in the form of a confession read by the State, follows: While working on the afternoon of Monday May 21, 1934, the negro made up his mind to rob former Senator Crockett, in order to obtain money to buy shoes.
>
> That night, armed with a telephone pole bolt, Holland says he hid himself at the home of Mr. Crockett. Driving up about that time Mr. Crockett placed his car in his garage and as he came out walking the negro felled him with a blow on the head, with the bolt.
>
> "I never got a chance to go through Mr. Crockett's pockets to search for money," states the negro's confession, "because just then a light flashed on the back porch of the Crockett home. I ran away hid the bolt under a colored school house, changed my clothes and went to my home."
>
> In confession assault with intent to rob and assault Mr. Burton on Saturday night, June 9th, the negro said he met Burton on the street and told him someone was stealing his (Burton's) chickens.
>
> "I went with Mr. Burton to his home and then to his backyard. Then I pointed a screw driver at him and told him to put his hands up. Then I grabbed him around the neck and searched him but found no money. Finally Burton yelled for help and I ran, I was finally caught that same night by Willard Burton and Mr. Craigmile two of the crowd that was searching for me."[287]

---

[287] *Marylander and Herald*, "Negro Sentenced to Penitentiary," Oct. 19, 1934

Chapter 11. Eastern Shore Cases

Arthur Collick and Charles Manuel (Pilchard Murder)

Collick executed and Manuel sentenced to prison 1940 for crime in Stockton, Maryland

> *"Jeering and taunting the cowering women, the men danced about them, dangling a rope in their faces and shouting, 'How would you like to have this around your neck?'*
>
> *"They dragged Lillian Black and her 14-year-old daughter Martha, through a window of the wrecked jail, shoved them around, demanded that they describe how the Pilchard murder was committed, and finally shoved them into automobiles and headed for Stockton, scene of the crime."*
>
> *February 14, 1940*
> *The Baltimore Sun*

In February of 1940, white farmer Harvey W. Pilchard was murdered in his home near Stockton, Maryland. Pilchard's wife was home at the time and to escape harm and also shot, hid on the roof until the alleged attackers left the home. Harvey Pilchard died from the shotgun wounds.

The Baltimore Sun of February 14, 1940 reported mob action.

Snow Hill, Md., Feb. 13 – An enraged mob of shouting men smashed into the jail here tonight and abducted two screaming Negro women suspected of having been companions of the men who murdered Harvey W. Pilchard and shot his wife Sunday night.

Jeering and taunting the cowering women, the men danced about them, dangling a rope in their faces and shouting, "How would you like to have this around your neck?"

They dragged Lillian Black and her 14-year-old daughter Martha, through a window of the wrecked jail, shoved them around, demanded that they describe how the Pilchard murder was committed, and finally shoved them into automobiles and headed for Stockton, scene of the crime.

The screams and cries for mercy of the victims of the mob could be heard above the roar of the milling hundreds as a caravan of more than 200 automobiles speeded off to the little town nine miles away from this county seat.

There was no interference with the mob as it moved against the jail, first sawing through the bars of the windows of the windows and then ripping out the whole metal frame and bursting into the jail proper, where the cell block containing the suspects was smashed and they were dragged out.

Mob Law on Delmarva

The only persons of authority present were Gerald Bowen, the jailer, and his wife, who were helpless against the assault of the enraged mob. Other officials, including Sheriff J. William Hall, his deputies and State policemen, were nowhere to be seen.

The Negro women were arrested by two civilian possemen shortly after noon when they emerged from a murky swamp near Stockton with Arthur Collick, who is wanted as "definitely implicated" in the murder. Collick escaped, but the women, their feet bloody and bruised, gave themselves up.

A few minutes after the broaching of the jail, Lieut. Andrew T. Connor of the State police, drove up to learn what had transpired. With two patrolmen, Connor, who has been in charge of the State police concerned in the two-day man hunt, started in pursuit of the mob.

At the same time, word came from Col. Beverly Ober, State police head, who was getting reports on developments in Baltimore, that Lieut. Ruxton Ridgely had been ordered to follow the crowd and to effect the re-capture of the women "at all costs."

A force of twenty-five State policemen was reported converging on the scene.

Angry undercurrents that began during the late afternoon took form about 8 o'clock when the first signs of the mob-to-be were evidenced around the jail.

At first there were cries and shouts of "Turn them over or we'll tear the building down brick by brick." No heed was paid within the structure to these demands and the temper of those outside began to grow violent.

The cries became hoarse shouts. Those behind pressed forward and a five-foot fence surrounding the jail toppled over under the weight. Some, more aroused than their fellows, stood on each other's shoulders and reached up to the gratings protecting the windows. It was a ten-foot stretch.

Tiring of their efforts at the front, the press became heaviest at the rear of the building. Finally a grating was pulled down, and fists were shoved through the bars to shatter the glass on the other side.

Now, apparently trouble-bent, the crowd shouted gain and again, "Let us at them!" They started calling for George Selby, Negro held for investigation in the case, who was arrested at Pocomoke City and who had been jailed at a place which authorities refused to name.

Some of the more venturesome moved up to the front door. Incessant pounding failed to bring an answer and jeers and catcalls welled up.

Alternately they called for "Those damn Negroes" and some one stated derisively that he "had a rope that would do the trick."...

The article continues about the mob driving away with the women.

...They started for the town where the murder took place.

Chapter 11. Eastern Shore Cases

> During the melee Sheriff Hall and Lieutenant Connor were not in evidence. In their stead, two State Patrolmen whom the lieutenant later took with him in pursuit of the mob, were waiting at a nearby store.
>
> They said they were without orders and that until they received some notification from their superiors they were not in position to interfere with the humanity surging around them.

Reports the newspaper, Lieutenant Ruxton Ridgely and Sergeant W. H. Weber had flown to the scene of the mob violence to take command of the rescue. Four state policemen pursued the mob members to Stockton.

> Col. Beverly Ober, commander of the State police, was informed by short-wave radio from Stockton that Sergt. W. H. Weber had been injured in the fight in which the officers used clubs and pistols.
>
> Two shots were fired by State officers when Sergeant Weber was knocked down, Colonel Ober was told, striking a Stockton man in the leg.
>
> The women were shoved into a police car and spirited away to an undisclosed destination for safekeeping. Colonel Ober said that he was rushing a State police surgeon from Baltimore to treat Sergeant Weber, the extend of whose injuries were not known immediately....

With Collick still at-large, suspects George Selby and Charles Manuel were smuggled off of the Eastern Shore by police and placed in the Harford County jail at Bel Air.[288] After a five-day search, Collick was arrested and transported to the Bel Air jail.[289] Collick had been caught near Girdletree. Collick and Manuel were indicted on charges of murdering Pilchard, robbery and assault and intent to kill Mrs. Pilchard. Collick was also indicted on the charge of rape and intent to rape. George Selby was not indicted.[290]

The Baltimore Sun of August 2, 1940 reported that Arthur Collick received the death penalty at the trial in Towson, and Charles Manuel was sentenced to life imprisonment.[291] Collick was executed in the Maryland Penitentiary on September 13, 1940.[292]

---

[288] *The Baltimore Sun*, "Police Think Negro Suspect Has Escaped," Feb. 15, 1940
[289] *The Baltimore Sun*, "Shore Negro Jailed; Court Meets Today," Feb. 17, 1940
[290] *The Baltimore Sun*, "Two Negroes Indicted for Shore Murder," Feb. 28, 1940
[291] *The Baltimore Sun*, "Death Meted to Negro for Shore Murder; Second Defendant Given Life Sentence In Killing Of Farmer, Pair Found Guilty of Slaying Harvey W. Pilchard And Attacking Wife," Aug. 2, 1940
[292] *The Baltimore Sun*, "Negro Is Executed For Farmer's Murder," Sep. 13, 1940

Mob Law on Delmarva

Mrs. Lillian Blake Collick, 32, common-law wife of Arthur Collick, fugitive suspect in the killing of a white Stockton, Md., farmer, and her daughter, Martha, 14, who were rescued from a mob of more than a thousand enraged whites, Tuesday night, after members of the mob took them from the jail at Snow Hill, shoeless and footsore from their flight through the swamps. They are shown in protective custody of Sheriff J. William Hall of Worcester County and Chief of Police A. W. Brittingham of Pocomoke.

Figure 34 Lillian Black Collick and daughter Martha

The Baltimore Afro-American[293]

---

[293] *The Baltimore Afro-American*, Baltimore, MD, "AFRO Cameraman Shows Principals and Scenes in Near-Lynching at Stockton, on the Eastern Shore of Maryland," Feb. 24, 1940

Chapter 12. Other Notable Cases

There are cases that did not involve mob law directly, that could be determined. A few are of specific interest.

Benjamin Goslee (Darby Case)
Set on Fire 1914 in Hebron, Maryland; Darby, white, sentenced to three years imprisonment

This horrific case was not a mob action case but is included here, on the burning of Benjamin Goslee in Hebron, Maryland. The October 10, 1914 edition of the *Salisbury Advertiser* mentions a recent case, called the Darby case of Hebron which was tried in Salisbury. Darby, white, was sentenced to three years in the Maryland penitentiary for setting a man on fire.

> "Stoops leaving the room heard Darby trying to get the old darkey up from the sofa but failing to arouse him Darby decided to pour a little coal oil over his body and set him on fire, which it is said he proceeded to do. The old negro was soon awakened by the blaze and running from the house threw himself on the ground in agony, trying to extinguish the blaze."
>
> *July 9, 1914*
> The Wicomico News

On Wednesday the Circuit Court took a recess on account of the necessity of opening court in Snow Hill on next Monday. Since last week the court has passed sentence upon several minor criminals. The most important of these criminal cases was the Darby case from Hebron. Darby was found guilty of setting fire to an old negro whom he had made drunk, and was sentenced to three years in the Maryland penitentiary.[294]

According to *The Wicomico News* of July 9, 1914,

> One of the most horrible practical jokes ever recorded in the history of Wicomico County was perpetrated on an old inoffensive colored man named Benjamin Goslee, at Hebron, Saturday last, which resulted in the old negro's death from being burned almost to a crisp. The facts as near as can be learned are as follows:
>
> Joseph Darby and George Stoops, of Hebron, were indulging in a little too much Fourth of July whiskey. Benjamin Goslee, an aged colored

---

[294] *Salisbury Advertiser*, "Circuit Court Closes; For A While – Decisions Rendered This Week," Oct. 10, 1914

man of Hebron, passing the place where the men were celebrating the day of American freedom, was called in to get a drink. He was probably given several glasses of whiskey and becoming stupid, laid down on a sofa in the room. Stoops leaving the room heard Darby trying to get the old darkey up from the sofa but failing to arouse him Darby decided to pour a little coal oil over his body and set him on fire, which it is said he proceeded to do. The old negro was soon awakened by the blaze and running from the house threw himself on the ground in agony, trying to extinguish the blaze. Stoops and Darby secured a blanket and finally succeeded in putting out the fire, not, however, before the poor old man had been practically burned to death. He was taken to his home and died in great agony Monday morning.[295]

As reported in July 7th edition of *The Baltimore Sun*,

Darby talked freely of the incident while in jail today [July 6th]. He said he threw the oil on the sleeping negro and touched off the match, but he did not realize what he was doing at the time. Stoops refused to talk, except to say he was present and was under the influence of whisky.

Goslee made a dying statement at the hospital [article reported he had been taken to the hospital in Salisbury]. He was unable to tell much about what happened, but said that the men were his friends and he knew of no reason why they should try to harm him.

Goslee was well thought of in the Hebron neighborhood. Stoops has no relatives in Wicomico. He came here as a berry picker a few years ago and lives in a shanty some distance from Hebron.

Darby belongs to an old family near Hebron and has a wife and several children. One of his brothers is former Constable John Darby.[296]

Dennis and John Frank Furbey

Arrested March 1923 for crime in Dorchester County, Maryland
Not everything is known about this case and hopefully someone can come forward with information and fill in the gaps about this story. This case involved the murder of a boat captain in Cambridge. Two black men who had worked as crew members were arrested for the crime. One crew member, John Frank Furbey (referred to as Frank) was tried and convicted and sentenced to life imprisonment, in 1923, and began his sentence at the State Penitentiary in Baltimore. It is not clear at this

---

[295] *The Wicomico News*, Salisbury, MD, "An Aged Colored Man Set Afire For Fun; Benjamin Goslee Given Drink and Kerosined and Set Afire as Joke; Aged Negro Burned So Badley He Died Monday," July 9, 1914
[296] *The Baltimore Sun*, "Old Negro Set on Fire; His Clothing First Soaked With Oil From A Lamp; Two Men Accused of Murder; Joseph Darby and George Stoops in Salisbury Jail – Had Been Drinking With Darkey," Jul. 7, 1914

Chapter 12. Other Notable Cases

writing why the case of Dennis Furbey, his brother also arrested, was dropped.

The next year, the case came back into public eye when curious circumstances led to the arrest of a white man for the crime of murdering the boat captain. The man, who had an alibi, nonetheless was arrested. The last that was located in the newspapers was that he had been released on $5,000 bail. Newspaper accounts seem to suggest the man might have hired someone to murder the captain. Other mysteries surround this case, such as the ownership of the gun to commit the crime and how the person firing the gun found it in the first place. Questions remain as to if the white man arrested was indeed tried, or if another assailant was identified and if Furbey was freed or continued his sentence.

There is a John F. Furbey (spelled Ferby), age 50, in the 1940 U.S. Census, at the Maryland Penitentiary. A World War I registration was located of a John F. Ferby [sic], giving his date of birth as December 28, 1886, his home as Cambridge. The 1920 U.S. Census identifies a John F. Ferby as a boarder with Ida Jackson, on Pine Street, age 28, married and born in Virginia, and listed as a shucker at an oyster house.

On March 25, 1923, Captain Ishmael Willey, a well-known captain from Cambridge, Maryland, was found murdered in his boat, the bugeye *Sadie F. Lewis*. Reportedly, he had arrived at Cambridge, with the intent of putting ashore one of his crew members, Dennis Furbey, someone Willey "had had considerable trouble during the trip, the man not only refusing to work but being surly and impudent as well and declaring that he intended to do just as little as possible." The crew had included two men: John F. Furbey, known as Frank, and his half brother, Dennis Furbey. Willey was found dead in the cabin of his boat which was anchored at the H. M. Fountain & Co. wharf in Cambridge.

Frank Furbey had been employed by Willey for eighteen days, and Dennis had been working for Willey since the 5th of March. Frank, arrested on the 26th and held in the Cambridge jail, had lived in Cambridge for about fifteen years, on Edgewood Avenue, although Frank reported that his family had been staying with his sister-in-law on High Street extended while he was away working, and that he was with his family during the time of the crime. Authorities began a search for Dennis Furbey. The crime was believed to have involved robbery of Willey, although the money Willey was reportedly so worried about being stolen and was secured in the cabin safe, had been untouched, the safe not opened nor the money taken. Dennis Furbey was arrested on the afternoon of the 26th in Crisfield.[297]

The March 31, 1923 edition of *The Crisfield Times* reported the following.

> Dennis Furbey, colored, wanted by the Cambridge authorities in connection with the murder of Capt. Ishmael Willey, a Cambridge oysterman last Sunday night, was arrested upon leaving the train at Pine Street station in Crisfield, Monday afternoon. The arrest was made by Chief of Police Kirwan as Furbey left the train, having just come to Crisfield from Cambridge. The sheriff of Dorchester County came to Crisfield for the negro and took him back to Cambridge on Tuesday, where he was lodged in jail. Both he and his brother, John F. known as Frank Furbey, give detailed accounts of their movements Sunday afternoon and evening and while there are some discrepancies they are said to be trivial.
>
> While the negroes are held on suspicion, nothing has been found to implicate them except their conduct before being discharged and Captain Willey's fear that they would cause trouble. A coroner's jury Tuesday morning found that Captain Willey came to his death at the hands of some persons unknown. Dennis Furbey claims that he did not know of Captain Willey's death until he was arrested in Crisfield.[298]

The March 8th edition of *The Daily Banner* described the case still a mystery as who had fired the gun killing Willey, and reported that the two brothers were still under arrest and held in Cambridge. The mystery centered on the use of the gun found to have been used to kill Willey. The newspaper reported that the gun used to murder Willey had belonged "to Captain Parks, of the sloop *Pearl*, alongside of which the *Sadie F. Lewis* had been moored. The gun was purchased a year or so ago by Captain Parks' son from Mr. George W. Meekins." It was believed stolen.[299]

The May 4th edition of *The Daily Banner* reported on the trial for John Frank Furbey and that the jury delivered the verdict for both of "'Guilty of Murder in the First Degree Without Capital Punishment.'"[300]

The May 12, 1923 issue of *The Crisfield Times* also reported on the conviction and sentencing of John Frank Furbey. The newspaper further explained that "Dennis Furbey, his brother, of Crisfield, indicted at the

---

[297] *The Daily Banner*, Cambridge, MD, "Ishmael Willey Murdered Last Night On Boat In Cambridge Harbor," Mar. 26, 1923
[298] *The Crisfield Times*, "Crisfield Negro Held for Murder, Dennis Furbey Arrested Here Monday Afternoon," Mar. 31, 1923
[299] *The Daily Banner*, Cambridge, MD, "Willey Murder Still a Mystery, Many Wild Rumors Afloat Concerning The Case But At The Time This Issue Goes To Press No Arrests Have Been Made Except The Negroes Arrested Monday," Mar. 28, 1923
[300] *The Daily Banner*, Cambridge, MD, "Furbey Guilty of 1st Degree Murder," May 4, 1923

Chapter 12. Other Notable Cases

same time [as his brother], was discharged." The article also reported, "All during the trial courthouse was filled to overflowing and throughout the cross-examination [John] Furbey was one of the coolest and most composed men ever tried in Cambridge."[301]

John Frank Furbey was imprisoned, but new evidence which re-opened the case, and on December 13, 1924, *The Baltimore Sun* reported.

> Philip J. Zill, 706 McHenry street, yesterday was arrested in Baltimore by Dorchester county authorities and taken to Cambridge, where he is held for investigation in connection with the murder of Ismael Willey, captain and managing owner of the bugeye *Sadie Lewis*, March 23, 1923.
>
> For the murder of Captain Willey, who was found shot to death in the cabin of his boat moored to a Cambridge wharf, Frank Furbey, colored, was convicted in April, 1923, and sentenced to life imprisonment in the Maryland Penitentiary, where he now is incarcerated.
>
> Zill is a brother-in-law of the murdered man. His arrest followed accusations made in a letter a few days ago addressed to "The Judge, Cambridge, Md.," and signed "A Friend." The letter was turned over to Judge John R. Pattison, who ordered an investigation.
>
> The writer of the letter, according to A. Stengle Marine, State's Attorney for Dorchester county, is Zill's 14-year-old stepdaughter, a Mrs. Bonghi, of Baltimore. In the letter she asserted that her stepfather had frequently boasted in the presence of her mother and herself that he had had Captain Willey "done away with."
>
> As a result of the investigation instituted by Judge Pattison, Mr. Marine and Levin H. Mowbray, Sheriff of the county, came to Baltimore and arrested Zill at the clothing establishment where he was employed as a tailor.
>
> On their arrival at Cambridge last night, Mr. Marine said they had visited and questioned Mrs. Zill, her daughter, Mrs. Bonghi, and also the negro prisoner in the Penitentiary.
>
> Mrs. Zill, according to Mr. Marine, said she was the widow of Melvin Willey, a brother of the murdered man, and that she and Zill were married several years before the fatal shooting. She said, it is alleged, that Zill was jealous of Captain Willey.
>
> Shortly after the murder, according to Mr. Marine, she said her husband boasted that he had had Captain Willey done away with. On many occasions afterward, it is alleged, he made the same boast, particularly whenever he had been drinking.
>
> Mrs. Bonghi, Zill's stepdaughter, according to Mr. Marine, told substantially the same story. She admitted writing the anonymous letter

---

[301] *The Crisfield Times*, Crisfield, MD, "Convict Furbey of Killing Oysterman, Verdict of Guilty Brought In At Cambridge, Crisfield Brother is Given Freedom," May 12, 1923

to the judge at Cambridge, according to Mr. Marine, and said she did so because Zill had attempted to force his attentions on her.[302]

The December 17, 1924 edition of *The Baltimore Sun* reported that Zill was released on $5,000 bail for a hearing January 16, 1925.[303]

Luther Moore
Accomack, Virginia, 1924, sentenced to five years for attempted murder

The Crisfield Times of March 15, 1924 reported the following.

> Luther Moore, a negro who attempted to shoot James Hartman on the latter's farm near Temperanceville early last year and who was sentenced shortly after to a twelve month's stretch on the road gang, was brought back to Accomac Tuesday night by T. G. Kellam. Moore was working with a State road gang in Augusta county and Constable Kellam went for him Monday night. Upon his arrival here he was placed in the county jail at Accomac, where he will remain until brought up to be tried for attempted murder.[304]

The Peninsula Enterprise of April 26, 1924, reported that Luther Moore was convicted and sentenced to five years for attempted murder.[305]

Junius Evans
Arrested September 16, 1924, Milford, Sussex County, Delaware

The Crisfield Times of September 13, 1924 reports the following.

> Junius (Duke) Evans, colored, alleged slayer of Christian Christenson, well-known poultry raiser of near Milford, Del., who escaped from Police Chief Martin, of Seaford, Del., nearly three weeks ago, is still at large. The desperado, for whose capture a large reward is offered, was hunted on the day following his escape by a large armed posse, and bloodhounds were used in the search, but although a number of promising clues have been followed, to date the quest has been in vain. In the few days following the general hunt, in which police and posses from several counties of Maryland and Delaware took part, several suspects were rounded up, and the State Police of Delaware were kept

---

[302] *The Baltimore Sun*, "Kinsman Held in Murder of Bugeye Captain, Man Arrested Here In Connection With Crime In March, 1923," Dec. 13, 1924
[303] *The Baltimore Sun*, "Zill is Released In Bail For Hearing January 16, Man Charged With Implication In Murder of Oyster Boat Captain," Dec. 17, 1924
[304] *The Crisfield Times*, Crisfield, MD, "News Brief," Mar. 15, 1924
[305] *The Peninsula Enterprise*, Accomac, Virginia, "April Term Of Court Not A Busy One As Usual," Apr. 26, 1924

Chapter 12. Other Notable Cases

busy responding to calls from those who thought they had captured the negro, but in every case it proved to be the wrong man.[306]

The September 16, 1924 issue of *The Evening Times* of Salisbury, Maryland, reports the following.

> Wilmington, Del., Sept. 16 – Junius "Duke" Evans, a negro charged with the murder of Christian Christenson, a Sussex County poultry man near Milford several weeks ago, was captured at noon today as he was standing in the doorway of Greenbaum's canning factory in Seaford.
>
> He readily admitted his identity, pleaded for mercy, as he was in evident fear of being lynched and and was at once placed in an automobile and rushed to the Workhouse at Greenbank, near this city.
>
> Evans said he has been working in the canning factory for ten days as a laborer. Meanwhile an intensive search for him had been continued in every part of the state.
>
> The poultryman was fatally shot by Evans, it is alleged, when the former surprised the negro prowling in his poultry yard on the night of August 16. Evans escaped into a nearby swamp.
>
> A search for the fugitive through lower Delaware and the Eastern Shore of Maryland then followed. Arrested twice, he managed to escape his armed guardians. He was shackled with handcuffs when the last escape was effected.[307]

William Randall

Acquitted November 23, 1931, Easton, Talbot County, Maryland

The November 24, 1931 issue of *The Baltimore Sun* reported,

> Easton, Md., Nov. 23 – William Randall, 40-year-old Kent Island Negro, was acquitted today when arraigned for trial, without a jury, in Circuit Court here, charged with attacking Mrs. Florence V. Dashiells, 60, of Kent Island.[308]

---

[306] *The Crisfield Times*, Crisfield, MD, "Eastern Shore News in Brief," Sep. 13, 1924
[307] *The Evening Times*, "Suspected of Slaying Milford Man; "Duke" Evans Is Captured At Seaford Canning Factory At Noon Today; Had Worked Incognito for Past Ten Days; Negro, Admitting Identity, Is Rushed To Sussex Workhouse To Prevent Lynching," Salisbury, Maryland, Sep. 16, 1924
[308] *The Baltimore Sun*, "Negro Is Acquitted On Charge Of Attack," Nov. 24, 1931

Mob Law on Delmarva

Change by Degree

The slight tilt of the angle and summer becomes winter
The loosening of the throat turns a yell into a whisper
A shift in inflection confers judgment or acceptance
The change of one word affects the meaning of a sentence

The sun's slow slip past the horizon turns day into night
A look that says I'm sorry can turn wrong into right
The gaze up from devastation reveals heavens on high
And the course of humanity alters in the blink of an eye

Stranger to friend with one word that you speak
A slight bend in a bone can change strong into weak
A turn of a phrase changes why not into why
A twitch of the body reveals truth from a lie

Lowered degrees in the air can turn life into death
A movement of clouds can change dry into wet
The cock of the head turns a bored look into interest
The movement of an eye can change victim to witness

Time measured not by days but by the tick of the clock
The sturdy brick wall built by placing one block after block
The journey of a mile formed by one step after step
Every letter of a book probes life's mysteries in depth

One degree off course sends a ship to different lands
A small twist in a breeze can destroy mountains of sand
A lifetime lengthens with every breath that you take
Shifts in point of view can alter the decisions we make

The whole of our being rests on the slight angles of life
And a myriad of subtleties that turn darkness to light
So look for the changes, ones not by leaps but by degree
To the degree that the challenge sets your mind free

Linda Duyer

Chapter 13. Reflection

Finally, if I could impart one wish for all of us who study, experience or effect history, it is that we expand our critical thinking skills. Question not only the facts – the details, the nature of the sources and the absence of them – but examine the questions and statements themselves. Why ask the question? Might there be underlying reasons for questions or statements? Avoid assumptions. Question it all, and question yourself. Question history and your place in it.

Earlier in this book I described several of my memories about my family. What I failed to say was that I have had my own demons, my own history, my own perceptions and thoughts about people. I had fears and angers and if I am honest, I still have some of them. I know those feelings and my perceptions during my life affected how I interacted with people – who I associated with, who I avoided, who I chose to get to know, and more. I have alienated people, isolated myself, and lost opportunities to get to have relationships that could have changed my life for the better. Had I early on bothered to get to know the people of Salisbury, the course of my life might have been different.

When I think back on all my thoughts and fears, I can see that they shared a cause. They existed because of my inadequate view of history. I was mis- and un-informed. I was affected by the beliefs and outlooks of others who also knew little about history or about other groups of people. I did not know the whole story; I still don't.

But with every new piece of history I learn and every new conversation I engage, something inside of me changes. My point of view is altered. Each lesson teaches me something I didn't know, and it's as if someone says, "Stand over here, you can see it differently." My choices change, I think of new questions. I still have misconceptions, I still have fears, but now I know that with every new lesson I can see the world more clearly and I feel a little stronger.

So every lesson has the potential for creating change, positive change. The lessons are subtle, incremental, changing our view and the course of our future by degrees.

Mob Law on Delmarva

Bibliography

Alnutt, Brian E. 2005. ""The New Excursions": Recreational Outings among Philadelphia African Americans, 1876-1926." *The Pennsylvania Magazine of History and Biography* (The Historical Society of Pennsylvania) 129 (1): 73-104.

Arnold-Lourie, Christine. 2008. "A Madman's Deed--A Maniac's Hand: Gender and Justice in Three Maryland Lynchings." *Journal of Social History* (Oxford University Press) 41 (4): 1031-1045.

Barnes, Brooks Miles. 1906. *The Gallows on the Marsh: Crime and Punishment on the Chesapeake.* Hickory Press.

Barnes, Brooks Miles. 1984. "The Onancock Race Riot of 1907." *The Virginia Magazine of History and Biography* 92 (3): 336-351.

Blackmon, Douglas A. 2009. *Slavery by Another Name.* New York: Anchor Books.

Delaware State Archives. 2008. *An Ancient Punishment -- The Whipping Post Last Used in Cecil in 1940.* http://cecilcounty.wordpress.com/2008/08/01/an-ancient-punishment-the-whipping-post/.

—. 2010. *Enforcing the Law.* http://archives.delaware.gov/100/other_stories/Enforcing%20the%20Law.shtml.

—. 2011. *The Whipping Post.* http://archives.blogs.delaware.gov/2011/12/02/the-whipping-post/.

Downey, Dennis B. 2005. "Racial Lynching, History, and the Filmmaker's Craft; A Roundtable Discussion of Stephen Labovsky's In the Dead Fire's Ashes - The Lynching a Town Forgot." *Pennsylvania History: A Journal of Mid-Atlantic Studies* 72 (3): 269-274.

Downey, Dennis B. 2013. "The "Delaware Horror," Two Ministers, a Lynching, and the Crisis of Democracy." In *Lynching Beyond Dixie, American Violence Outside the South*, by Michael J. Pfeifer, 237-260. Urbana, Chicago, and Springfield: University of Illinois Press.

Dray, Philip. 2003. *At the Hands of Persons Unknown, the Lynching of Black America.* New York: The Modern Librar.

Ford, Harry Pringle. 1910. *History of the Manokin Presbyterian Church.* Philadelphia: James M. Armstrong, Printer.

Gibson, Edward A. 1995. "Roots of My Peers: Neal V. Delaware and its Effect on Jury Selection in America." *San Francisco Law Review*, 111-118.

Historical Amnesia. 2009. *90th Anniversary of Race Riot in Wilmington, Delaware.* November 18. Accessed January 15, 2014. http://janvoogd.wordpress.com/2009/11/18/90th-anniversary-of-race-riot-in-wilmington-delaware/.

Ifill, Sherrilyn A. 2007. *On the Courthouse Lawn.* Boston: Beacon Press.

2004. *In the Dead Fire's Ashes, The Lynching A Town Forgot.* Produced by Stephen Labovsky.

Lay, Shawn. 2005. *Ku Klux Klan in the Twentieth Century.* July 7. http://www.georgiaencyclopedia.org/articles/history-archaeology/ku-klux-klan-twentieth-century.

Maryland State Archives. 2004. *October 6, 1908 Preliminary Report: Exhibits portion, Maryland State Lunacy Commission.* Accessed January 10, 2014. http://msa.maryland.gov/msa/speccol/sc5400/sc5492/html/almshouse_gallery_revised.html.

McGuinn, Henry J. 1939. "Equal Protection of the Law and Fair Trials in Maryland." *The Journal of Negro History* (Association for the Study of African American Life and History, Inc.) 24 (2): 143-166.

Mears, James Egbert. 1957. *Miscellaneous Items among the Freedmen's Bureau Records, Relating to the Virginia Eastern Shore.*

Miller, Randall M. 2005. "Lynching in America: Some Context and a Few Comments." *Pennysylvania History* 72 (3): 275-291.

Moore, Joseph E. 2006. *Murder on Maryland's Eastern Shore: Race, Politics and the Case of Orphan Jones.* History Press.

Patrick-Stamp, Leslie. 1995. "Numbers That Are Not New: African Americans in the Country's First Prison, 1790-1835." *The Pennsylvania Magazine of History and Biography* (The Historical Society of Pennsylvania) 119 (1/2): 95-128.

Ramsay, Meredith. 2013 Revised Edition. *Community, Culture, and Economic Development: Continuity and Change in Two Small Southern Towns.* Albany: State University of New York Press.

Rodgers, Marion Elizabeth. 2006. "H.L. Mencken: Courage in a Time of Lynching." *Nieman Reports.* Summer. Accessed January 30, 2014. http://www.nieman.harvard.edu/reports/article/100441/HL-Mencken-Courage-in-a-Time-of-Lynching.aspx.

Skinner, Cal. 2011. *The Lynching My Father Saw on the Eastern Shore of Maryland.* July 17. http://mchenrycountyblog.com/2011/07/17/the-lynching-my-father-saw-on-the-eastern-shore-of-maryland-part-3/comment-page-1/.

Smith, Asbury. 1985. *More Than A Whisper.* Gaithersburg.

Smith, C. Fraser. 2008. *Here Lies Jim Crow: Civil Rights in Maryland.* John Hopkins University Press.

1993. *The Great Depression: Program 6, "To be somebody".* Produced by PBS television.

Vincent, Keith. 2010. *Courthouse History.* http://courthousehistory.com/.

Wennersten, John R. 1992. *Maryland's Eastern Shore: A Journey in Time and Place.* Centreville, MD: Tidewater Publishers.

Williams, Yohuru. 2013-2014. ""Revenged in the Most Terrible Manner": The Lynching of African American Civil War Veteran William "Obie" Evans." *Delaware History* (Historical Society of Delaware) 33-60.

Williams, Yohuru. 2005. "A Tragedy with a Happy Ending? The Lynching of George White in History and Memory." *Pennsylvania History* 72 (3): 292-304.

Bibliography

Williams, Yohuru. 2001. "Permission to Hate: Delaware, Lynching, and the Culture of Violence in America." *Journal of Black Studies* 3-29.

Worthington-Smith, Hammett, and Hammett Worthington-Smith. 1994. *Stephen Long (1865-1921), The Man An Educator*. Salisbury: University Press, Salisbury State University.

Mob Law on Delmarva

Index

"Grey Eagle", 46
Ades, Bernard, 241
Adkins, Judge, 238
Adkins, Judge W. H., 219
All Saints Church, 44
Allen, MD, 169
Almodington plantation, 44
Almshouse Farm, Somerset County, MD, 28
almshouse, outside Princess Anne, MD, 48
Amos, Justice of the Peace Frank, 82
Anderson (Granger), Charles, 200
Anderson, Charles, 200
Anderson, Sheriff, 187
Andrews, Capt. Thomas, 137, 138
Andrews, William, 47, 166
Annapolis, MD, 214
Antioch M. E. Church, Princess Anne, MD, 59
Antioch Methodist Episcopal Church, Princess Anne, MD, 54
Archer, Deputy, 187
Armstrong, Walter, 141
Armwood, George, 10, 39, 106, 240, 249, 253
Arnett, Rev. Henry Y., 235
Atlantic City, NJ, 41
Attix, Frank, 82
Augusta County, VA, 73
Austin, Chief Marion, 107
Bagwell, Dan, 77
Bailey, George, 47, 114
Bailey, Judge, 225
Bailey, Judge Joseph, 241
Bailey, Judge Joseph L., 222, 229
Baker, Clara, 227
Baker, Frank "Home Run", 226
Baker, Mrs. Norman, 226
Baker, Sheriff Edward, 83
Ball, Justice William S., 120
Ballard, Earle, 230
Ballard, John, 230
Ballard, Kate, 230
Baptist Temple, Crisfield, MD, 59
Barnes, Brooks Miles, 12, 42, 48, 76, 77, 86, 113, 183
Barnes, Frank, 160
Barnes, Mrs. Robert, 183
Barnes, Robert, 183

Barnes, Samuel S., 191
Barnes, Wilbur, 231
Bartlett, Constable E. W., 226
Bartlett, Kate, 122
Bateman, Samuel J., 230
Beauchamp, Roland, 95
Beauchamp, Senator, 107
Beauchamp, State Senator L. Creston, 256
Beauchamp, State Senator L. Preston, 257
Beck, State's Attorney, 231
Beckford Plantation, 44
Bell, John Handy, 162
Berlin, MD, 173, 186, 240
Bethel, DE, 96
Bethel, MD, 235
Bevans, Andrew, 223
Bevans, Luther, 223
Birth of a Nation, 52
Bishop Helen, 189
Bishop, Helen S., 175
Bishop, Rev. E. A., 175
Bishop, William E., 104
Black, Addie, 243
Black, Lillian, 261
Black, Martha, 261
Black, William, 141
Blackmon, Douglas A., 8
Blockson, Harry, 97
Boland, James, 107
Bond, Wells, 223
Bonghi, Mrs., 269
Boonsboro, MD, 173
Borden, Frank, 256
Bowen, Gerald, 262
Bowland, James E., 106, 259
Boys' Village of Cheltenham, 67
Bradshaw, Mayor William H., 258
Bradshaw, Perry, 151
Bradshaw, Sheriff, 208
Brady, Sheriff William, 98
Brady, Warden Patrick J., 230
Brainard, Frank (or Baynard), 152
Brandywine Springs, DE, 176
Brannock, Chief of Police Daniel, 63
Brave, 114
Bridgeville, DE, 80, 234
Brocton, Jailer, 156
Brooks, Buck, 151
Brooks, Isabella, 220

Mob Law on Delmarva

Brown, Amanda, 235
Brown, Edward H., 174
Brown, Elaine, 17
Brown, George, 162
Brown, Michael, 93
Brown, Sheriff, 205
Brown, Sheriff George W., 183, 204
Brown, State's Attorney Madison, 232
Brown, T. L., 215
Brumbley, Fred, 255
Brumbley, Margaret, 255
Bryan, George C., 116
Bryan, Rev. J.E., 137
Burke, Levin, 223
Burton, J. Wesley, 260
Burton, Samuel L., 86
Burton, Willard, 260
Bush, Celia, 135
Butler, Henry, 234
Butler, State's Attorney Charles J., 212, 213
Byrd, Gordon, 50
Calk, 82
Cambridge, MD, 41, 51, 62, 133, 135, 136, 203, 207, 225, 242, 266
Camden Riot of 1904, 79
Camden, DE, 79
Camp Hall, 92
Camp Meade, 51
Campbell, Deputy, 187
Cannon, George, 96
Cannon, Henry, 114
Cannon, Levin, 136
Cannons Crossing, DE, 235
Cape Charles, 76
Cape Charles, VA, 48, 88, 90, 184
Carey, Assistant Fire CHief Raymond M., 54
Carey, Orrie J., 54
Carey, Policeman Orrie J., 228
Carey's Purchase, 28
Carrol, Alice, 51
Carter's Creek, VA, 154
Carver, Constable Edward, 47
Carver, Constable Ned, 160
Carver, Edward, 48
Caulk, 81
Centerville, MD, 236
Centreville, MD, 74, 104, 126, 145, 158, 173, 188, 200, 232, 238
Cephas, Frederick, 135
Cephus, Oliver, 182
Chambers, Samuel, 130
Chelton, George, 52, 221
Chesapeake Canal, 120
Chesapeake City, MD, 120, 165

Chester, PA, 181
Chestertown, MD, 14, 147, 205, 231, 237, 238
Choptank Klan, 59
Christenson, Christian, 270
Christian, Justice, 140
Church Hill, MD, 15, 236
Clanahan Shop, 236
Clanahan, Mr., 236
Clark, Enoch S., 210
Clark, Mildred, 210, 211
Clayton, DE, 150, 181
Cloak, John, 111
Cochran, Governor John Price, 130
Coleman, James R., 205
Collett, Rev., 134
Collick, Arthur, 261
Collins, George, 130
Collins, State's Attorney Stephen R., 238
Collins, William, 114
Conley, Charles, 188
Connor, Liet. Andrew T., 262
Connor, Lieutenant, 263
Conquest, Alfred, 162
Conquest, Leonard, 162
Conquest, Sylvanus, 86
Constable, Chief Judge Albert, 212, 213
Constable, Sr., Albert, 31
Cooper, Capt. J. Frank, 154
Cooper, Deputy Sheriff A. E., 210
Cooper, Stephen, 152
Copper, Robert W., 90
Corwell, Arthur, 175
Council, Constable Marion C., 105
Coursey, Justice of the Peace Robert, 232
Coursey, Justice Robert, 104
Courtney, Arthur, 47, 154
Craigmile, Mr., 260
Cramer, William, 78, 180
Cressfield, Justice G. F., 121
Crisfield, MD, 53, 98, 184, 193, 204, 215, 226, 258, 268
Crockett, Senator James M., 260
Crossley, Nathan B., 158
Crothers, Omar D., 207
Crownsville, MD, 230
Culver, Deputy, 221
Cumberland, MD, 84
Cummins, Policeman Joseph, 181
Curry, Sheriff, 140
Cutler, Joseph, 223
Dailsville, MD, 207
Damman, McLee, 155
Damman, Walter, 155

Index

Darby Case, 265
Darby, Constable John, 266
Darby, Joseph, 73, 265
Darlington, MD, 141
Dashiell, Sheriff, 169
Dashiell, State's Attorney Harry C., 229
Dashielle, Dr., 161
Dashiells, Florence V., 271
Daugherty, Chief of Police John H., 194
Daugherty, John H., 259
Daugherty, Patrolman Harry, 106, 258
Daugherty, Sheriff Luther, 54, 107, 229, 250, 258
Davis, Ferris J., 179
Davis, George, 237, 240
Davis, Green K., 240
Davis, Nora, 179
Davy, Deputy, 140
Dawson, Rev. W. F., 59
Deal Island, MD, 60
Deals Island, MD, 154
Dean, Capt., 137
Dean, Sallie, 10
Delmar, DE, 64, 95
Delmar, MD, 98, 203
Denby, Charles W., 117
Denniger, H. C., 150
Dennis, John L., 51
Dennis, Summerfield, 187
Denny, Annabel, 213
Denny, Mr. and Mrs. Elbert, 213
Denston, Mary, 249
Denton, MD, 10, 140, 173, 210
Deweese, William H., 174
Dick, Dr., 191
Dixon, Asbury, 187
Dixon, Thomas, 45, 51
Dodd, Justice T. S., 150
Doty, Ephraim, 140
Doty, Henrietta, 140
Dougherty, John H., 194
Douglass, Earle, 241
Douglass, Edward, 32
Dover, DE, 83, 179, 181
Driver, Moses, 197
Drummond, Mrs., 113
Dryden, Charles F., 229
Dryden, Deputy, 161
Dryden, Deputy Sheriff Charles, 106
Dryden, Deputy Sheriff Lewis, 228
Dryden, Deputy Sheriff Louis L., 54, 228
Dryden, Deputy Sheriff Norman, 106
Dryden, Officer, 161
Dryden, Sheriff Chas. S., 221

Dublin district, Somerset County, MD, 139
Duer, Judge, 109, 225, 229
Duer, Judge Robert F., 222, 251
Dugan, Deputy Albert I., 148
Dukes, Sheriff, 173
Dulaney, Mayor John P., 97
Dunton, Pete, 77
Dutton, James, 207
Easton, MD, 32, 51, 122, 124, 211, 213, 218, 226, 238, 271
Eastville, VA, 184
Elderdice, Rev. Chas. M., 58
Elizabeth City, NC, 198
Elkton, MD, 119, 141, 164, 207, 212, 233, 238
Elliott, Daniel J., 243
Emma Florence, 215
Emma Ford, 159
Emory, Charles, 151
Endeavor, 193
Erecliffe, 195
Evans Patrolman, 194
Evans, Capt. John, 215
Evans, Captain, 180
Evans, David, 259
Evans, Imperial Wizard, H. W., 60
Evans, Junius "Duke", 270
Evans, Junius (Duke), 270
Evans, State's Attorney William S., 164
Evans, William E. "Obie", 114
Everitt, Richard, 164
Farnan, Marshal, 197
Federalsburg, MD, 135, 210, 211
Felton, DE, 172
Ferguson, Charles, 92
Ferris Industrial School, 78
Fiddemon, Deputy, 125
Field, Bannel, 104
Field, Dillard, 104
Finney, Joe, 77
Fischer, Dr. P. R., 211
Fisher, Dr., 191
Flemming, Harry, 258
Fletcher, Magruder, 142
Fooks, Hiram, 29, 117
Fooks, Sheriff Dewitt Clinton, 129
Foreaker, Deputy Sheriff John W., 83
Fosque, John M., 86
Foundes, John, 164
Foundes, Maggie, 164
Fountain, Fannie, 220
Fountain, George, 220
Fountain, Isaiah, 217

Fountain, William, 220
Frank, Leo, 65
Frankish, Beatrice, 188
Furbey, Dennis, 266
Furbey, Frank, 73, 266
Furbey, John Frank, 266
Gale, William L., 51
Galena, MD, 237
Gannon, Sheriff, 32
Gassoway, Charles, 104
Georgetown, DE, 32, 60, 100, 128, 216, 234
Georgetown, Salisbury, MD, 17
German Baptist Church, Boonsbory, MD, 173
Gibbons, Alva N., 162
Gibson, Carroll, 226
Gibson, Edward A., 131
Gillis, Ernest, 207
Gillis, Henry, 208
Gillis, Marguerite, 207
Girdletree, MD, 263
Gladding, Constable, 143
Goldsborough, Governor, 209
Goldsborough, Judge, 135
Goldsborough, T. Alan, 207
Goodman, Sheriff, 231
Goslee, Benjamin, 73, 265
Goslee, Constable Albert, 156
Goslee, G. A., 154
Gosser, Margaret E., 131
Gov. Robert M. McLane, flagship of the Maryland Oyster Navy, 183
Granger, Charles, 201
Grano, Frank, 10
Grantner, Charles, 200
Gray, State Detective, 188
Grays Hill, 31
Green Bank, DE, 176
Green, Asbury, 145, 201
Green, man, 120
Green, Mrs. George, 99
Green, Patrolman, 78, 180
Greenbank workhouse, 234, 271
Greenbaum's canning factory, 271
Greensboro, MD, 140
Greenwood, DE, 80, 203
Greenwood, John H., 148
Griffin, Burgess, 104
Griffin, Deputy Sheriff Samuel, 173
Griffith, Walter S., 120
Grubb, Secretary of State Ignatius G., 130
Gunby, Alonzo, 223
Gunby, Noah, 67

Gunning, Samuel, 102
H. M. Fountain & Co. wharf, Cambridge, MD, 267
Hagerstown, MD, 239
Hall, Jack, 223
Hall, Sheriff, 263
Hall, Sheriff J. William, 262
Hamburg, Policeman, 102
Hamilton, Jacob, 111
Hampton, VA, 89
Handy, John, 162
Handy, John (alias John Handy Bell), 162
Handy, Mary, 243
Hard, John, 104
Hardy, Mr. W. C., 140
Harland, Justice John M., 131
Harrington, DE, 173
Harris, Eugene, 179
Harrison, John, 152
Hartman, Luther, 270
Hatfield, Leonard, 97
Hawkins, Detective, 198
Hawkins, Dr. J. H., 53, 58, 61
Hawkins, State Detective, 188, 198
Hawkins, State Detective J. H., 83
Hawkins, State Detective James L., 182
Hayes, Buck, 104
Hayman, Celeste, 51
Hayman, Eldon, 250
Hayman-Bingham, Carlyn Juanita, 250
Hearne, U.S. Commissioner Louder T., 225
Hebron, MD, 265
Helen Avetta, 195
Henny, slave, 111
Henry, Charles, 187
Henry, Dr. Z. C., 173
Henry, John, 186
Henry, Rev. E. J., 187
Henry, State Attorney, 135
Hildred, 193
Hill, Dr., 206
Hill, Dr. J. Heighe, 73
Hill, Dr. James, 151
Hill, undertaker, 171
Hines, George, 124
Hines, Wm., 124
Hitch, Clarence, 229
Holden, George, 162
Holden, John, 113
Holland, John, 31
Holland, Judge, 171
Holland, William, 260
Hollis, Fletcher, 181
Hollis, Magistrate, 27

Index

Holman, George, 162
Honey, Howard, 82
Hoopers Island, MD, 136
Hopkins, 82
Hopkins, Sheriff William, 226
Hopkins, Walter, 81
Hopper, Judge P. B., 212, 213
Hopper, State Attorney, 158
Horn's pier, 74
Hotel Steckle, Clayton, DE, 181
Hotel Townsend, 74, 93
Houston Cemetery, 17
Houston, Charles H., 257
Howard, Commander Thomas C. B., 183
Howard, Richard, 223
Hudson, George, 95
Hudson, Robert, 17
Hughes, Rev. R. C., 107
Hughlett, Thelma, 221
Humphreys, Jane, 117
Hurley, Carroll, 215
Hurtt, James W., 150
Hynson, Henry, 152
Ifill, Sherriln, 117
Ifill, Sherrilyn, 17, 217, 237
International Labor Defense League, 241
Jackson, Helen, 59
Jackson, Howard, 98
Jackson, Ida, 267
Jackson, Ralph, 208
Jackson, Waldo, 208
Jackson, William, 74, 158
Jacobs, Dr., 150
Jamar, Dr. John H., 32
James V. Daiger, 154
Jarvis, Sheriff, 184
Jenkins, Lizzie, 135
Jenny, slave, 111
John Wesley Methodist Episcopal Church, Princess Anne, MD, 45
Johns, Magistrate Francis, 82
Johns, Squire, 82
Johnson, Aaron, 211, 214
Johnson, Capt. Benj. F., 114
Johnson, Deputy, 187
Johnson, Jack, 93
Johnson, Joseph, 101
Johnson, Rev. J. L., 58
Johnson, State's Attorney Edward H., 224
Johnson, Thomas, 100
Johnson, William, 104
Jolley, James, 18
Jonabe, Bailey, 215
Jones, Constable Charles H., 181
Jones, Georgia, 45
Jones, James, 255
Jones, John, 119
Jones, Justice Edgar A., 106
Jones, Rev. E. H., 64
Jones, Sam, 255
Jones, Samuel, 172
Keating, Commissioner Thomas J., 105
Keating, Judge, 239
Keene, Eliza J., 137
Kellam, Constable T. G., 270
Kellam, Constable Tankard G., 86
Kelley, Deputy Amos R., 148
Kelley, Mrs. Benjamin T., 166
Kelley, Officer, 149
Kemp, Isaac, 47, 160
Kemp, James M., 172
Kennedyville, MD, 147, 149, 237
Kennerley, Deputy Samuel W., 167
Kenney, Herman, 169
Kent County, MD almshouse, 30
Kent Island, MD, 271
Kenton, DE, 82
Kiah, Dr. T. H., 108
Kiah, Mary, 51
Kiah, Principal Thomas Henry, 51
Killgore, Dr. Bob, 59, 61
Kimbleville, PA, 142
King, Garfield, 75, 169
King, William, 181
King's Creek, MD, 191
Kingston, MD, 183
Kinnamon, Deputy Sheriff Howard, 227
Kirwan, Chief of Police, 268
Knight, Patrolman Harry, 197
Knights of Mary Phagan, 65
Knox, William, 92
Ku Klux Klan, 12, 53, 57, 223, 227
Kyler, Justice Ambrose, 143
Lake, George, 133
Lane, Jr., William Preston, 254
Lankford, Dr., 191
Lankford, Dr. Henry M., 204
Lankford, William S., 199
Latham, Samuel B., 150
Laurel, DE, 74, 94, 203
Lawrence, Fred, 123
Laws, Ernest, 23
Lea, Governor, 83, 92
Leager, George J., 158
Lee, Constable T. Emory, 141
Lee, Euel, 237, 240, 248, 253
Lee, Warden, 209
Lee, William, 42, 183, 192

Mob Law on Delmarva

Leech, Gussie, 188
Legg, H.C., 118
Legg, J. H. C., 238
Leipsic, DE, 114
Leitch, Gussie, 188
Leonard, Mattie, 241
Leonard, Purnell, 241
Leonard, Warden John F., 209
Lewes, DE, 73, 92
Lewis, Deputy, 187
Lingo, Alfred P., 216
Linton, George Kirwin, 32
Litton, George Kirwin, 32
Lloyd, Judge, 192
Loat, Jim, 132
Long, Stephen, 67, 73
Loveall, William, 85
Lusby, Edgar, 237
Lusby, Elizabeth, 237
Lynch, Mr., 120
Lyric theatre, 58
Mabel, David, 206
Mabel, Norman, 205
Mackey, Sheriff, 164
Mackie, Arthur, 141
Manda, Philip, 152
Manokin, MD, 249
Manuel, Charles, 261
Marine, State's Attorney A. Stengle, 269
Marion Station, MD, 255
Marion, MD, 166
Marlin, Rev. Dr. Henry B., 140
Marshall, C. W., 51
Marshallton, DE, 176
Martin, John E., 198
Martin, Police Chief, 270
Martin, Sheriff, 137
Marvel, Chief of Police Arthur, 85
Maryland Oyster Police, 183
Maryland State Lunacy Commission, 29, 30
Massey, Magistrate, 186
Matthews, Ralph, 39
Mays, Helen, 241
McClendon, Howard, 106, 258
McCready, Frank, 160
McCready, Mary E., 144
McCready, Mrs. Obediah, 142
McCubbin, 76
McDermott, Police Sergeant, 78
McDermott, Sergeant, 180
McDowell, Rev., 51
McGee, Captain, 198
McGlotten, Sam, 135
McKee, Deputy, 206

McKee, Sheriff William H., 205
McNeal, Deputy, 187
McNeal, Deputy Sheriff J. G., 187
Meekins, George W., 268
Melson, Sheriff, 144
Melvin, Sheriff, 179
Mercer, James, 180
Mercer, James A., 78
Meredith, Henrietta, 200
Merrill, Harry, 54, 228
Merritt, James, 121
Metropolitan Methodist Episcopal Church, 44, 51
Middleton, Capt. Charles, 215
Middletown, DE, 102, 130
Milbourne, Mr. S. T., 135
Miles, Arthur, 197
Miles, Arthur (or Artemus), 197
Miles, Sheriff, 116
Miles, Wesley, 202
Milford, DE, 270
Miller, Charles, 160
Millington, MD, 151, 232
Mills, Sidney, 223
Millsboro, DE, 217
Milvand, Chief of Police Harry H., 102
Minnie V., 215
Mitchell, Clarence, 253
Mitchell, Dr. H. Arthur, 32, 33
Mitchell, Frank, 32
Monroe, Rev., 134
Moon, Dr. I., 87
Moore, Leander, 180
Moore, Luther, 73, 270
Morris, R. G., 117
Mortimer, Constable, 211
Moses, Alexander, 140
Mowbray, Sheriff Levin H., 269
Mt. Pleasant M. P. Church, Crisfield, MD, 58
Mt. Vernon, MD, 185
Murphy, Celia, 135
Murphy, Cornelius, 135
Neal, Dr., 124
Neal, William, 131
Neary, James, 85
Nelson, Howard A., 244
New Castle County Workhouse, 26, 189
New Castle, DE, 64, 133
Newbill, Frank, 155
Newbill, Dr., 155
Newport, DE, 176
Nicholson, Holmes, 100
Nicholson, Rev. John L., 100

Index

Norfolk, VA, 48, 85, 184
Norris, Dr. R. R., 204
Nutter, Rev. John, 204
O'Brien, Rev. Theo. A. H., 129
O'Dunne, Eugene, 218
O'Toole, Kate, 130
Ober, Col. Beverly, 262, 263
Ocean City, MD, 41, 240
Odessa, DE, 132
Onancock riots, 12
Onancock, VA, 73, 76, 86, 142
Page, Judge, 48
Page, Judge Henry, 166
Paraway, James, 205
Parker, George, 162
Parks, Captain, 268
Parks, Magistrate, 198
Parks, Special Deputy Gustavus, 137
Parson, Stansbury E., 85
Parsons, Ben, 241
Parvis, John, 82
Passwaters, Robert, 182
Paswaters, Robert, 182
Patterson, Judge, 230
Pattison, Chief Judge John R., 222
Pattison, Judge, 225
Pattison, Judge John R., 269
Paynter, Harry, 216
Pea Neck, MD, 211
Pearee, Judge James Alfred, 206
Pearl, 268
Pearson, John, 136
Pearson's Corner, DE, 179
Pendleton, G. L., 220
Pendleton, George H., 214
Peninsula Times, 87
Peregrine, slave, 111
Perkins, Constable Louis B., 232
Perkins, Herbert E., 207
Perryville, MD, 165
Peters, Colonel Clarence, 122
Philadelphia, PA, 130, 150, 244
Phillips, Margaret E., 202
Phillips, Sheriff, 245
Phillips, Sheriff William, 202
Pilchard Murder, 261
Pilchard, Harvey W., 261
Pilchard, John, 67
Pilchard, William, 67
pillory, 25
Pilot, 137
Pinkney, Ninian, 117
Pitt, James, 197
Pitt, James H., 197
Plumber, Sheriff, 152
Plummer, Deputy Frank, 148
Plummer, Deputy William B., 148
Pocomoke City, 90
Pocomoke City, MD, 191, 199, 203, 260, 262
Pocomoke, MD, 73, 160, 184, 224
Pogoet, Harry, 101
Pogoet, Mrs. Harry, 101
Pondtown, MD, 149
Potter's Field, Salisbury, MD, 74, 171, 248
Potts, John, 152
Powell, Bailiff, 81
Powell, Clayton, 82
Powell, Frances, 183
Powers, Dr. Frank, 222
Presbyterian meetinghouse, Princess Anne, MD, 44
Preston, MD, 32
Prettyman, William, 85
Price, James, 104
Price, John, 104, 121
Price, Lemuel, 104
Price, Marshall E., 10
Princess Anne Academy, 108
Princess Anne Academy Band, 50
Princess Anne Silver Cornet Band, 50
Princess Anne, Maryland, 202, 255, 258
Princess Anne, MD, 28, 39, 43, 106, 114, 139, 154, 161, 166, 170, 185, 192, 194, 196, 202, 215, 221, 228, 244, 250, 253, 259
Pruitt, Deputy E. J., 129
Pryor, Bob, 82
Pryor, Robert, 83
Pungoteague, VA, 113
Purnell, Howard, 17
Purnell, Margaret, 127
Purnell, Sheriff Randolph, 242
Purse, Henry, 132
Queen Anne, MD, 220
Queenstown, MD, 159
Queponco, MD, 23
Quillen, Edgar, 96
Quillen, Mayor, 241
Rabowsky, Oscar, 241
Randall, William, 271
Ratledge, State Detective James P., 83
Reckord, Brig. Gen. Milton A., 254
Red Hannah, 26
Red Summer, 66, 103
Redden, James, 132
Reed, James, 73, 193, 259
Reedsville, WV, 114

285

regulators, 77
Regulators, Onancock 1890, 77
Rehoboth, DE, 42, 73, 92, 161
Revell, Washington, 202, 203
Reynolds, Taylor, 141
Richards, Attorney General Robert E., 81
Rider, Justice, 156, 162
Ridgely Violence, 1931, 105
Ridgely, Lieut. Ruxton, 262
Ridgely, Lieutenant Ruxton, 249, 263
Ridgely, MD, 105, 172
Riots,, 94, 97
Riots, Centreville 1919, 104
Riots, Delaware 1905, 80, 84
Riots, Delmar 1914, 98
Riots, Middletown 1915, 101, 102
Riots, Onancock 1907, 86
Riots, Rehoboth, Delaware 1908, 92
Riots, Seaford 1915, 100
Riots, Wachapreague 1899, 77
Riots, Wilmington 1910, 93
Riots, Wilmington 1919, 103
Ritchie, Governor, 68, 232, 253
Robinson, Governor Robert P., 234
Robinson, Judge, 145, 152
Robinson, Levin P., 10
Robinson, Mayor Walter B., 100
Roe, Walter, 152
Rogers, Charles, 95
Rogers, R. Hinson, 238
Ross, Annie May, 220
Rouen, Constable, 124
Rouen, Thomas, 124
Rounds, Frank, 47, 114
Rowe, Dr. Monmonier, 154
Rowlett, Taylor, 164
Royal Oak, MD, 211, 213
Ruffle, Patrolman, 102
Ruth, Ella, 27
Ruth, Theodore, 27
Sadie F. Lewis, 267
Sadie Lewis, 269
Salisbury Advertiser, 41, 75
Salisbury Armory, 253
Salisbury, MD, 17, 39, 41, 75, 95, 99, 105, 169, 191, 202, 203, 242, 253, 265
Schuyler, Harry, 226
Schwarz, Dr. William F., 222
Scott, Bishop, 132
Scott, Constable, 186
Scottsboro trials, 242
Seaford, DE, 80, 84, 94, 97, 100, 115, 182, 197, 203, 216, 270
Seebley, Tom L. (or Zelby), 104

Selby, George, 262
Selby, Joseph, 84
Selby, Mrs Frederick, 186
Seward, Sheriff T. Frank, 232
Sharptown, MD, 61
Shaw, James A., 150
Sheldon, George, 221
Sheppard, "Wish", 211
Sheppard, Aloysius "Wish", 210
Shepperd, Philip, 82
Shields, Roy, 108
Shockley, Deputy, 187
Shockley, Joseph, 180
Shockley, Joseph A., 78
Shockley, Moore, 78
Short, Braden, 87
Short, Linden L., 84
Showell, Jenkins, 127
Showers, Lemuel, 73, 193
Silcox, John, 147
Silcox, John W., 150
Silcox, Nettie (or Nellie), 147
Simmons, Clara, 134
Simmons, John M., 33
Simmons, William J., 65
Simpers, John, 31
Simpers, John M., 33
Simpson, Bertha, 217
Skinner, Cal, 236
Skinner, Roy, 236
Slaughter, Eliza, 220
slave auction block, 51
Slemons, Deputy Sheriff, 139
Slocum, James, 208
Smith Island, MD, 183, 215
Smith, Dr. J. T., 222
Smith, Ernest, 122
Smith, George, 141
Smith, James, 213
Smith, James R., 212
Smith, Peter, 130, 175
Smith, Robert J., 213
Smith, Sheriff R. Hopper, 146
Smith, Theodore Thomas, 162
Smith, Thomas, 162
Smith, William H., 48, 167
Smyrna, DE, 82, 111, 132, 181
Snow Hill, MD, 10, 51, 186, 199, 223, 224, 240, 261
Snowden, John, 214
Solomons Lump, Smith Island, MD, 183
Soulsby, Sheriff Charles M. T., 220
Spence, Harry, 98
Spence, Justice James, 141

Index

St. Andrews Episcopal Church, Princess Anne, MD, 44
St. George's Episcopal church, Pungoteague, VA, 113
St. Michaels, MD, 211, 212, 217
Stanton, DE, 176
Steamer Urbana, 118
Steinmetz, Elnora, 235
Sterling, Deputy Sheriff James B., 229
Sterling, Sheriff, 162, 215
Stevens, James, 117, 139
Stevens, Sheriff, 211
Stevensville, Dr. Dawson O., 211
Stewart, Adam, 172
Stewart, James, 248
Stitchberry, Mrs., 218
Stitchberry, Sheriff, 219
Stockley, Olin, 94
Stockley, Otto, 95
Stockton, MD, 261
Stoops, George, 265
Stroud, Bailiff, 191
Stump, Judge, 145
Swanson, Governor Claude A., 88
Sweezey, Colonel, 222
Tabernacle, Cambridge, MD, 62
Tangier Island, VA, 98
Tasley, VA, 87
Taylor, Alonza, 223
Taylor, Capt. Washington, 98
Taylor, Henry, 47, 154, 199
Taylor, Jack, 117
Taylor, James, 147
Taylorville, MD, 240
Temperanceville, VA, 73, 270
Temple, Sheriff James, 210
Thomas, James, 85
Thomas, Rev. M.H., 137
Thomas, Rev. W. H., 136
Thomas, Sheriff, 121
Thomas, State Detective Oscar, 216
Thompson, John, 96
Tilghman, Police Justice P. M., 195
Tiller, Joshua, 232
Tink, Henry, 199
Tolsen, Mrs. Howard, 145
Topping, John, 87
Townsend, DE, 80, 82
Townsend, Deputy, 98
Townsend, Deputy E.O., 203
Townsend, Sheriff, 199
Towson, MD, 263
Trappe, MD, 123, 217, 226
Trehearn, Mary, 139
Truitt, George W., 187
Trussell, William, 84
Tull, Dr., 191
Tull, Gordon, 192, 229
Tull, Sheriff, 50, 98, 154, 202
Tull, Sheriff Harding P., 202
Tull, State's Attorney Gordon, 202
Turner, Chief of Police Benjamin, 181
Turner, Sheriff T. B., 146
Twigg's store, Allen, MD, 169
Tyler, Jack, 29
Unidentified Man, Queen Anne's County, 118, 236
Unidentified murder victim, Salisbury, MD, 247
Uzzle, James D., 87
Vaughn, Dr. Edward M., 102
Veasy, C. A., 160
Venn, W. D., 181
Vickers, Constable T. H., 133
Vickers, Sheriff John T., 237
Vickers, State's Attorney, 205
Vickers, State's Attorney H. W., 206
Wachapreague, VA, 77, 88
Waddy, Mary E., 106
Waggaman's Purchase, 28
Wainwright, Dr., 162
Walker, John, 84
Walker, W. Irving, 158
Wallace, Constable William, 82
Walls, Edgar, 95
Walls, State Detective Frederick A., 95
Ward, Mary, 141
Warfield, Governor, 32, 183, 205
Warwick, MD, 120
Washington Hotel, 50
Waterloo, Somerset County, MD, 28
Waters, Littleton, 51
Waters, Samuel G., 128
Waters, State Attorney Henry J., 156
Watson, Edward, 48, 191
Wayman, Bishop A. W., 152
Webb, Rev. Martin, 125
Webb, Samuel, 162
Weber, Sergeant W. H., 263
Wells, Lindsey C., 117
Wells, William, 47, 114
West, Warden Ernest, 240
Westchester, PA, 218
Westmoreland, 210
Wheeler, George, 124
Whiekes, Mrs. E. R., 148
whipping post, 25
White, Benjamin, 93

Mob Law on Delmarva

White, George, 78, 131, 175, 188, 234
White, Hattie Nutter, 51
Whitman, Margaret, 124
Whitney, Robert, 94
Wickers, Judge, 152
Wickes, Judge, 145
Wicks, Judge Lewin, 239
Wicomico Hotel, 18
Willey, Captain Ishmael, 267
Willey, Charles, 211, 212
Willey, Lulu, 212
Willey, Lulu S., 211
Willey, Melvin, 269
Williams, Annie, 243
Williams, Charles, 136
Williams, Constable, 179
Williams, Constable R. Kemp, 140
Williams, George, 96
Williams, Harry, 243
Williams, John, 162
Williams, Matthew, 10, 17, 39, 105, 237, 240
Williams, Olivia, 243
Williams, Yohuru, 26, 114, 130, 131
Williamson, Constable John P., 105, 232
Willing, Capt. James, 137
Wilmington, DE, 27, 32, 78, 93, 101, 103, 150, 180, 181, 188, 234, 238, 271
Wilson, Charles W., 117
Wilson, Dick, 76
Wilson, Jacob, 136
Wilson, James T., 95
Wilson, Judge, 135
Wilson, Walter, 32
Wilson, William, 47, 114
Windsor, Capt. W. D., 154
Wise, Wilbur, 223
Wond, Right W., 117
Wooden, Eugene, 201
Woodland, Justice, 133
Worcester County almshouse, 30
Worthington-Smith, Hammett, 67
Wright, Constable James D., 181
Wright, Mollie, 94
Wright, Sewell, 139
Wright's Auditorium, 97, 100
Wyoming, DE, 79
Young, Rev. Charles H., 136, 137
Young, Rev. Nathan, 29
Zelby, Tom L. (or Seebley), 104
Zill, Philip, 73, 269

www.ingramcontent.com/pod-product-compliance
Lightning Source LLC
Chambersburg PA
CBHW031309150426
43191CB00005B/142